The Reminiscences of
Vice Admiral Roland N. Smoot
U. S. Navy (Retired)

U. S. Naval Institute
Annapolis, Maryland
1972

Preface

This manuscript is the result of a series of tape recorded interviews with Vice Admiral Roland N. Smoot, U. S. Navy (retired). These interviews were conducted by Commander Etta Belle Kitchen, U. S. Navy (retired) in the Admirla's home at Laguna Hills, California in the period between November, 1970 and March, 1971. They were done under the aegis of the Oral History program of the U. S. Naval Institute, Annapolis, Maryland.

Some minor emendations and corrections were made by Admiral Smoot to the original typescript. The entire manuscript was re-typed subsequently. The reader is asked to bear in mind that, as with all oral history memoirs, he is reading a transcript of the spoken word rather than the written word.

A subject index has been compiled and is appended for the convenience of the researcher.

DECLARATION OF TRUST

The undersigned does hereby appoint and designate as his (her) Trustee herein, the Secretary-Treasurer and Publisher of the United States Naval Institute to perform and discharge the following duties, powers, and privileges in connection with the possession and use of a certain taped interview between the undersigned and the Oral History Department of the United States Naval Institute.

1. Classification of Transcript.

(X)a. If classified OPEN, the transcript(s) may be read or the recording(s) audited by the qualified personnel upon presentation of proper credentials, as determined by the Secretary-Treasurer of the U. S. Naval Institute.

( )b. If classified PERMISSION REQUIRED TO CITE OR QUOTE, the user will be required to obtain permission in writing from the interviewee prior to quoting or citing from either the transcript(s) or the recording(s).

( )c. If classified PERMISSION REQUIRED, permission must be obtained in writing from the interviewee before the transcribed interview(s) can be examined or the tape recording(s) audited.

( )d. If classified CLOSED, the transcribed interview(s) and the tape recording(s) will be sealed until a time specified by the interviewee. This may be until the death of the interviewee or for any specified number of years.

2. It is expressly understood that in giving this authorization, I am in no way precluded from placing such restrictions as I may desire upon use of the interview at any time during my lifetime, nor does this authorization in any way affect my rights to the copyright of my literary expressions that may be contained in the interview.

Witness my hand and seal this 28th day of May 1971.

I hereby accept and consent to the foregoing Declaration of Trust and the powers therein conferred upon me as Trustee:

6/1/62

VICE ADMIRAL ROLAND N. SMOOT
UNITED STATES NAVY, RETIRED

Roland Nesbit Smoot was born in Provo City, Utah, on May 7, 1901, son of Brigham Roland and Margaret A. Nesbit Smoot. He was appointed to the U. S. Naval Academy, Annapolis, Maryland, from his native state in 1919. Graduated and commissioned Ensign on June 7, 1923, he subsequently progressed in rank to that of Rear Admiral, to date from January 1, 1951 and Vice Admiral to date from July 20, 1958, having served in the temporary rank of Commodore from April 6, 1945 until November 5, 1945. On June 1, 1962 he was transferred to the Retired List of the U. S. Navy.

Upon graduation from the Naval Academy in 1923, he joined the USS CHASE, a unit of Division THIRTY-FIVE, Destroyer Squadron TWELVE, Battle Fleet. Detached from the CHASE, in May 1925, he had six months' instruction at the Submarine School, New London, Connecticut, before he was assigned in January 1926 to the USS S-7, operating with Submarine Division TWELVE, as Navigator. In April 1927 he transferred to the USS S-26, attached to Submarine Division ELEVEN, and served as Her Engineer Officer until April 1928.

He was under instruction in mechanical and diesel engineering at the Postgraduate School, Annapolis, Maryland, and continued the course at the Pennsylvania State College, receiving his Master of Science degree from the latter in 1930. He had further instruction at various activities, between June and October 1930, after which he joined the USS V-5 (later renamed the USS NARWHAL), and remained aboard that submarine until June 1933.

Following duty as an Instructor in Engineering at the Naval Academy, he reported in June 1935 aboard the USS MARYLAND, operating with Battleship Division FOUR, Battle Force. In May 1938 he was assigned to the Navy Yard, Pearl Harbor, Territory of Hawaii, as Shop Superintendent, and in December 1939 assumed command of the USS AULICK, on neutrality patrol in the Caribbean. He commanded that destroyer until October 1940 when she was turned over to the British at Halifax, Nova Scotia.

Ordered to return home, he had fitting out duty in the USS MONSSEN at the Navy Yard, Puget Sound, Washington, and assumed command of that vessel upon her commissioning on March 14, 1941. After a brief shakedown cruise, the MONSSEN was on convoy duty in the Atlantic until March 1942, when she was ordered to the Pacific as one of the escort ships of the carrier HORNET, which transported Major General James H. Doolittle's flyers to within eight hundred miles of the Japanese coast, for their famous strike on Tokyo on April 18, 1942.

Under his command the MONSSEN also participated in the Battle of Midway; the assault and occupation of Guadalcanal; the First Battle of Savo Island; and the Battle of the Eastern Solomons. He was awarded the Gold Star in lieu of a Third Bronze Star Medal, with authorization to wear the Combat Distinguishing Device "V." The citation follows in part: "For meritorious achievement... in action against enemy Japanese forces in September and October 1942...When the ALHENA was torpedoed on September 30, he drove off the attacking submarine, removed the wounded from the sinking vessel and, by his expert shiphandling and seamanship contributed materially to the saving of the ship..." He also received

Vice Admiral R. N. Smoot, USN, Ret.

a Letter of Commendation, with authorization to wear the Commendation Ribbon, for action while in command of the USS MONSSEN during the period April to October 1942.

In December 1942 he reported for duty with the West Coast Sound Training Squadron, San Diego, California, and in June 1943 became Commander of that squadron with additional duty as Officer in Charge of the West Coast Sound School at San Diego. For meritorious service in this assignment, he received a second Letter of Commendation, with authorization to wear the Bronze Star on his Commendation Ribbon.

Between March and October 1944 he had successive duty as Commander Destroyer Division FOUR, with additional duty as Commander Destroyer Division SEVEN; Commander Destroyer Squadron FOURTEEN, with additional duty as Commander Destroyer Division TWENTY SEVEN; and as Representative of Commander Destroyers, Pacific, in the forward area. In October 1944 he assumed command of Destroyer Squadron FIFTY SIX, with his flag in the USS NEWCOMB, and later in the USS R. P. LEARY. He was awarded the Navy Cross, the Legion of Merit, with Combat "V," a Gold Star in lieu of a Second Bronze Star Medal with Combat "V," a Gold Star in lieu of a Second Navy Cross, and the Bronze Star Medal, with Combat "V." He is also entitled to the ribbon for and a facsimile of the Navy Unit Commendation awarded the officers and men of the USS NEWCOMB. The citations follow in part:

Navy Cross: "For extraordinary heroism as Commander, Destroyer Squadron FIFTY SIX, in action against major units of the enemy Japanese Fleet during the Battle of Surigao Strait, Philippine Islands, in the early hours of October 25, 1944...Launching a deadly torpedo attack with precise timing on a formidable column of Japanese battleships, cruisers and destroyers, (he) surprised the enemy and rendered him vulnerable to the smashing blows of our heavy Naval Units..."

Legion of Merit: "For exceptionally meritorious conduct...during the battle of Leyte Gulf and the landing on Leyte, from October 16 to 29, 1944; and during action in Lingayen Gulf and the landings on Luzon, Philippine Islands, from January 6 to 16, 1945..."

Gold Star in lieu of Second Bronze Star Medal: "For heroic service as Destroyer Screen Commander and Commander Destroyer Squadron FIFTY SIX during the amphibious assault on Iwo Jima, from February 16 to March 7, 1945...(He) delivered intense and accurate gunfire into targets of opportunity, thereby rendering effective support to our forces ashore..."

Gold Star in lieu of Second Navy Cross: "For extraordinary heroism... against enemy Japanese forces in the vicinity of Okinawa, Ryukyu Islands, from March to May 1945...A superb leader and seaman, cool and decisive under fire, (he) maintained his command in a high state of combat readiness, thereby contributing essentially to the success of the Okinawa Campaign..."

Bronze Star Medal: "...As Commander of several Destroyer Squadrons and as a Representative of Commander Destroyers, Pacific Fleet...during operations against enemy Japanese forces from February 1944 to May 1945..."

Navy Unit Commendation: "...Operating in the face of continued and persistent air attacks...the USS NEWCOMB blasted Japanese shore emplacements, screened our attacking transports and effectively laid support barrages for amphibious assaults. As the Leader of Destroyer Squadron FIFTY-SIX in the historic Battle of Surigao Strait, she spearheaded a three-section night torpedo attack, boldly closing the battleship YAMASHIRO terrific broadsides to aid in sinking the powerful man-of-war...Culminating her brilliant combat service in a furious engagement with seven enemy suicide planes determined to destroy her, the NEWCOMB, staggering from the first suicide crash and slowed by loss of steam, shot down a second plane and was immediately smashed amidships by a third. She fought on relentless with her remaining guns in manual control to blast three more attackers into the sea and damage the last Kamikaze..."

In July 1945 he assumed command of Task Flotilla FOUR, Destroyers, Pacific, and acted as Screen Commander in Fast Carrier Task Force assaults on the Japanese homeland, commanding the troop transports and screening ships which effected the first landings on Japanese soil at Yokosuka, Japan. He became Port Director and Senior Officer Present Ashore (Administration), under the Commander THIRD Fleet at Yokosuka, Japan. "For exceptionally meritorious conduct..." in the above assignment, which extended to October 1945, he was awarded a Gold Star in lieu of a Second Legion of Merit.

Returning to the United States in November 1945, he reported as Director of Officer Personnel in the Bureau of Naval Personnel, Navy Department, Washington, D. C. He remained there until February 1948, and following temporary duty as Chief of Staff and Aide to Commander Task Force EIGHT FOUR, he assumed command in January 1949 of the USS NEWPORT NEWS. Relieved of command of that cruiser in January 1950, he had seven months' service as Chief of Staff and Aide to Commander Cruisers, U. S. Atlantic Fleet. In August 1950 he was assigned to the Office of the Chief of Naval Operations, Navy Department, and on July 23, 1951, assumed the duties of Assistant Chief of Naval Personnel (Personnel Control), in the Bureau of Naval Personnel. He remained there until August 1953, when he assumed command of Cruiser Division THREE. On May 1, 1954 his title was changed to Commander Cruiser Division ONE, and on July 7, that year, became Commander Mine Force, U. S. Pacific Fleet.

In December 1955 he reported as Assistant Chief of Naval Operations (Personnel), Navy Department, and in August 1957 transferred to duty as Deputy Chief of Naval Operations (Administration). In July 1958 he was designated Commander United States Taiwan Defense Command, in the accompanying rank of Vice Admiral. "For exceptionally meritorious conduct...(in that capacity) from August 1958 to April 1962..." he was awarded the Distinguished Service Medal. The citation further states in part:

"With the Chinese Communist bombardment of Kinmen and Matsu commencing shortly after Vice Admiral Snoot assumed command of the Taiwan Defense Command, thrusting upon him the grave responsibility of advising the Nationalist Government on matters of defense and resupply of these islands, he quickly and efficiently welded the United States ground, naval, and air forces assigned to him into an operational unit affording support to the Nationalist Chinese Armed Forces in such measure that the Communist threat was thwarted. Throughout his

Vice Admiral R. N. Snoot, USN, Ret.

tenure of command, he has demonstrated outstanding leadership, an intimate knowledge of the requirements of the Nationalist Chinese Defense Forces, a broad understanding of the interrelationship of Far Eastern affairs, and an unusual ability to foster good relations among the United States and other nations, thereby enhancing the prestige of his country throughout Southeast Asia..."

On June 1, 1962 he was transferred to the Retired List of the U. S. Navy.

In addition to the Navy Cross with Gold Star, the Distinguished Service Medal, the Legion of Merit with Gold Star and Combat "V," the Bronze Star Medal with two Gold Stars and Combat "V," the Commendation Ribbon with bronze star, and the Navy Unit Commendation Ribbon, Vice Admiral Snoot has the American Defense Service Medal with Bronze "A"; the European-African-Middle Eastern Campaign Medal; the American Campaign Medal; Asiatic-Pacific Campaign Medal with one silver and two bronze stars (seven engagements); the World War II Victory Medal; Navy Occupation Service Medal, Asia Clasp; National Defense Service Medal; and the Philippine Liberation Ribbon with two stars. He has also been awarded the Military Order of Aviz, Grand Officer, by the Government of Portugal.

His usual address is 109 First Avenue, Salt Lake City, Utah. He is married to the former Sally C. Ridgely of New Orleans, Louisiana, and they have two children, Roland N. Snoot, Jr.; and Sally D. Snoot.

NAVY - Office of Information
Biographies Branch
1 June 1962

Interview # 1

Vice Admiral Roland N. Smoot
615A Avenida Sevilla
Laguna Hills, California

by E. B. Kitchen
November 1, 1970

Miss Kitchen: The Institute's awfully happy that you're willing to do a biographical series of interviews Admiral, because your career is so distinguished that it will be a fine addition to the Oral History Library, and I appreciate seeing you.

I'd like to start our interview with some vital statistics. Would you care to provide those for me as a beginning.

Admiral Smoot: I was born in Provo City, Utah, a town about forty miles south of Salt Lake City, on the 7th of May, 1901. I spent most of my young pre-school period in that city, where my father was a chemist in some company that I don't even remember now. We left there and traveled throughout the western states for many years, ending up in Idaho Falls, Idaho, where I graduated from grade school. From there we went to Salt Lake City, where I attended high school. And from there I went to the Naval Academy in 1923. There's nothing very important that I remember in those days.

Q: Before we leave those days, I want to refer to your name as "Smoot," because it is illustrious in the history of Utah.

Smoot: Yes. It was a Mormon family. My grandfather joined Brigham Young in Pennsylvania, I understand. I'm not sure about these details. But anyway he went with him to Nauvoo City, Illinois, where Brigham Young really became the leader after Joseph Smith was killed in Nauvoo City, Illinois.

Brigham Young liked old man Smoot pretty well, I guess. So he made him sort of a first lieutenant, and he stayed with him all through that long and arduous trek across the plains to Salt Lake City, where he is reputedly to have said, "This is the place," and there settled.

By the time they got there, there were many more ladies than there were gentlemen. So Brigham Young decided that the only way to maintain a community and see that it was properly maintained was to authorize plural marriages. Hence from that point of view and just plain ecology and human nature, it was authorized that polygamy would be a part of the communitys regular affairs.

But he established certain pretty rigid rules. If a man took a second wife, he had to show that he could keep her in the same manner that he kept his first one. And if she wanted to live separately, he had to provide her a separate house.

I speak of this primarily because my grandfather did have three wives and thirty-three children. So you can imagine that I've got a lot of cousins.

Among the most illustrious of the family was Senator Reed Smoot, who was the second son of the third wife. My father was the youngest son of the third wife. There were six members of that family, three girls and three boys. They're all long since passed on now.

Uncle Reed was 36 years in the United States Senate, and spent the last 15 of those 36 years as Chairman of the Finance Committee. He was a very strong man, very highly respected, and one for whom I had the greatest admiration.

My father was a technical man and ended up being the Superintendent of the Utah-Idaho Sugar Company in Salt Lake City, Utah. They had 23 or 24 factories that made beet sugar, as opposed to cane sugar.

One of the things that defeated Uncle Reed, on his last go for the Senate, aside from creeping age which was catching up with him too, was the famous "Smoot-Hawley" Act which he sponsored and worked for. It had to do with tariff matters. Among them of course was the protection of the Utah-Idaho Sugar Company sugar beet, because at that time Cuba was just cutting the life out of them with cane sugar. Sugar is sugar and there is no difference between the two, although there was an awful argument about it. Anyway he was accused of a little bit of family protection matters.

Q: He was protecting the people who elected him.

Smoot: Sure he was. It was a big industry in Utah. But nevertheless they used it to serve a personal matter and he was defeated and he died shortly after that.

Q: You remember him, I'm sure.

Smoot: Oh yes. I stayed with him on many occasions. As a matter of fact, it was he who gave me my appointment to the Naval Academy. It was an uncontested and "principle" appointment. All I had to do was to pass the exams, which I never had any trouble doing, except in one interesting case which was purely youthful. I don't know that it's important enough.

Dad had decided that instead of graduating from high school the best course was for me to go to Annapolis and take preparatory instruction. I entered a fabulous school called "Wilmer and Chews." I had no trouble ever with school work, school was easy for me, particularly mathematics which has always been my speciality. But I didn't think too well one day.

I got through with these eleven sets of examinations. They take a period of one whole week. You spend four hours in the morning and three in the afternoon on examinations for five straight days. I did everything fine and was amazed when the information came out that I'd failed one of the exams. It was geography, of all things, which I thought was the easiest one of the whole bunch.

They spoke about the fact that in the mathematics department and in navigation and all the ones that had anything to do with science in the letter that my father received - they were all outstanding marks, but the geography was just so poor they couldn't accept me. I failed, and it just about broke the old man's heart.

I couldn't believe it. I wrote back to Wilmer and Chews and asked them to send me a copy of the exams, and I would try to remember what I said and how I answered the questions.

The whole thing was - I had taken the exam in history and my concentration was on early American history and the thirteen original colonies. The geography exam followed that afternoon. One of the four main questions in geography was, "Trace the waters that you would go through in visiting all of the colonial possessions of the United States by ship."

So I just took a perfectly delightful trip right from Maine down to Florida through the thirteen original colonies. I was still doing history. They were talking about the current colonials possessions - Alaska and Hawaii and all of those. It would have been so easy. It was such a stupid answer that I just imagined that they gave me a failing mark on that.

I had to take the exams over again in April. Because my uncle was a Senator I received a "principal" appointment again uncontested. And I went back and passed the exams in April, and entered in June.

Q: I think that's an interesting footnote to your career.

Smoot: It shows that there wasn't much concentration in my youthfulness, and that proved to be the case in some of my later work at the Naval Academy.

I enjoyed the Naval Academy. I was a good student, always was. I liked student work, liked college work. I wasn't a mixer, wasn't a joiner.

I was raised in a female dominated family, very strongly female dominated family. When you're raised that way, as you grow older the idea of conformity to all things is dominant.

Such influence serves to stultify your imagination. I found this to be a terrific obstacle and a terrible thing that I had to overcome during the course of the years later on, when imagination and originality and thinking becomes very important to your advancement in your career in every way. Not only in your career, but in your association with other people which is a great part of a career. And this was later to become my most important function in the Navy - personal relations.

Raised with this influence one has to fight terribly to have the courage to stand up for ones own convictions.

Q: You think that's the result of a female domination?

Smoot: No doubt about it, because I had to fight it for a long time - really until I was married and found out that females were quite different from my mother.

My wife taught me confidence and introduced the concept of friendship between people as opposed to enmity.

Q: Up until that time you had felt subordinate to others?

Smoot: Oh I should say so. People in authority particularly were fearsome to me. And I treated them as fearsome people.

This doesn't give your contemporaries and those above you much confidence in you, does it? It's a terrific battle to overcome. It's an awful handicap for a young fellow, terrible handicap.

My father was really quite a henpecked man, not very strong, but a brilliant man, and should have gone much further than he did.

You see I'm starting off with considerable belittlement of myself, and you will find this true in all I do. Mrs. Smoot gives me the devil for this.

Q: But don't you feel that since you became so extremely successful in the Navy and participated and made such wonderful contributions you got over that?

Smoot: I wonder if I did. I some times wonder if it was me, or the people that worked for me.

Q: Nobody does a good job unless the people who work for them do it, but you have to have leadership for them to do the good job. You do know that naturally.

Smoot: Then I some times wonder, "What is leadership?" Leadership is a very complicated thing.

I found that the way I practiced leadership was first of all to make people understand that I was a human being, that I was interested in their personal welfare, particularly interested in their family, their weaknesses as well, but they would always have me back of them. And that they would have my loyalty no matter what happened.

I disliked intensely having to put people on report, having to bawl them out, or things like that. I don't like to do that.

I don't mind confronting anybody when it's very obvious that they've made a deliberate mistake but basically I think leadership, mine at least, has been based on the fact that I always believed those who worked for you are going to try to do their best no matter whether they like you or not.

But because of their own future and their condition and everything, they're going to try to do their very best. And any mistakes they make really aren't their fault. They didn't do it purposely. Maybe it's their fault from a physical or mental weakness, but they didn't make mistakes deliberately. So you have misjudged them if you've put them into a place where they can't do their job well. You haven't been very smart as a leader.

So if subordinates do something that's bad, that implies an attempt to cheat or trying to get by with something, then I can give it to them. But I never liked it, I usually liked to give them the benefit of the doubt. I feel it was my fault because I put them in a job they can't do, find somebody else to do it.

Q: You were saying, in my view, the finest characteristics of a leader. And I'm sure that you will agree that one of the finest characteristics of leadership is knowing your job better than anybody else.

Smoot: You have to know that, or at least think you do. However I don't go for that completely, because there are certain jobs that I took that when I had command I didn't know, except superficially. I didn't know gunnery very well, my gunnery officer knew it. I knew what I wanted, and when I wanted it and if I didn't get it he found out about it. But I didn't know gunnery as well as he knew gunnery.

Q: But you didn't need to know gunnery to know how to do your job. You needed to have somebody who did know it.

Smoot: What is Command anyway — it's just the ability to make the best out of the people that are working for you.

Q: Your comment is extremely interesting.
So through the Academy days, you did enjoy it?

Smoot: Thoroughly, because I liked scholastic work.

Q: Did you enjoy being away from home for the first time?

Smoot: Oh boy, did I ever, I loved getting away from home. That was the happiest day in my life — when I left home.

Q: That's kind of sad.

Smoot: Yes, sure it is.
I tried to run away once, but I didn't have the fortitude to go up to the Recruiting Officer — this was in World War I — and lie about my age. I got right up to the door and then I thought he's going to say, "Go on home kid and go to bed."

Q: How old were you then?

Smoot: Fourteen, it was 1915 during World War I.

Q: Off the tape you surprised me by saying you were not raised as a Mormon.

Smoot: No, I wasn't. My father married an Episcopalian, and so he was really ostracized from the church. It wasn't any kind of a disgrace. The family accepted my mother and it was perfectly all right.

We were brought up as Episcopalians, me and my sister. This was not forced upon us and that became a difficult thing in the family, what religion we were going to take. Theoretically both mother and dad left it up to me and my sister, but we didn't make a choice. Because of the location it was easier for us to to go an Episcopal Church than it was to go to a Mormon Church. We were in Idaho. Church and Sunday School became important and there were no Mormon churches close to us. There was an Episcopal Church so we were raised as Episcopalians mostly because of propinquity more than anything else.

So Mormonism, as such, I learned more about from the bedside of my wonderful aunt, the wife of the Senator, in Washington when I was a Midshipman and used to visit her in their home in Washington. As a matter of fact that's where I did a lot of couring of my future bride at that place. My aunt taught me more about Mormonism than I ever learned from my own parents. But it isn't a dominating feature of my life whatsoever, not at all.

Q: Shall we go on from your graduation from the Academy then.

Smoot: I graduated 41 in a class pretty close to 900. One of the reasons that I didn't stand higher was because I was a little bit careless in some of my scholastic work. It was easy for me and I took it too easy.

I was called up before the Superintendent one time. I'll never forget that as long as I live, because he was just about that much below Jesus Christ as far as a Midshipman was concerned. When I stood there at attention he beckoned me to come and stand beside him. I announced myself and he said, "I'd like you to explain this. This came from the Academic Board. The four main subjects which you have here in your case go like this - in mathematics you stood two, in marine engineering and naval construction you stood five, in English and history you stood 350, in Spanish you stood nearly 900. It's very obvious to us that you're not the least bit interested in really good work and doing what you're capable of doing, and we don't want your kind in the Navy."

Of course this scared the devil out of me. This was coming from real authority, with my background and everything, this was a frightful thing. So I was just dumbfounded, I had nothing to say. So he said, "Well since you have nothing to say - this is now January and you have until the middle of February, mid-term examinations, to bring your marks up reasonably and show that you can do what we know you can do, or you're going to be dropped." So I did.

But it was typical of the whole way I went through the Academy. Things were easy for me, and I didn't take anything seriously. I'd just slide through. It was fun, I enjoyed it. Studying was fun. I spent an awful lot of time tutoring my classmates in mathematics, so that lost me a lot of time for studying.

Consequently I graduated much lower than I could have, which was probably good. After graudation I immediately wanted to go into the Engineering Corps of the Navy, and become an Engineering Specialist.

The first official letter I wrote after graduation was a request to follow engineering and become a naval engineer. Of course the selections for that were taken from the first ten percent of the class, and I was below the ten percent of the graduating class. The next fellow above me who requested it got it, and I didn't get it.

The whole thing was that I wasn't particularly interested in going to sea. I was interested in being an engineer, and a Naval Engineer particularly. And I just didn't make it, because I was a little careless in my scholastic work.

Subsequently it turned out that I was very happy about that, because the function of Command became important to me as I grew up and matured and realized what it was. I never would have had the experience of Command in the Engineering Corps.

After graduating from the Naval Academy I was motivated primarily and solely by one thing, and that was to get some kind of assignment where me and my brand new bride could at least see each other as much as possible.

The destroyers of the Pacific Fleet at that particular time spent quite a bit of time in Long Beach and San Diego. And those were beautiful places and cheap places to live, and we didn't make much money. So that's what I requested and that's what I got.

Those were my motivating circumstances. I didn't particularly want destroyers. I wanted something that would let me have a little more time at home. I really wasn't fundamentally a good naval officer to start with.

Q: You were young, and one would wonder at that age how much judgement anyone has.

Smoot: That's very true. But I still look back on it now and with the experiences I had, I wonder why I continued. I really do. Because fundamentally I love the technical things in life, and I love routine. I love to know that tomorrow and the next day and the day after that I will be doing something that has to do with the advancement of science or something like that. Instead of not knowing where you're going to be next week, and how long you're going to be away from your family.

People have asked me in my retirement, "Why don't you live by the ocean, you spent your life on it." The ocean to me is a restless monster that takes you away from your home and takes you to sea, and involves killing and shooting and noise and tension. This is the sea. I like to go down and thumb my nose at it.

The thing that gives me a feeling of stability and comfort, all that I've wanted all my life, are these lovely hills out here that I can look at from our window.

Q: I think it's interesting that you analyze yourself that way.

Smoot: Oh boy, there's no doubt about it. Under those circumstances it's remarkable that I did as well as I did. It's remarkable to me because I didn't like it.

Q: Was your tour of duty on the CHASE then very exciting?

Smoot: No, it was very unhappy. I didn't like it at all. I disliked it intensely, had no loyalty towards it at all, disliked my skipper terribly.

Q: Shall he remain nameless?

Smoot: Yes, that's better. He was a fine fellow. I knew him later on and he was fine. He didn't do very well in the Navy. He got to be a Commander, but he was a fine fellow.

It was just me. I didn't like anything about it, because it took me away from my wife. I didn't like destroyers because I got seasick. And I was immediately put into a job, shall we call it "George" - everything that was left over. And I ran the mess and made a mess of it.

I disliked it intensely and put in for everything that I could put in for to get off of that ship - schools of all kind. That's really why I went to submarine school.

Q: You were there for two years.

Smoot: I couldn't get off any sooner, I had to stay two years in the CHASE.

Q: Did you think you'd learned very much at the end of the two years?

Smoot: Not much, I wasn't mature enough yet to really learn anything. I was interested only in getting off of it.

At submarine school I first became serious. I first began to realize that this was a career. And submarines fascinated me. There was something about the third dimension that fascinated me. Furthermore I was a school boy again.

There's where my first child was born. For a present to my wife she asked me that I stand 'one' in my class and I did. It was as simple as that. I could do anything I wanted to do scholastically, and did.

Q: May I say with that sort of inspiration behind you that may be one reason why you've been as successful as you have.

Smoot: I think so, I think it had a lot to do with it.

Q: I think for a wife to ask that present is extremely perceptive, and surely helpful to you.

Smoot: It was. And it wasn't hard at all to do it.

Q: I started to ask you what person influenced you, and you have given me the answer before I asked it.

Smoot: She did, very deeply and always has. That was the first one, but that made me serious. To be able to do what she asked me to do and do it with ease gave me the insight of how easy really it is to do what you want to do if you put your mind to it.

Q: You were born with the grey matter to permit you to do it too.

Smoot: Probably one of the inspiring things that helped me there also, in addition to Mrs. Smoot, that has been a great inspiration to me all along, was that Admiral King was head of the submarine school at that time, and a greater man I've never known.

As a matter of fact I've tried to analyze the four five-star Admirals that we've had in this Navy. I think it's the most fascinating thing in the world when you look back on it and you see that you have a man like King - a terrifically "hew to the line" hard martinet stony steely gentleman; the grandfather and really lovable old man Nimitz - the most beloved man I've ever known; the complete and utter clown Halsey - a clown but if he said, "Let's go to hell together," you'd go to hell with him; and then the diplomat Leahy - the open handed effluent diplomat Leahy. Four more different men never lived and they all got to be five-star Admirals, and why? What have they got in common?

Q: What is your analysis?

Smoot: Leadership. The ability to make men admire them one way or another. Leadership is an awful collective word, but I don't know any other word to describe it.

Q: Inspiration is part of it I suppose.

Smoot: I suppose so.

Q: I was going to ask if there were any other comments or anecdotes that you had concerning submarine school.

Smoot: Because of my first child being born there I'm here today. I was assigned to go out on fleet submarines at that time in rotation, and my rotation was on the S-51. You may remember that she was sunk in a collision.

The night that I was supposed to go my oldest child decided that that was when he was going to be born. I called up the school executive officer and said, "I'm taking my wife to the hospital. Can I shift with somebody?" A young fellow named Pino, out of the class of '21 who was in my school, went in my place, and he died. He was lost, and I'll never get over it, but I didn't know.

That's the only incident that happened, otherwise it was just a routine affair.

I think for the first time Mrs. Smoot and I began to socialize a little bit. We began to enjoy, in addition to each other's company, company of other people. Before that we were pretty much circumscribed - intra-vamily only.

And we were growing up enough now to begin to realize that it was fun with other people, other couples, and to bring families up together. So the value of social contacts became important to us at that time. We were growing up a little bit, is what it was.

I loved submarine duty. I loved the first ship I went to. I didn't particularly like the skipper. But I loved it because I went right into engineering, and I loved engineering. I was on the S-7, that was January 1926.

Roper, the skipper, was an awfully nervous man, and of course he made everybody else nervous when he was around. So I didn't particularly like him. But he was all right, I got by with him.

Q: Is that the Roper who later became Admiral Roper?

Smoot: No, he didn't go very far, too nervous.

Submarine work was very interesting. I liked it. We were home more than we were in destroyers. I liked that part of it too. But I also began to take a little interest in my work for the first time. I began to realize it was a career.

An incident happened here, I'll never know why it happened. But anyway the S-7 with all of its group, I forget the rest of the submarines, were shifted to the East Coast. A group of submarines that were on the East Coast were brought around to the West Coast. In Panama I suddenly received orders to go to the S-26, which was coming from the East Coast to the West Coast.

It was just wonderful. Mrs. Smoot was on her way to New London, when I had to send a telegram to her family and send her on the way back to Coronado, which was wonderful.

Roper never never forgave me for that. Nothing would satisfy him that I didn't go to some friend and use my uncle as influence to get transferred to another ship and go back to the West Coast again. It wasn't true. I didn't ask for a thing, heavens no. And why would he say that, because I'd already spent an awful lot of my meager Ensign's money on sending my wife and young baby to the East Coast. She was on a train. I wouldn't have done that if I thought I was going to get exchanged, but that didn't satisfy him.

He made my departure from that ship awfully miserable and unhappy. Again I left that ship with a very bad taste in my mouth. It set me back quite a bit.

But then I reported to my new ship, the S-26, and here was the beginning of my naval career, on the S-26. This was fine, this was wonderful. Why? Because we were tied up at the dock in Colon. I went aboard and the executive officer was a delightful man, just perfectly delightful. He has since died, I can't even say his name now. He was an awfully nice fellow.

He said, to me, "You're going to have the first watch and get her underway, and take her out to sea. And you're going to dive her, so just get yourself all set for it. If you haven't been used to that on the S-7, you will on the S-26."

Well it scared the devil out of me because Roper never gave anybody the authority to dive or con the ship.

The idea of getting up there and saying, "Back full," and whatever you do, and take a ship out to sea, me by myself, it was the most wonderful thing in the world and I thorougly enjoyed it. Furthermore I dived it, I had the time of my life.

The skipper never said a thing to me. He just sat there, looked at me, and had nothing to say. I thought, "Well for goodness sake."

It suddenly came to me, "I'm part of a team, a member, I'm not 'George' anymore." It just thrilled the devil out of me. And it was really the beginning of my career.

This was in 1927, four years out of the Academy, I suddenly realized that I had a career and I could be a part of it, and maybe go somewhere.

Again I look back on this as a significant factor of leadership. Roper wasn't a leader. Roper was purely a doer, and scared to death of his own authority.

A man named Forrestal – he isn't the Forrestal who later became Admiral because he died shortly after leaving the S-26 – was the skipper. He was a kind fine fellow who knew how to get the best out of a young kid. He and the executive officer were just marvelous, and I thoroughly liked this new duty.

I became important then. I became the Chief Engineer of that ship, and I became the Navigator. More important than anything, the other officers began to show me a little respect. They liked me. It never occurred to me before that I was important enough to be liked or not to be liked. It hadn't occurred to me. But they did, and I became a part of the team. I woke up, that's what happened. I suddenly began to grow up.

Q: And you were given the opportunity. You were permitted to develop instead of being restricted.

Smoot: And it was delightful, I thoroughly enjoyed it.

Q: And that lasted for a year?

Smoot: Yes, just a year.

Q: Were you still putting in letters to go to school?

Smoot: I asked for postgraduate school, yes. It wasn't awfully important to me, I didn't care. What I wanted now was to get Command of a submarine. I wanted Command more than anything on earth.

Q: Were you still an Ensign? When did you become a J.G.?

Smoot: I became a J.G. on the S-7. I took the examination while the S-7 was in the shipyard at Mare Island, and got a letter of commendation out of the examination for J.G. Everything above a 3.4 was a starring mark. That was just another significant thing - that I was a student and not an officer at that time.

I made J.G. then, in 1926, on the S-7. Then in '29 I made Lieutenant. They were more of less automatic, you just had to pass the exam. There was no selection in those days, it was just automatic.

Q: So you went to P. G. School in Annapolis.

Smoot: Liked it, thoroughly enjoyed it. The course was Internal Combustion Engines, Engineering. It was one year at Annapolis and one year at Pennsylvania State College. That was the first year that they put postgraduate people in Penn State, and it was pretty grim.

The living conditions up there were pretty bad for a J.G. with two children and no money, pretty grim. We found some living quarters. When I look back on it now, it's really something. We lived over a garage to start with. We had a two room apartment with two children - noise, miserable, smelly. It was the only thing we could afford, and the only thing we could find. Then that place was condemed because of bed bugs, isn't this awful? So then we got another place over a grocery store and that was pretty good, and convenient.

But those were kind of hard times, tough times for a growing family. But I thoroughly enjoyed the work.

Q: Where did you study?

Smoot: I studied at home. Sal was wonderful with the kids, I don't know how she did it. She was marvelous with the kids.

Studying wasn't difficult for me, never was. I never had any trouble studying. I could assimilate Engineering and Mathematics very easily. I was usually way ahead. So it wasn't difficult.

We had some good social fun up there too.

Q: Were you introduced to any new ideas at Penn State?

Smoot: Yes, when we first went up there, because the curricula at Annapolis for the first year ended in July and school didn't start at Penn State until September. But they ordered me up there in the summer anyway.

So I wrote back and said, "What am I going to do all summer long? This is like leave. I've got to do something." They said, "We'd entertain a request for leave if you want it, but you're on duty now and there isn't anything to do."

So I went in and saw the Dean of the men. I asked to have an appointment with him, and I asked if there was anything that I could do in the way of scholastic work to prepare myself for the course. He said, "Well no, it's a pretty tight curricula. We do have some summer courses that we give up here. Ask my gal to give you the list of summer courses, and if anything interests you, let me know and I'll see what I can do about getting you into it."

So I saw this word "Horography." I said, "What's that?" He said, "It's the history and technique of clockmaking. It's a three week course and it will cost you fifteen dollars, because it isn't authorized. It doesn't come under the Navy program. That's the tuition for the three week course."

I'll never forget the gentleman who supervised the course. His names was De Juhaaz. He was Austrian, fascinating man. He spoke with a broken accent. He gave me three of the most fascinating weeks I've ever had in the "history and technique of watchmaking." You end up with a little hack watch. For your fifteen dollars you get a little hack watch that you take all apart and put back together again and a little set of instruments and a loupe glass — all of that for fifteen dollars, plus an ability to fix watches which I did for years and years.

Q: It's a shame that we can't get a picture of this magnificent clock on the tape. I'm sure that it has taken a technician to keep it going.

Smoot: It has, it's really something. That is a beautiful thing, and I've had a lot of fun with it.

To get back to P.G. School, when the work started up there it started in real earnest. This was a civilian institution which I wasn't used to. They do it their way and they don't tolerate any foolishness because there is money in it. You do it or else. It was an easy and interesting course and well worthwhile. I thoroughly enjoyed it.

Q: Did you have a dissertation?

Smoot: I wrote a thesis for the Master's Degree. I had another little lesson on that.

I remember taking the finished thesis into this wonderful professor of ours who had been teaching us, the head man of our group, for the whole year. I was so proud of that paper and had worked so hard on it. He said, "Leave it with me. I'll have an hour tonight to read it."

The next morning he called me in, and it was torn in a thousand pieces on his desk. He said, "Now go back and write what you really want to write, and don't try to be a student. I'd like you to give it some thought that comes out of your mind, and not out of a book."

This set me back. This was two weeks before graduation and I'd been working three months on that thing.

Q: That was rather a hard blow, wasn't it?

Smoot: Yes, but one of the best lessons I ever had. He was right, I had written my thesis just like a school boy, right out of the book. Just something he already knew, and he wanted something original.

So I really went to town. It was tough. The last two weeks were really rough on me, but a great lesson from a great man.

These incidents stand out like a tremendous light in later years - not very significant in isolation but how great and big they are to the overall picture of what you do and how you do it over a life time.

Q: It's so important to have it in a biography too, otherwise it is a sterile piece of paper.

Smoot: This man really shook me up.

I consider his influence, plus almost getting kicked out of the Naval Academy and getting my great and wonderful thesis torn up in front of my face, as three of the most significant factors in the difficult process of my growing up.

Q: What was the title of your thesis as submitted and accepted?

Smoot: THE THEORY AND APPLICATION OF INDICATOR CARDS. I can't remember the exact wording, but it has to do with the timing of diesel engines, the technique of timing diesel engines. It's important.

Q: And there were new ideas in it?

Smoot: The one that was accepted had new ideas. I began to think about it and never opened a book. I just sat down and said, "Well what have I learned? And how can I use it if I go back to a submarine? What good is it if I've got to talk to an enlisted man who's actually going to do these things, and how am I going to tell him how to interpret these things if I can't give him the book?"

So I started thinking in terms of the enlisted man, the man that's going to work for me, and what he thought of. They thought it was good and it turned out all right.

Q: I shouldn't editorialize, but it would appear to me that that might be the beginning of your creative thinking.

Smoot: I guess so, as good as any place right there. It was quite a shock. Those two things to me were awful shocks in my life. I didn't think anybody did that. And maybe that was the point where I ceased being a school boy, probably right there.

Q: And were you able to take and put into application what you had learned?

Smoot: Yes, that's another thing that was quite important to me. They sent me to the NARWHAL, and they made me Chief Engineer. The NARWHAL had a brand new set of diesel engines that had never been used before. And they were quite important to get them going because the NARWHAL was an awfully expensive submarine. It was terrificly big. There was an awful lot of criticism in Congress that that was too much money put into one thing. And we had to make a success of it, and engineering was awfully important to make it.

So I think I contributed a little bit to it. At least I feel that I did in that I was able to get the battle efficiency pennant in engineering that year. Whether that means anything or not I don't know.

Q: But it's important in your career.

Smoot: It was important in my career, it helped me an awful lot. I had a good set of engines, and there never was a time when we couldn't go where we were supposed to go and be there first, never. So I think maybe I learned something, and maybe I used it.

I certainly had a wonderful gang in that black gang of mine, they were marvelous. We were a team again and I loved it.

And I loved the skipper, famous old Babe Brown, 240 pounds soaking wet, had to stoop to get through the hatches in the submarine, a fearless and wonderful man, a great football player, and a delightful lovely wife. They just mothered us like we were their own. They were just marvelous.

So I began to feel part of a team now, and important. I was on that ship for three years, and it was three years of very wonderful and interesting experience.

Q: Do you recall any particular incidents that should be a footnote to history?

Smoot: We made the deepest dive at that time. We went down deeper than any submarine had ever gone. But that's a matter of record and not too important, just that we did.

I'll never forget it because my station for the dive was in the engine room. We had installed vertical and horizontal battens, because we didn't know how much this hull would take. It was a different shaped hull, it was an oval shaped instead of round. It was a big ship, and it had an awful lot of flexibility this way. There were a lot of engineering features about it that weren't too well known.

When we did go down we had a lot of important people aboard. I was watching these battens in there. As we went down the markers went this way, something was going to give.

Q: Can you describe that, because your fingers won't show on the tape?

Smoot: There were two little markers. What it looked like was that the pressure of this thing was just collapsing this ship, very slowly. And you could watch it happen with these two pointers approaching each other as we got deeper. There was a big red spot in the middle, and if it got too close to that you were supposed to yell, "Stop." It never got any closer, but there were a few moments of creaking and cracking and worrying about that.

1 Smoot - 32

We had one little thing that happened. It sounded like a shotgun went off in the engine room, just back of me. It was a small valve that blew. We had a stream of water coming in there with considerable pressure, but the boys had it cappaed off in a minute. There never was any danger.

Q: Do you remember the people aboard that day?

Smoot: Not really. From the Bureau of Ships there were civilian technicians. I'm sure we had the Division Commander aboard, and other officers from ComSubLant.

Q: The NARWHAL was the first of a series?

Smoot: One of the three great big submarines, and the last they built like that. They were called V-boats.

Q: Was that the end of the S-boats? With the building of these three, the S-boats had stopped at that point?

Smoot: Yes, and that was the end of the V-boats too. They started going back to small boats - smaller, higher speed, deeper diving. This great big thing was too big and it took too much of a crew to run it - we didn't need that. And what was the advantage of it? Nothing, except that it could go a little deeper than anybody else at that time. Then they got them very shortly after that that could go much deeper. But it had more endurance on the surface, that doesn't amount to very much during war time. It didn't carry anymore batteries and any more submerging ability than any of the smaller ones. Sixteen torpedoes was all it carried. So it really wasn't any advantage to it, and they suddenly realized it, and that was the last of them.

But it was three years of good duty, mostly out of San Diego.

Interview # 2

Vice Admiral Roland N. Smoot   by E. B. Kitchen
Laguna Hills, California   December 6, 1970

Miss Kitchen: At the end of our last interview Admiral, you had left submarines and now you are going to go back to Annapolis where you became an instructor. I know you loved being a student How did you feel about being an instructor?

Admiral Smoot: I enjoyed that very much. Actually I had a bent and a great desire to have been an instructor in school for a long time. I'm a natural student and always have been. The art of teaching had been a challenge to me, so I enjoyed it. It was easy, as far as teaching was concerned, because they put me into Mechanical Engineering, Thermodynamics, and Mathematics. Those of course are all engineering type of subjects which come easy to me and which I enjoy teaching.

I found that there wasn't anything particularly significant about teaching at the Naval Academy, except the fact that you do have complete disciplinary control of the students. There never was any problem.

The biggest problem to me was typical of all types of teaching - how you get across complicated subjects in classes that are divided across the board in mental acuity from the brightest

Midshipman down to the dumbest. Your effectiveness shows in the results that you see at the end of the month in the marks that come out.

Consequently we found that among the professors in these technical subjects we tended to develop quite a lively competition between the groups that we taught in watching particularly how the lesser gifted Midshipmen responded to your method of teaching.

I don't think that it ever had any significant emphasis or weighted on my career one way or the other, because I don't think I was any better or any worse than the average of the instructors at the Naval Academy. But it was lively and it was interesting.

Naturally, at this time, we were becoming a little more mature. Our children were older. We entered the social life of the Navy with great enthusiasm and with a great deal of pleasure. And we began meeting more senior officers and their wives and families. This imbued us with a great deal of spirit of wanting to go on and remain with this great service, because we loved it and saw some wonderful people from a different angle for the first time.

I thoroughly enjoyed the Naval Academy and would like to have gone back and taught again later, or take up some other kind of work at the Naval Academy. I liked university type of work, always have. But other things intervened.

Q: Then you went to the MARYLAND.

Smoot: Yes.

At this time the Navy was introducing for the first time a type of a competitive promotion system. Up to that time, officers had to just live long enough and not get in trouble to get promoted.

At the time the selection system went into effect, which was about the time that I went to the Naval Academy, it looked like our class and the one ahead and in back of us might make Commander when we were late in our fifties maybe. That's the way it looked.

The Navy Department recognized that, so for the first time a selection system was introduced, whereby the officers records in a certain grade and year group went before a selection board, and the process for selecting up or selecting out went into effect. This, of course, put a greater premium on ones performance as an officer that you didn't have before.

Q: At this time, did you go personally or was your file submitted?

Smoot: Your file was submitted. Your fitness report file went before the Selection Board.

So a balanced type of duty became very important. We found out, particularly where you were going up to Lieutenant Commander and Commander the specialists sort of suffered in relationship to the man who had a broad across-the-board series of duties.

So with my having spent so much time in small boats, destroyers and submarines, it behooved me to get in the big ships category for awhile and learn something about it.

So I struck hard and fast for battleship duty, and was able to get it, and went to the MARYLAND. Because of my work at Postgraduate School I was immediately assigned to the Engineering Department. They put me in the Boilder Division, and I didn't like it at all. I didn't enjoy a minute of it.

So I knuckled up to a few of the people on deck that I knew that were senior to me and finally got myself transferred to the Gunnery Department, which I thoroughly enjoyed.

Q: Did you find you were able to use the skills which you had learned in your P.G. work?

Smoot: Yes, of course. Ninety percent of postgraduate work, even though it was engineering, diesel engineering specifically, is mathematics and the use of mathematics. A great deal of it was.

We had very crude instruments in our ordnance bag at that particular time. I thoroughly enjoyed the innovation of certain types of usable things that could be used to correlate navigation and gunnery and help the skipper out on deck. Basically the crude instruments devised really were fundamental uses of the slide rule principle being adapted to gunnery, which later was put into the mechanized type of directors.

Q: You speak of the fact that ancient methods of position keeping on the bridge were bad enough when they were used on sailing ships and impossible for speeds of the then components of the field which were stimulating and challenging problems which you enjoyed solving.

Smoot: It was very interesting. They were still using the old "stadimeter" to keep position with these ships. And that's all they had. We didn't have radar at the time.

In fog they'd put the fog buoy over the side on a 500 yard line and tow it. We'd just try to keep it right on the bow of the ship so that you knew you were following the ship ahead of you. This was pretty crude.

Q: You knew there must be a better way.

Smoot: And there was, and it soon came forth. Of course very shortly after that radar was invented, and we started to get the use of it then. And of course all of the instrumentation for keeping position and everything went out the window because it was all on radar.

Q: What was the home port of the MARYLAND?

Smoot: Long Beach.

Q: So I imagine you enjoyed coming back to the West Coast again.

Smoot: Yes, we did. I enjoyed that duty very much and enjoyed the skippers we had.

We had three captains during my time aboard. Each one entirely different, each one likable in his way, each with his own theory of leadership, and I quite admired working for them.

We had an executive officer during two of the three years I was aboard who was very unpopular, but this teaches the young fellow to get along with various and sundry kind of people, get along or else that's all. In particular with greater competition coming along in the Navy for promotion it behooved us to get along with our seniors, like 'em or not.

Q: It puts a different aspect on your performance of duties, doesn't it?

Smoot: Entirely different.

Q: Do you have any other comments on the MARYLAND, or shall we go on to your next shore station?

Smoot: I saw a great deal of difference between what they call the big ships sailor and the small ships sailor.

The small ship navy was interesting to me for your closeness to your sailors and closeness to your officers.

The big ships are compartmented so much, they are so big and so overwhelming that a lot of the personal touch becomes difficult. And here of course you begin to learn about the way big organizations run. You can't do everything, the skipper can't be all things to all hands aboard. And you begin to see that the successful skipper is the skipper who can delegate authority, and he will let the person below him do what he is capable of doing and if he fails he's out, and if he's good he goes up.

Whereas on the small ship it's a team that's very close and you never move that everybody else doesn't know exactly what you're going to do and why you're going to do it. It's usually all held right in the palm of the number one man, the skipper on a small ship. He's good or he's bad. He's liked or he isn't liked depending upon what he is.

The skipper on a big ship can be good or bad, and you hardly know it when you're down on the level that I was until you do something wrong. Then you know it. Personal leadership is more dissipated in the big ship.

Q: I think you made a comment that – it didn't make too much difference whether you knew a particular job because the enlisted man under you knew it better. And you had a comment from a senior officer that taught you something. Do you remember what you told me about that?

Smoot: He said, "Maybe he, the enlisted man, knows more about it, but if things go wrong it's the officer in charge who is responsible."

Q: I thought that was an interesting comment. It's certainly true. Your next duty ashore was certainly a change from anything you had done before. Did you ask for that duty?

Smoot: At the shipyard in Pearl Harbor. Yes, I asked for that duty. Actually I was asked for (for the first time) by Captain Hird, the Commanding Officer of the shipyard. He was called the Captain of the yard. We had an Admiral out there who had the District. The Captain of the yard was Captain Hird, a very lovable and wonderful man. He asked for me. I had known Harry Hird at P.G. School. He was one of my instructors.

Q: That was flattering.

Smoot: It was, for the first time being asked for where a job was good. To go out there in this wonderful paradise of the Pacific and get a job that you enjoy, and one where you're paying back for your postgraduate work was good all around.

My assignment was Shop Superintendent, a completely fascinating job, and for the first time related to civilian employment also. Civil Service became a big part of my life, as a matter of fact I was a member of the Civil Service Commission of the Island of Oahu. I enjoyed it, and I learned a lot.

Q: How many civilians were there at the shipyard at that time?

Smoot: This will be vague to me, but I'd say there were about 11,000. It was pretty small, it wasn't a big yard.

In fact while I was there, for the first time, we brought out destroyers from the Pacific Fleet that normally went to Bremerton or Mare Island. We started getting destroyers from the Fleet. Previous to that we used the shipyard primarily for submarines and the mine layers and the mine sweepers that were stationed in Pearl Harbor. But now we started getting some of the Fleet types of ships out there, and later on cruisers.

Q: This was in 1938. Was there any attempt to enlarge the shipyard?

Smoot: Yes.

Q: That was your responsibility?

Smoot: Not necessarily, no. It was the shipyard commander's responsibility.

Q: I know as Shop Superintendent you would have been involved with the shops. When I say enlarge I mean enlarge every part of the yard.

Smoot: Yes indeed. I wasn't senior enough at this time to get in on the top secret information that was going on, but they knew that there was trouble brewing in the Pacific and that Pearl Harbor would be a key base. And consequently there were directives out to Civil Service and everything else to start building up a force.

They were building larger docks. They had started that two years before I arrived. And a new drydock was being built while I was there, and larger dockside spaces for repairs and upkeep and docking of ships, and a larger Supply Department.

I'm sure this was all in anticipation of and based on the intelligence that indicated trouble was brewing in the Pacific. And none too soon I assure you, because we were really scratching for space when we did get into trouble.

But it reflected on me very little; only to the extent that I, in my meetings with the Civil Service Commission of the District, was able to survey the entire capabilities of the whole islands, all the island chain - of people that could fit in to the labor force, in what capacity, their technical knowledge and technical ability. We were able to build up quite a perspective employment list for the shipyard. We, of course, knew that we'd go into competition with civilian shipyards and civilian labor forces everywhere. But they recognized the fact that when the chips are down and we need a force, we'd get them. We had to have them. All this was laid down in plans for the coming trouble.

Q: Did you have anything to do with training the civilians there? I'm sure they were not equipped to come in and do a technical job.

Smoot: Yes, I did. Strangely enough I found out that there wasn't much there in the way of an apprentice type of school.

Apprentice work for a shipyard is very important, because of the specialized type of work that we do. So we hired a man, I've forgotten his name now, who was an instructor. And we set up a small apprentice school. In fact I gave a lot of my time to it, in night instruction and setting up the curricula and arranging for the space for these things. I quite enjoyed it.

Q: It would seem to me that that would fit naturally into your taste and your ability.

Smoot: Yes, I quite enjoyed it. And it turned out to be quite a large and rewarding thing. Because later on when we needed any kind of specializied type of work, supervisory work particularly, we would go right to the apprentice school and pull them out whether they were ready or not and get them going. We had to.

Q: These were people who were native to the Hawaiian group?

Smoot: Not necessarily. We hired the foreign type also. We did discriminate against the Japanese, we had to. It was difficult to do because of the way the Civil Service lists are made up, and the way one chooses people to man forces from Civil Service lists. The Japanese people out there wanted to know how come they were skipped. We just disregarded it.

Q: Did you have meetings, did they try to make it a political issue?

Smoot: Yes, they did indeed. Not so much with me as they did with the Governor.

Q: How did you handle it?

Smoot: We just kept putting them down the bottom of the list. They didn't make enough of an issue of it to get us into any trouble. We knew what was going on, we just couldn't take those people, and we knew that.

As I say I didn't have any security ratings then. Consequently they just told me to use the options, but skip the Japs. By the rules you must select one out of three, but we had to disregard this to a great extent because so many on the list were Japanese.

Q: There was such a large population of Japanese at that time. You did, I presume, have some difficulties.

Smoot: Yes, we did.

Q: Did you ever have any shortage of personnel?

Smoot: No, we had no problem at all. We had an awful lot of people who wanted to come out from the United States too. But we didn't need them at the time, because Civil Service didn't want to usurp the privileges of the people that were on the list out there, except in special highly qualified and high ratings in Civil Service. Some times we had to go to the mainland for supervisory people.

Q: Where did you live when you were in this job?

Smoot: We lived in the shipyard, lived in quarters for the first time in our career. We never had lived in quarters before. The enjoyment of it made a lasting effect on all of us.

We had a perfectly delightful little maid. This was the first time we had a live-in maid too. We lived in the manner in which we would like to become accustomed, it was delightful.

We really had eighteen months of lovely duty out there, useful and educational, both socially and professionally to me. To get into civilian work and shipyard work was very very inspiring and interesting type of duty.

Q: It's the kind of job that on a piece of paper doesn't look like much, but I was in a shipyard myself on my first duty and I know it's in a complete world of it's own.

What time in your career were you selected and promoted to Lieutenant Commander?

Smoot: I was promoted to Lieutenant Commander when I went to Pearl Harbor. My name went before the Board and I was selected for advancement to Lieutenant Commander just before we went out there. I was there in Hawaii as a Lieutenant for about six to eight months before I made my number for Lieutenant Commander.

Q: To go on to your next duty - then you really had Command, didn't you? Let's make that date definite.

Smoot: Yes, December of '39.

War was on the horizon then, guns were booming theoretically and figuratively. We could see things were going to happen. Mr. Roosevelt had started the neutrality patrol. They were taking the old destroyers and other types out of mothballs.

Command at this point became important in my life, at least I thought so. I needed Command. I'd never had Command at sea, and I needed it. So I went after it.

Although Harry Hird wanted me to stay there, because he saw the problems that were arising and wanted to keep as much of his experience around as he could. He understood that I was a line officer and I had now partially paid my duty for my postgraduate work.

The thing to do was to go to sea. All my contemporaries and my classmates were starting to get Command, and I wanted it. So I put in for it and got orders immediately, right away, to the AULICK, an old World War I destroyer in mothballs down in San Diego.

Q: Was it still in mothballs at the time you took Command?

Smoot: Oh Lord yes. The thing that I saw when I finally arrived was the most interesting thing. When we arrived in San Diego I got myself all gussied up, complete with sword and gloves, and went out to the destroyer base. I finally reported to the Commanding Officer, a famous old Commodore.

He said, "Well, go see the executive officer." So I saw the executive officer, then the executive officer sent me to the shipyard commander. I finally ended up with somebody who was a commander. He said, "AULICK, AULICK, oh yeah. Oh that's down there towards the kelp bed somewhere," very casual.

Here I am all dressed up - blues, sword, cap, and gloves. I wandered down through the mud and mire and looked out there and here was this red thing tied to the dock - no mast, no stacks. This was the USS AULICK - my first Command.

And just about that time up from the hold, coming up from the bowels of the engine room, came the dirtiest filthiest looking human being. He took off an officer's cap and slammed it down on the deck and leaned over and yelled some epithets down to the bottom of the place that would scare the devil out of anybody, and that I can't repeat here. He was telling them what he thought of them, what they were doing and weren't doing, and he let them know how without any question. He looked up and saw me and then he said, "Oh my God." This was my future Engineering Officer.

This was my introduction to my ship. What a mess she was, what a frightful mess. But they all looked the same, covered with birddroppings for years and years, 18 years of bird droppings.

Q: There was no provision for mothballing them after World War I?

Smoot: They had mothballed them, but not the way we do now. They were just given a good coat of red lead, the hatches were battened down, the stacks and masts were taken off, and the openings covered. Then a coat of red lead and years of bird droppings constituted the protection.

Q: Where was the crew at this time?

Smoot: They hadn't all gotten there. We just started to get a few. We had the Chief Engineer and the Executive Officer. We had two Chiefs, a Deck Chief and an Engineering Chief, and five or six men. That's all. But they started coming in pretty fast.

Q: Tell me when you went home and took off your sword.

Smoot: I took my sword off before I ever went aboard. As a matter of fact I didn't feel like going aboard. But the Chief Engineer said, "Are you Commander Smoot?" I said, "Yes." He said, "Well, the Executive Officer is here somewhere, and I'm sure he wants to see you because we got word that you were going to come today." So finally the Executive Officer came up. He was just as dirty.

I learned that this was nothing unusual, we all had to pitch in and do it, all of us, including the skipper. We did everything.

Everything was just smeared with grease down below, just covered with grease. That's the way they preserved them, with just tons of grease. So we had to take it all off with steam so we could get everything down to bare metal and start painting.

Q: Was the Engineering Department able to function - the equipment?

Smoot: No, most of it was up in the shipyard. The turbine rotors and everything movable were in the shipyard. And that brings out another interesting story that will develop later about the AULICK.

We worked and worked day and night. And we had a wonderful Division Commander, who I got to know very well later and who I worked with later too. It was during the war, as Commander Destroyers Pacific. He was really the Navy father of my life, one of the greatest, Reggie Kaufman.

He reported to us as our Squadron Commander about March. We were supposed to get underway and go to Mare Island and get the last few things fitted on the ship, and then go down through the Panama Canal and go up and be part of the Neutrality Patrol of President Roosevelt's.

So he had set certain dates for us to have our turnover - the first time the engines turned over at dockside. We worked night and day to meet those dates, because this fellow was impatient and he let you know it.

The day came and we had steam on the lines and we were ready to turn over. So I ordered, "All ahead one-third," and everything went just fine. We took strain on the lines, and we put more power on and held her. And it just went fine.

Then I said, "All stop," we wanted to test the backing engines. So, "All back," and nothing happened, nothing happened.

So I got impatient and started yelling around there. The Division Commander got impatient, "What's the matter?"

So finally the same old dirty Engineer came sticking his head up out of the same old hatch and looked up and said, "Captain, something's wrong, it won't back. I think I know what it is."

What they had done was put the starboard low pressure rotor in the port casing, and the port L.P. rotor in the starboard casing - incredible but true. We had power to go ahead because of the high and intermediate turbines, but no backing power at all.

Q: Had this been done in the shops?

Smoot: This had been done on the ship with our own force at dockside. Our own force had done it. Of course the shipyard helped naturally. I don't know why they didn't notice it. It isn't too difficult to see how you could do that. The rotors fit either casing.

Of course when we had steam on to go ahead, we were going ahead under the high pressure and the intermediate pressure turbines. We weren't getting any help out of the low pressure turbines, we found that out when we started going in reverse.

So that meant tearing that whole engine room apart to take that whole great big low pressure turbine out of there. When you tear it apart you just have to see it to realize what you have to do — it's a terrific job.

The Division Commander came up on the deck and said, "All right. This is Friday. We're getting underway Tuesday. You have this ship ready to go with us on Tuesday."

Normally it's about a two week job. He was giving us the week-end and Monday, that's what he was giving us. This was late Friday.

We did it, the whole shipyard turned to. My crew never got a bit of sleep.

When we backed away from the dock Tuesday morning, there was a big roar that went up from everybody. To get rid of the AULICK was quite a relief to the Base Commander.

Q: To make the picture complete — I'm curious to know what uniform you wore during this period.

Smoot: Mostly khaki. During the working hours everybody worked in dungarees, including myself. I wasn't afraid of getting my hands dirty, why should I be? I was right with them. There wasn't a place on that ship that I didn't crawl in and see and inspect and help and do things when I could. I just became part of the crew.

Q: I am guessing when the AULICK was underway that there couldn't be anything wrong with it that you didn't know what it was all about.

Smoot: No, this is true. I knew everything about that ship. All of us did. I had a good crew, a very fine crew.

Q: You spoke of the fact that the engines were up in the shipyard and that would come in later —

Smoot: It had to do with this backing, that was the incident.

Everything was up in the yard. We had troubles finding a lot of the things. We never did find our own ship's bell. We had to get a new ship's bell and have it engraved and everything, USS AULICK. We never did find it, don't know where it is to this day.

Q: She had been there 30 years, is that correct, from 1918 to 1938?

Smoot: Yes, as far as I know.

All of the antenna, all of the rigging, the masts and the mast structure, were all up in the shipyard. All that had to be brought down. An awful lot of it was rusted and gone, and we had to get new equipment.

It was a very frustrating ordeal to go through, but really challenging. We were always working against a deadline.

Q: How many ships went up to Mare Island?

Smoot: Eight of us, there were eight ships in that squadron, two divisions. The squadron commander was Reggie Kaufman, as I have mentioned.

Famous Reggie Kaufman – who later in his duties during the war had command of all the destroyers in the Pacific during the height of the attack in the Pacific. Then after the war he went as the Commandant of the Fourth Naval District in Philadelphia. After retirement he became the President of one of the big civilian hospitals there. Strangely enough it was in the red and he put it in the black, and made a great success out of it. He was a wonderful man, wonderful wonderful man.

Q: And he is the man whom you call your Navy father?

Smoot: My Navy father, yes. There are stories about him later that I'll tell you, when he got me out to command one of his squadrons in the Pacific.

Q: I'll be anxious to hear more of him.

Smoot: He was just a fabulous man.

Q: But we're still now just in San Francisco.

Smoot: From here on until we got into the Caribbean it was more or less perfunctory type of a Navy operation. The trip going to Panama, with those eight destroyers, was a fabulous trip.

There was hardly a day that went by that one of us wasn't towing another one, trying to keep the squadron underway. They had all come out of mothballs, all had come right from that group of ships.

But Reggie Kaufman with his leadership, his impatience, and everything, you knew that here was a man that was going to help. There was no doubt about it he was going to help you. But God pity you if you let him down, don't ever let him down. He was the greatest person to me right from the very beginning.

We got there, we got through the Canal, and we finally got to Houston. By this time we all thought we were pretty good sailors. I'd never had Command before, and practically all the skippers on the ships had never had Command before.

I was the fourth ship in line coming in to Houston. Reggie Kaufman, who was a Commodore at that time, a four-stripe Captain, was in the leading ship. He went alongside the dock. We went up the River and made a big turn to the left and came down stream and tied up to a big commercial supply dock, well arranged to tak any kind of ship, it was fine. These isn't much tide in those things. You've got a river current, a very slight river current.

I didn't think there was much to making that landing at all. It was going to be my first landing, because when we went up to Mare Island we were put alongside docks by tugs. So this was my first landing, and I wanted to make an impression on my Division Commander.

So I very gently conned the ship up stream and made a big 180 degree turn and came alongside and backed downed and tied up. I no sooner tied up then there were two hoists on the flag ship calling for me, the Commanding Officer, to report aboard immediately.

When I went over there here was Reggie just roaring. He said, "You call yourself a destroyer skipper, and you make a landing like a cream puff. Now get that ship underway and go back down the river, and come back and make landings until I hoist affirm at the yardarm. And when you make a proper landing like a destroyer should make I'll hoist affirm and you can tie up."

What had I done? I tried to figure it out. I went back and I yelled at the Exec, I said, "Get this ship underway. Let's not act like a bunch of cream puffs, let's make a landing." See - I was repeating my Division Commander.

I didn't know what the devil to do. So I talked it over with the Exec on the way down the river. "What do you suppose he wants?" The Exec said, "Well maybe Captain we ought to do it a little faster. Should we try that?" I said, "Well, if it's speed he wants let's give him speed."

So I came up that river at twenty knots. When I got up to the point where I thought I should make my turn, I backed full on the inboard engine with full left rudder. And that ship just spun around on a dime and hit the side of the dock just as gracefully and neatly as you ever saw and we got lines over and tied up with no fuss at all. Reggie hoisted two "affirms" and two "first repeats." So I went aboard and found that I was accepted as a tin-can C.O.

Reggie proved to be quite a politician in Houston from the point of view of personal relations with a city that was totally unused to the Navy. He had the whole city of Houston in his hand in no time. He arranged for baseball fields for the crew, and he got to know the Mayor and all the leading people

He had what he called a social condition A, B, and C, which he hoisted by flag. We really got to know him, and had a wonderful time there.

Q: Was Houston your home port when you were doing Neutrality Patrol for the Caribbean?

Smoot: While we were doing Neutrality Patrol, yes.

Q: How long were you there before you went up to the Atlantic?

Smoot: I was there about three months. Then we had three or four months of Reserve cruises. I was made a Division Commander at this time, and took the Division out of Houston. We took two groups of Reserve officers and crews to sea for periods of six weeks cruises, where we would go to Miami, down to Cuba, down to the Caribbean, to shoot the guns and come back, then dump the Reserves off and take another group.

Q: What was involved in the word Neutrality Patrol?

Smoot: One ship was always underway cruising down the coast of Mexico, and that was about all there was to it. We only wanted to see the foreign ships that went into Mexico. It was off Mexico, all the way down past Yucatan.

We took our turn. When we didn't have our turn cruising on patrol, we were doing such jobs as Reserve training and training ourselves for war.

Q: Your trips, as far as the Neutrality Patrol was concerned, were off Mexico. Then the trips that you went out toward Cuba were with Reservists for training for them and for you.

Then when did you go up to Halifax? Did you have any duty along the Atlantic other than just taking the ships up to turn them over to the British?

Smoot: Yes, we went to Norfolk for the installation of some more modern anti-submarine gear. It was the first time we started getting more sophisticated type of anti-submarine gear. Up to that time we had none at all. We just didn't have any echo sounding at all. How you were ever supposed to find a submarine I don't know.

Q: Had you known of this gear and what it could do?

Smoot: Yes. It was the first kindergarten type of an attempt at echo sounding, echo ranging, and a guided type of instrumentation for dropping the depth charges. It was the first time.

Up to this time the only thing we could do was to follow a given procedure and a given routine and drop depth charges on stop watch, that's all, in a given pattern. If you ever got a submarine under those conditions you were just lucky.

Q: Was there any attempt to restyle the destroyers before they were turned over to the British, as far as the internal arrangement of the ship was concerned?

Smoot: No. Of course the first thing that we did was to get rid of the confidential material. All of the new material as far as gunnery and anti-submarine warfare was concerned was taken off. Our torpedo warheads were also removed. The guns were left on, just as they were, with the ammunition.

We wondered why they were so specific about having the torpedo warhead locker clear with nothing in it at all. We found out very soon afterwards that that was their liquor locker. There's more to it than that.

The ships went up to Halifax. I think we took four up at that time, where we made the preparation to turn over to the British. There was a great deal of ceremony to it, and quite a few interesting and continuing parties and social obligations that went with it, which was fine. We thoroughly enjoyed it.

But there were quite a few things that the British wanted done before they actually came aboard and took charge. Most of them were perfunctory and didn't amount to very much. We had done most everything.

Matters of how they handled their books and classified material were entirely different from ours, quite more meticulously done as a matter of fact. I really think we could have taken a lesson from them.

One of the things which they took so much time about was to be sure that the torpedo war head locker was properly prepared. This was done sort of on their own cognizance, on their own time, and without us really knowing what was going on. We worked together in their shipyard quite well, but this was one place we were told not to go.

So we decided that this is something new and mysterious that's going on down there in this torpedo locker. What in the world can they be doing down there? What are they putting in?

Finally it just developed, and this is more or less anti-climatic. One of the things which you do and remember about transfer of a ship - here you are an American Navy that has been famous for spartan like views, as far as liquor is concerned, aboard ship for years and years and years. Then you leave, have the ceremony, turn the ship over, the new skipper salutes and says, "I take Command sir."

Then he invites you back aboard and you go down into that doggone locker and find it now is a beautiful bar, and they start giving you some whiskey on your own ship that you just left just a minute ago. I think if I forget everything about the turnover I'll never forget that particular phase of it. The rest of it was nothing compared to this event.

Q: So then you came back and got yourself another ship?

Smoot: Yes. I knew when I went up there that I was going to be assigned to a new ship. It was promised to almost everybody who had one of these old wartime destroyers. They were promised that when it had served its purpose, they'd get a new ship.

So they assigned me to the MONSSEN, which was then under construction in Bremerton. But I had to go back to Washington before I went out to Bremerton. I had plenty of time to get out there, and I had my orders in hand.

But I had to go back to Washington. A classmate of mine was on the Detail Desk at that time and he had been trying to get hold of me. I knew why he'd been trying to get hold of me, because almost every skipper that came back from this turnover to the British, this turning over Command of our ships to the British, was commandeered to take another group up there and turn it over because they knew the ropes. I knew this was what he was trying to get hold of me for.

Nevertheless I had my orders in hand, this was his mistake -- to give me my orders. Going to Washington was purely incidental to picking up my family, who were left in Washington.

You always have to go through the halls in the Department. There's always things you want to do and last minute arrangements, but I kept very clear of the Detail Department. I stayed far far away from it, as far as possible. And that night I got in the automobile and went out of town, just as fast as I could. I got about thrity or forty miles outside of Washington and stopped. We spent the night there with friends.

The next morning I called the Bureau. I said, "Neil you wanted to talk to me?" He said, "Oh yeah. I want you to take Command of one of the divisions thats going up to Halifax, take it up there and turn it over. It's just routine. It will only last for a month or two, and then you can go out and pick up your ship."

I said, "Why didn't you tell me that before Neil? I'm already half way on the way across the continent. I got into my car and really went to town." He said, "Oh well, never mind." I said, "Do you want me to come back?" He said, "How long will it take you?"

"It will take quite a while, I'm pretty far out." He said, "Where are you exactly?" I said, "Oh gee, I don't even know. I'm calling you from a friend's place. We've stopped for the night," which was right. I didn't tell him anything, I didn't know how far it was. It could have been eighteen or twenty-five miles. He said, "All right, if you're already underway I'll get somebody else."

So I never did go back there. But this shows how things can be done.

The MONSSEN was a new ship, and it was a great experience in putting a new ship in commission. You've got everything new, it's like moving into a new home. There's no describing it, you never know it until you've done it.

Q: Quite a contrast to the AULICK.

Smoot: Oh yes, quite a bit.

She was a good ship and I had a good crew and I enjoyed the time aboard her very much. The commissioning ceremony was very short and quick and served it's purpose only to get the ship out of the yard, because it was war time now. This was March of '41. So we were getting close, the war clouds were already on the horizon.

Q: Was your crew regular Navy?

Smoot: No, I can't say that. More than half of the officers were regular Navy. I had an officer complement of twelve, which was low. It later went up to eighteen. I think six of us were regular Navy and the other were Reserves. I imagine that the crew was about the same, but it was a good crew.

I had eighteen months of pretty interesting ~~highlighted~~ service on that. We went down the coast to San Diego, fitted out with torpedoes down there, then immediately went to the east coast.

Q: You were on convoy duty in the Atlantic then for a year before you went back to the Pacific. You were commissioned in March of '41, and you didn't go back to the Pacific until March of '42. Do you recall that convoy duty?

Smoot: It isn't so significant that I remember anything about it, until we went to Iceland. Before that I remember one major convoy job where we assembled the combat ships in New York and met the convoy coming out of Halifax. Then we took them as far as Iceland and were met by the British, and they took over and we came back. And I only did that once.

Q: Where were you at Pearl Harbor, December of '41?

Smoot: I was up in Iceland when that happened.

I had done coastal convoys, going up and down from Norfolk to New York. Those don't seem to stick very much with me because there was no incident at all. We just zigzagged and took some commercial ships and discharged them. We never went in to port. We went back to our regular supply base and got more fuel and went out again. We did a few of those.

Then in August I remember a big conference that was called in New York or ~~Norfolk~~, where the Task Force was organized that went to Iceland with the battleships - took the battleships up to Iceland.

That was an experience that I'll never forget, those days in Iceland. I've always understood why they have the Marines there and why they have the Navy and the Air Force, but I never did understand why they have the Icelanders there at all. That's the most barren, drab, inhospitable piece of land in the world. It is just awful, with the foulest type of weather.

They anchored us up in a lagoon that's unpronounceable. We used to call it "havafajava." It would be perfectly lovely weather, that is if 32 degrees can be lovely weather. It would be clear, lovely skies, absolutely clear. You'd look upon a great big mountain over to the left there and you'd begin to see snow, sort of flurrying up around the top of the mountain. Then you'd look at your barometer, and you could actually see that barometer dropping, it would go down so fast.

The wind in the next ten or fifteen minutes would go from zero up to ninety, so fast that an awful lot of us drug anchor and went aground. We got pretty expert at keeping ourself from going aground.

You couldn't get out because the King's guard was always closing the gate all the time. The gates were always closed. So to try to get out was an act of Congress, it really took something to get out of that place. You had to really be on a mission and you had to notify them ahead of time, and they'd open the gates and let you out.

Q: Why was that?

Smoot: The German submarines - to keep them from coming in. It was wide open. The German submarines could come up there and launch, so they had to keep a net up there for the submarines. So it was pretty safe from that point of view, but not safe from the weather. It was miserable, miserable weather, just frightful.

I got ashore once, just once. We went down to Reykjavik and had a miserable Norwegian dinner, cold stuff, in the number one hotel there. Nobody spoke to us, they were cold on the streets, they didn't like us at all.

They just never did like us, they don't like us now. I don't know why they don't, but they don't. I think they're suspicious of all people except the people that live there.

We stayed there and our main job was meeting convoys, escorting them over to England, meeting them and escorting them back to New York.

I never made a Murmansk run, never once. I started on one but it aborted for some reason or other and didn't go. I guess they got word that there was going to be a real shenanigan about it, because there was. The big German ships came out at that time, so we didn't go.

The only thing that we fouled up there was weather. I had one incident where one of our destroyers was torpedoed, about 300 miles south of us. I was called late at night, over the local circuit, by the Division Commander who had picked on my ship. The SOP there had said, "Send a destroyer down there and get this ship and bring it in port." So he picked me.

I got underway and had a devil of a time to get the King's guard to open the gate to let me out. It was dark as could be, oh boy was it dark. All we knew was just a general location of where this ship was. We had a pretty good idea of where it was torpedoed, we didn't know what he'd done since then except before his radio went out he said he was heading towards
That's all we had.

So I was in the dark, but I got that ship before dark that night. I found it. I didn't have any radar at that time. But we were lucky.

I had finally gotten radio contact with her and said, "Can you give me a puff of smoke? We know we're somewhere around you, but I don't know which way to turn now. I don't know if I've passed you, I don't know anything. Give me a puff of smoke." And we saw it, he was about thirty miles away.

To bring him back - he was badly damaged and lost a lot of men - I was afraid if I towed him his ship would break in two. The weather was bad, high seas. I lashed myself alongside that ship. We lashed ourselves together. I took him on the port side, because he got his torpedo on the starboard. That torpedo had blown straight up, and had split the deck. She was just like two ships. She was so weak amidships that if she got broadside to the sea she would have broken in two. Her keel was holding her together, and her deck armour was shedding most of the water. She did have some armour, not very thick, but it was quarter-inch stuff and that was holding her together.

I can't remember the name of the ship, but the skipper was Dana, in the class ahead of me. There were a lot of casualties aboard. The blast of the torpedo when the submarine had hit them had destroyed a lot of their medical supplies. They needed blood, and we had lots of volunteers who went over to give blood. Blood plasma was the main thing they needed. They ran out of that, and they ran out of ours.

So I sent a message back to please send a plane out and drop some plasma in a floating bag that we could pick up. That's normally very simple. They just fly over your bow and they drop it, and it has a long line attached. The bow usually catches that line and you hook it aboard.

The message went to our forces, and they had a Navy seaplane there that brought it out. I imagine we were within 200 miles of Iceland, so it took only an hour and a half to come out.

That thing dropped, and dropped just a little bit too close to the bow, stringing out the line that we were supposed to grapple and get aboard. It got fouled under the ship, and around the anti-submarine sound head. We could see it down there under water. We tried everything to pull that thing aboard. We grappled it, but we were afraid if we really put strength to it and pulled on the winch and tried to pull it aboard, we'd tear it apart and lose it.

So one man volunteered to go over the side in that water. I said, "You wouldn't last two minutes." He said, "I come from Michigan and we used to go with that group of "polar bear" people into the Michgan water every Christmas and New Year's. I can take any water." So I said, "Well all right, if you think you can. But I want you to get real bundled up in your diving suit. And I want you tied with good line, plenty of line, good heavy line. I don't want just a heaving line. I want something that can lift 180 pounds aboard, if we have to lift you aboard."

And thank goodness I did, because he hit the water and went out just like that. He just wasn't used to it. So we pulled him aboard.

We had to give up on that. And by this time the beating had busted the bag and it had gone, so we never got it.

In another hour another plane came, and he dropped the plasma properly and we got it. But it just goes to show what would happen if you had an accident and you got in that water up there. You just have no chance, not a chance. You're just immobilized in just a few seconds.

Q: The bravery of the man in offering is certainly remarkable.

Smoot: Very brave, but not very wise on my part. I should have known better, but he convinced me he could do it. And fortunately we got him aboard. He got a free half glass of liquor too, given by the doctor. That was one incident.

There were a lot of other little incidents, I don't know whether they're pertinent or not.

We went out when the TIRPITZ was coming through. We lined up across the whole fiord there, the Danish Straits. We lined up across there with the British and the Americans. That's right between Greenland and Iceland.

We had the word that she was coming down. She had gone up the coast of Norway and was heading west and was going to come down through those Straits between Iceland and Greenland. We deployed the whole fleet up there.

And we got into one of the worst blows that I've ever seen. My anemometer blew away at 119 knots. So I don't know what that weather was. Of course you couldn't see anything. At this point I still didn't have radar.

The battleships had radar and they could tell us where we were with respect to them, but in the weather we got lost and separated. We had an awful time getting back together.

It started in the daytime and lasted about three days. It was miserable. This was the worst storm I've ever been in in my life. I've been in typhoons and everything, but I've never been in anything like that. I don't know what that wind got up to.

Fortunately as far as destroyers are concerned I found out and the rest of us did, we were all good enough seamen, to keep our head into the wind and to keep our decks closed and don't let anybody go on deck, and don't open anything up so that the water gets down on your distribution systems and you lose control of the steering. The main thing is to keep your head into the sea, and find the speed that gives you the least beating.

We found that keeping our engines at seven knots gave us the best ride, but the battleships couldn't take it. They had to go faster, and they left us, and we lost them. So the destroyers were left behind.

Q: Isn't that a frightening experience?

Smoot: It's terrific. It's just the most horrible thing in the world to go through something like that.

We found out afterwards that though we were headed into the wind, which was out of the northeast, and were steaming seven knots, the difference between our actual position and our dead reckoning position showed that we were blown astern at the rate of about eight knots. So that we were going astern all the time, although we were making headway.

But this kept us in pretty good shape. And as far as the destroyers were concerned we had no damage and no trouble.

The battleships had bad trouble. The waves were so bad. On some of those old battleships they had catapults, on number three turret, the highest turret on the ships. These catapults were torn off and the planes were lost. It was terrible. And it broke deck fittings and took so much water over the side, because they were so frequently in phase with the waves, and water got down below.

Q: Do you recall the actual date of this, in the winter of '41?

Smoot: It was probably sometime in October or November. It wasn't long after that that the 7th of December came along.

As a matter of fact with the advent of Pearl Harbor, the battleships were all gathered together and mine was one of the destroyers that escorted them back to the Coast on their way to the Pacific.

Q: How did you learn of Pearl Harbor?

Smoot: All by radio.

We had a blow that night, not very bad, but I was up on the bridge. It was in the late afternoon. I was sitting up on the bridge. We had been ashore that day. The weather was coming up a little bit, so I was up on the bridge seeing that both anchors were out the way we wanted, and that the engines were warmed up and ready to go if needed. I was just sitting there talking to the officer of the deck. The radioman came up and handed me a radio message which said, "Pearl Harbor being bombed by Japanese. This is no drill."

Then of course things started popping. We started getting elaborations and details. Oh boy, before the day was over things looked mighty grim.

Q: What was your personal reaction?

Smoot: Couldn't believe it. I just wouldn't believe it. I couldn't believe that we would be caught that way, that our intelligence would let them get in without our knowing it.

Then of course the next thought was – well, it won't be long because we'll get them, we'll get them. They had to be pretty close, we'll find them, we'll get them.

I just couldn't believe it. I couldn't believe that we didn't have intelligence on that, and that we would have known when they got that close. And I'm still incredulous about it.

Q: Lots of books have been written pro and con on that too.

So then you did take the battleships back through the Canal?

Smoot: We went to New York first, then the destroyers went into Boston.

I've skipped an incident that was quite important in my life, during the period that we were doing convoy duty on the Atlantic Coast and before I went to Iceland. I think it was during that period; I was still on the MONSSEN. I think it must have been just before we went to Iceland.

My family had moved to Boston and we were getting prepared for this Iceland trip. As a matter of fact, we had made one convoy trip up there and had come back. I thought, "Oh Lord, I hope I never have to go up there to have any duty," because although we never went into the place we saw nothing but bad weather.

So we came back and we were in drydock in Boston getting the bottom fixed up and scraped and propellers relined, and doing little jobs that are necessary to do before you go out on another cruise.

I got word that I would be undocked the next morning, and to be prepared to go to sea on a special mission, and that I'd get information later what it was.

So we were all ready to go to sea, we were undocked, just my ship. I had my dockside test and everything went fine. The Engineer was perfectly satisfied and we were all lined up to go.

I finally got a message to rendezvous with the USS WASHINGTON, a new battleship, at a point at sea which required me to go through the Cape Cod Canal and meet her in the Atlantic Ocean at a given time. That was all right, I had been through the Cape Cod Canal before, there's nothing to that.

Everything was fine, and we started off. I left Boston, and went down through the Sound. It was getting on towards night. I knew I'd have to make the passage at night. I had to make it at that time to make my rendevouz the next morning, which was about forty miles south of the Canal.

As we started through the Canal it started to snow. Oh boy, did it snow. It was just terrific. You'd turn on your lights, and all it did was throw the lights right back into your eyes. So I couldn't see anything. There were no navigational lights in the Canal at that time at all, they were all blacked out for national security. They had little blue lights that sat way down close to the water. You couldn't see them until you were right on top of them. Of course I still had no radar.

The only thing that I could do was to use my sound gear, and the water was so muggy that I got echoes from everything. But at least I could tell if I was clear ahead, and I used that to the limited extent possible.

Finally the Navigator came to me and said, "Captain, I think we'd be foolish to try to go through. Even if we get through the Canal, which isn't too hard, going through the other end there are two places that open up very wide and then you have a narrow gap to go through before you come into that Sound." (Or whatever it is that's on the south end of the Cape Cod Canal.)

So I sent a message to the Task Force Commander and said, "Request delay in rendevouz, consider it dangerous to proceed." Message came back, "Not approved, make rendevouz on time." It ended up, "Good luck."

I didn't make it, I went aground. I hung up on a rock. I really hung up on a solid submerged crag. The ship rode up on it, pierced the hull, and went down on it. We had a sharp pinnacle of rock inside the ship, protruding into the forward peak tank almost three feet. The state of the tide was low, and I knew that eventually we'd float off. I reported my predicament.

I knew that if I swung to port I was sure I'd really make a mess of that ship. The wind was on the starboard bow. So for over two hours we continued full speed backing on the port engine, and it kept my head steady right the way I was.

I tried to get an anchor out. I could get a boat over the side, but it would have been foolish. I would have just lost it, and the crew. That kind of risk was too real. I didn't want to take a chance. I did drop the bow anchor, but I didn't let it run free, I just dropped it so that it was on the ground. I knew it was on the ground. I didn't want it to catch on anything in case I came off. I wanted to know that it was ready to go.

About dawn just as daylight was breaking the snow had stopped and it was quite a calm nice morning. I was able to see exactly where I was and what I had done. I had just missed the channel by not more than the width of the ship, that's all. I was outside to the left of the channel.

Suddenly we started backing. I let the anchor go down very slowly until it hit the ground. It hit ground and I stopped the engines. I stopped them just in time for the chain to take up, and take a little bit of grab on the bottom. But the stern of the ship went aground on the other side of the channel.

I really polished my propellers, but had no damage there at all, but they really polished in the sand - no rocks over on that side fortunately.

But there I was and now the tide was going out, and it left me high and dry there for another two or three hours. Here the bow was clear, and the stern held fast in soft sand. I was in a mess.

And so they had to cancel our rendevouz because inspection of our bow indicated it would be dangerous to go to sea. So with rising tide I came off the sand smoothly and I went back to the shipyard. I thought that was the end of my career, that was the end for sure.

At the Board of Investigation the serious thing was the matter of not making our rendevouz and going aground, which of course is inexcusable. You just don't go aground, but I did.

The Board gave me a reprimand, or a letter of censure is what it really is. The thing that saved me from getting a court martial, charged with hazarding the ship and failing to meet a rendevouz in time of war, which was very serious, was the fact that I had sent a request not to go through the Canal, that I considered it dangerous, and that request was denied. And I was proceeding against my own desires and judgement. This was outlined by the Board of Investigation, that it was considered my judgement was better in that case.

The Unit Commander with whom I was to have a rendevouz had a division of battleships and was then in the WASHINGTON. He was the Admiral who was lost at sea on a later occasion and was never found. Suspicion was foul play. He was a character. Even if I could remember his name, I wouldn't say it.

Q: He wasn't lost at this time? It had no relationship to this?

Smoot: He was lost at a later date. There was no relationship to this rendevouz. It was a perfectly clear night, he was out on deck, and he just never was found.

Q: Did you ever know what the rendevouz was about?

Smoot: No, never did, never got the orders or anything. Didn't know what it was about, and never found out. Went back and got myself fixed up, and it was very shortly after that we went to Iceland.

Q: Now you're back from Iceland, and going into the Pacific. You went into New York or Boston you said -

Smoot: Yes, we did. This was a real hurried trip, so there was no time for anything. We were to get out to the Pacific as fast as we could.

We went into Boston just for supplies, and minor voyage repairs that were necessary, but none of us had voyage repairs.

We resupplied and went through the Panama Canal and up to San Francisco, and departed from San Francisco for Hawaii, but we didn't know our mission until we were way out.

Q: Was the whole squadron together at this time?

Smoot: Yes, our whole squadron was together, the same eight ships were still there.

Q: Who was the Squadron Commander, do you recall?

Smoot: I can't remember.

Q: I know that you did escort the HORNET on Doolittle's raid. Can you give us some background on that, as to whether you knew where you were going and what you were going for?

Smoot: We had no idea what we were going to do until we were way past Midway. As far as I was concerned, down at our level, we just were told that we were going on a special mission that would take us very close to Japan, that's all.

But we didn't know Jimmy Doolittle was aboard until we were well out past Hawaii. I could be wrong on the details of this, really my memory is not so good on details.

Q: What I suspected was that you might not have known the purpose or any of the details, until maybe even learning of it afterwards.

Smoot: They told us about it, and we were briefed by a long letter that was handed to us at sea by courier destroyer going around from ship to ship like we used to do - transferring mail and supplies and personnel. When we were well out to sea and way beyond Pearl Harbor we were told what the mission was.

We'd known something about it, because here were these Army planes aboard the carriers. That's not normal, to say the obvious.

Of course they hadn't practiced taking off at sea. I'll never forget the first one that took off. When they took off we were in a circular screen and I was on the HORNET's port bow about six or seven thousand yards away. We were looking back at her from an anti-submarine screen position - standard at that time. I remember seeing the first of those planes going down the deck, and it looked like he was never going off. But when he did he took off almost straight up. He wasn't going to hit that water.

Those Army boys didn't like that, they didn't like that at all. But they went off with no problems at all. They all went off, there were no casualties as far as I remember, not on the take offs.

We were given further information later by mail passed at sea as to their mission and what they were going to do and what they expected of us. I think we got within 300 miles of Japan.

It was really, as far as we were concerned, quite anti-climatic because we launched them and then headed back to Pearl Harbor.

We did have one contact at sea, one surface contact in that whole trip. And it was just a lumbering old Japanese fishing vessel. One of the destroyers was sent over to investigate. They determined that they didn't have anything aboard and there wasn't anything they could do about it, so they didn't sink it. They should have sunk it, but they didn't. They didn't find anything, it looked like a plain old fishing vessel. But you can't tell. I think I would have asked permission to take the crew off and sink it, but they didn't. So I guess they knew what they were doing.

Q: What did you do then, turn around and come back to Pearl, after the Doolittle raid?

Smoot: Turned around and came back to Pearl Harbor.

There we participated in several quite high level conferences. This was the first time I began getting into some high level conferences where I met some of the future famous naval leaders like Nimitz and Halsey, and the aircraft carrier commanders who were then just young Rear Admirals like Marc Mitscher.

Q: Do you have a recollection of meetings in which you participated where Admiral Nimitz was present?

Smoot: Oh yes, several, because I had known Admiral Nimitz from my early submarine days. He was a submariner then and my division commander when I was a young officer.

Q: I don't think we mentioned that.

Smoot: No. It didn't really affect me, except as it applied later when he was famous.

The thing about him was that he did remember me, when I saw him the first time at a conference in Pearl Harbor. As I remember it, that's the conference that we had after the Jimmy Doolittle raid where we were briefed for the first time on the plan of action for the Coral Sea, and what we were to do about it if we could. We were pretty far away, and things were developing pretty fast down there, but they needed help.

I don't remember the carriers that we had. The LEXINGTON was already down there. She was there and we were going down to help her. I've forgotten which Admiral it was.

We hurriedly made all of our logistic preparations there in Pearl Harbor, and just rushed like the devil to get down to the South Pacific to help in the Coral Sea battle, but by the time we got down there it was all over. We didn't participate in it at all.

Q: Would you be more specific as to 'we'?

Smoot: My ship was moved around so much at that time that I don't remember. But when I talk about 'we' now and from now on it will be some kind of task groups, and for the first part of it it will be with carriers. Because I did work with carriers all during the first part of the Solomons campaign, up until the time that we actually entered the Solomons, and then I went over to the Landing Force.

So when I'm talking about 'we' on that trip down for the Coral Sea action I'm talking about a division of two carriers, all the supporting elements including one of the new battleships as I remember and the cruisers and destroyers support that went with it. The Task Force Commander was the boss, who would get us together on his flag ship, and all the skippers would be called and we would be briefed as to the coming operation. This required deployment as fast as we could all the way down to the South Pacific.

Incidentally this was the first time that I had crossed the equator, I believe.

As far as we were concerned, we didn't get into the Coral Sea action. It was all over by the time we got there.

I'm a little vague as to what we did then. We operated as a high speed Carrier Task Force Support Group for preparations and landings around - where were we then?

Q: I think you must have gone quite soon back up north to Midway, within a month.

Smoot: We did. But there were some interesting actions that developed at that time - never turned into any warfare as I remember.

What we were doing - and I didn't learn about it until later because I didn't have high enough clearance to know it at that time - was fooling the Japanese into making them think we were going to stay down there. The Japanese were pretty sure they had Midway in the bucket, and that there was only one or two carriers up there to meet them. That was the whole idea.

Late one night, I remember, after a contact report was made by a Japanese plane we drove him off. But we made sure he made the contact and saw us.

We were just lazing around heading south, going slow. Then we turned north, put on the speed, and headed north. We got to Pearl Harbor, fueled, provisioned, and got out just in time for Midway.

Midway was a disappointment to me, I didn't really get into it. Because for some reason or other they put me with the Supply Force, the tankers. So just about all I could do was sit around by the radio and listen to what was happening. I didn't see a thing in the Midway campaign. I just stayed with the tankers. It was a great disappointment.

I don't know why they did that to me, because while we weren't the newest type destroyer we were still quite modern. But we did not have radar yet, and we did not have the newest sound gear and the new sound equipment that goes with it. So I guess they did it because we weren't fully equipped yet.

It was after the battle of Midway that we went back in Pearl Harbor, and there we finally got our radar and the most modern equipment for anti-submarine warfare. That took a couple of weeks.

Q: Do you have any anecdotes at this time concerning Admiral Nimitz, either in the early days when he was a division commander or when you saw him in Pearl?

Smoot: It's hard to describe a man like Nimitz. He was one of the kindliest and most gracious gentlemen I've ever known.

I'd like some psychologist to explain to me some time how we could have four five-star Admirals with the stature and ability that took us through World War II that were four of the most different men in the world. I still get amazed about it.

Nimitz was one of the kindliest. I've never seen him ruffled or upset. Inspiring in his billiance, inspiring in his ability to let you feel that he has complete and utter confidence in you. He had those qualities of a leader that endeared him to you, at the same time you had great awe and respect for his ability.

I don't know that I've ever met a man who's impressed me more than Nimitz, from the point of view of just being a great wonderful man.

Quite different from the man I call my Navy father. He's entirely different. He was closer to me, but what a vibrant vital vindictive old son of a gun. He was something - Reggie Kaufman.

Q: Admiral Nimitz seems to be almost without any flaws.

Smoot: As far as I'm concerned he had none, and and as far as the Navy's concerned I think he stands at the top of the admired leaders. History will prove, as far as I'm concerned, that he was the greatest man.

Q: I'm sorry that you didn't get into the battle of Midway, but maybe it was for the best.

Now you've been at Pearl Harbor and had your ship modernized in every way.

Smoot: Pretty well fixed up now. Now things are heating up down in the South Pacific.

Q: You are about in August, going down to participate in the assault and occupation of Guadalcanal.

Smoot: That was quite an exciting affair. It turned out to be, as far as my experiences were concerned, the first time I became involved in hot warfare, my baptism of shooting to kill.

The Task Force was quite a large one. As I remember it was commanded by Admiral Turner. There were others - Fletcher was one. I could be wrong about the overall command.

By this time the destroyers had lost their identity with given squadrons and divisions. We had a Division Commander, yes, but you lost your identity as an entity in terms of a destroyer division. The division commanders and the squadron commanders were utilized as some kind of a task group commander for the given mission. You didn't serve as a squadron commander as such, except in matters of administration, and that almost went by the board during the war.

We didn't go direct to the Solomons; we went to Tongatabu. Close to the islands of Tongatabu there is a large lagoon that for the purpose of rehearsals, for the landing that we anticipated in Guadalcanal, served our purpose pretty well. So we had a full dress rehearsal for the landing in Tongatabu.

I had never been with amphibious forces before. And this was fascinating for me to watch, to see these people being lowwered from our combat transports and put in the water and go skitting off in little boats against a beach that was firing at them. . They even had blank shells over there to simulate the resistance.

My ship with many other destroyers was attached to a division of cruisers, and we served as that division of cruisers' anti-submarine screen and anti-aircraft screen. Our mission was to defend the landing force against hostile combat forces of any kind.

We were close enough in the rehearsals to see what was going on, and I found out afterwards that we would be close enough to see what was going on when we got into the real landing, even though we didn't actually support the landing in terms of firing at the beach. We didn't have that kind of armament to really do the work at the beach that was needed. Other destroyers that came out later than mine did have that, and they were used as the landing force support ships who went with the amphibious groups.

We were with the high speed task forces that supported the engagement. I was with this all during the Guadalcanal campaign. For the actual landing however I was detached from the aircraft carrier group and joined a task group that operated back and forth across the southern end of the entrance to Guadalcanal.

Admiral Norman Scott was our Division Commander. There was also a British cruiser in our group. And there were four destroyers, including my ship.

We had precise patrol areas designated when we went into the landing area – later to be known as "Iron Bottom Bay." We were going into real war now, my first experience at real war. This was the first counterattack that America had made, the first one in World War II.

The raid of Jimmy Doolittle's was a brave demonstration and it did a wonderful thing for our morale at home.

This Guadalcanal campaign was the first big thing we were going to do in terms of counterattack. We cruised those beautiful southern waters just as casually and unconcerned as though we were going to a Sunday School picnic. It didn't seem like war at all to me at first.

All during that quiet cruise from Tongatabu, all the way down the south end of the whole Solomons chain, and up on the west side of Guadalcanal, that great big island to the east of us full of Japanese, we didn't have a single incident.

There wasn't a plane. There wasn't a contact, there was nothing.

God was with us during the approach, because we had a complete overcast of clouds just about five hundred feet above us, complete dense white overcast of clouds, a perfectly calm night, not a ripple on the ocean.

We came down through the northern entrance to Guadalcanal. Everything went exactly according to plan. We took our positions, and made the landing. The landing was bitterly opposed, yes, but not initially as we thought it would be. I didn't see anybody getting shot at really, or hurt. We didn't have much to contend with as far as our position was concerned.

We could see the boys going ashore, and we could see the shooting and hear the shooting, but they soon disappeared into the jungle and we didn't see them anymore. It was a most prosaic type of thing. We had achieved complete surprise.

Then about two or three hours after the landing was made, and we were patrolling as ordered, the first group of Japanese bombers came in. Oh boy, we just turned the whole place loose. And I never saw so many bullets in my life going up against them. We knocked several of them down. I'll never forget that, it was the first time I'd seen a plane knocked out of the air by ground fire.

I was never severly threatened. We did have one strafe us, but the bullets didn't hit anybody or hurt anybody. They put a hole in the deck, but didn't hurt us. It was over before I knew it had really begun. They came in, dropped their bombs, and didn't hit anything or do any damage. They dropped their bombs on the beach, they didn't drop their bombs on us. They didn't come after us, they'd shoot at us on the way out.

So I thought, "So this is war. It's nothing." I would soon be dissuaded of that.

In another hour in came torpedo bombers, and they were after us. Just before that I had been called by the Group Commander to go down a channel behind a little island across the bay from Guadalcanal, the other one that they made a landing on. From a British ship I was to pick up an Australian naval officer who knew those waters like the back of his hand, and he was to guide me in behind this little island, where the Japanese had some Marines tied down across a bridge. They wanted my guns to shoot that bridge, and they'd tell me where to shoot in some of the caves.

So we took aboard this Australian officer, he did know the waters, and he told us where to go. We went around behind this island, Tulagi, or the small islands south of Tulagi that gave the Marines so much trouble.

We weren't behind there for more than fifteen minutes when the second raid came in. Of course we had procedures for raids. It was a question of whether or not I should go out and join the rest of the destroyers in the defense of the big ships against torpedo bombers or whether I should stay right there.

I just took a quick look at the situation and decided I could not get out in time anyway to do any good. While I was pretty well stymied over there as far as maneuverability was concerned, I could give a good account of myself if they decided to come after me.

We went on with the firing at this island, where the Marines told us to fire. We could see the shooting over there. This was my first sight of warfare.

I saw a Marine tank climbing up a hill, and I saw a group of Japs come out of a cave close by and pour gasoline over that tank and set it afire right in front of my eyes. Of course this was the first time that I realized what this was.

My Gunnery Officer saw those Japs running back, and he turned the whole broadside of the ship on that cave and blew it to smithereens. I hope we got them, I never did know.

We had to get out of there in a hurry after that anyway, because the Task Force Commander said that he wanted his group together before dark.

What good I did I don't know. I hope I sealed that one group of Japanese lives forever that got our boys, because that tank stopped right there and never moved again. The sight of war wasn't pretty under those conditions.

We began to learn the treachery and seriousness of the business. This was no fun, this was going to be real tough stuff.

Up to this time the only thing I'd had in my ship was one little hole from a rocochet from a bullet off the water, when this first raid came. That's all I'd had.

Then we cruised around all that day, and the next day the unloading went without incident, no more raids. It began to be very quiet.

We were called upon every once in a while for special bombarding, both on the Guadalcanal side and the Tulagi side. For some reason or other I seemed to be stuck over on the Tulagi side a lot of times. And there wasn't very much bombardment over there. The Marines had that place under control in jig time. So we stayed over there. This one little group that I was in stayed on the Tulagi side most of the time.

Then the third night we began getting word about a Japanese naval task force that was coming down from the north. This would be about the seventh or eight of August, as I remember.

During all the planning and arrangement for this the amphibious commander had called the senior group commanders of all of the fighting ships to a conference on his flag ship, which was near Tulagi close to our side. They were getting all the word all together. They were all being briefed as to how to meet this surface threat coming down from the north.

We didn't get much word about it, because every senior officer was in that flag ship. Not being at that level I really didn't know what was planned, except listening on the circuit we could hear and decode enough to know that there was a task force of Japanese navy ships, a big one, that was coming down through the slot and would be there about midnight. So we figured we were going to have a battle that night. This would be our first surface Navy battle.

Far be it from me to criticize what they did, but I never will understand why they disposed our forces the way they did. I just never will understand. To me it gave the Japanese every advantage.

They put a couple of destroyers up north of the entry into the sound. I remember one of them was the "Blue." A classmate of mine had command of it, a fellow named Williams. They patrolled back and forth up there, and they duly notified us when the Japanese ships came. They, the Japanese, didn't do anything about our two DDs, they didn't fire at them or anything.

Meanwhile we were disposed in four separate groups in a great big broad bay far away from the entry point, and none of us really knew what the other was doing. None of us were under any coordinated control at all. The senior Admiral of the whole group was ashore, or else he was at a conference somewhere. He didn't exercise any centralize command at any time during the engagement.

It ended up being a fiasco. The Japanese came in one entry, sunk and damaged a lot of ships, and went on out the other. And we shot at each other.

This was the first battle of Savo Island, and it was a fiasco. It was just a fiasco. It just showed how "unbattle-wise" we were as a fighting outfit.

Q: What was your position during this?

Smoot: Way down at the southeast side, south and east of Tulagi. We didn't get anywhere near anything. All we could do was see the fighting up north of us, and see the ships when they got hit. Nothing came close to us. We didn't fire a gun. In that respect we were fortunate, I suppose.

But to me why in the world - here is a perfect situation for a navy force to cross the T, and to dispose all his forces in one area, all together under one command, and let loose at the enemy, one by one, as they close the trap.

They, the Japs, had to come through a narrow inlet. We could have lined ourselves up and have picked them off one at a time. It would have been duck soup.

I guess the Japs realized at that time that we were pretty unbattlewise. And it was a terrible fiasco.

We were ready, we could have knocked them out. We could have out gunned them, we could have outmaneuvered them. We had them in a perfect position to cross the T. This is the classic Navy battle which we did later, and probably the last time it will ever happen, at Suragao.

Q: Were you aware of the frustrations at that time?

Smoot: I couldn't help but keep saying to my gang around the bridge, "Why in the devil don't we get into this? What are we doing down here waiting to be picked off one at a time? What's the matter with us?"

We could see all the shooting. And there we were just patrolling a square, with another group somewhere else patrolling a square. The only ones they got were two of our task groups up north of us. They got three of our big cruisers. It was just a fiasco.

Q: And they were afriad they were going to be followed, and nothing happened to follow them up.

Smoot: Nothing. It was a disgraceful allied defeat. That was a great lesson to all of the Navy. And it's a part of our history that I don't think we can be very proud of.

About two days later we all got underway and left the area.

Q: I have a reference to the battle of the Eastern Solomons later on in August. Do you have any recollections on that?

Smoot: That was an anti-aircraft battle. We were supporting the aircraft carriers and the Japanese planes went after them. They weren't too interested in the DDs.

We did have an attack on us. We had about three attacks on us, I guess. I've got some good pictures of those.

We were really dashing around and we were somewhat more battlewise at this time. We were spinning in circles, and firing and shooting.

It seems to me that one of our carriers did get hit at this battle of the Eastern Solomons, not bad, not sunk, but did get hit - had his deck ruined, and had to go back and get repaired.

None of the destroyers was hurt. I remember our guns were sure hot when we got through.

We alternated between high speed task forces and amphibious groups down there to relieve each other of the type of duty and give us a chance to resupply and to learn the other part of warfare. It was a good idea.

I was fortunate to get in that one battle and actually see an attack on our forces by a determined group of Japanese bombers. A lot of them hit the water, and it looked like they were starting that kamikaze business at that time. We didn't realize it, we thought they were hit. But I believe that one that did hit the side of the carrier, the one that got hit then, decided that was the way to do it. He went in with his plane and hit him and really messed him up.

Q: I think it was the SARATOGA.

My next reference is in September. The battle of Eastern Solomons was late August. Then I have a reference to September and October of the incident when you drove off Japanese forces that was attacking the ALHENA.

Smoot: After I reported back to the amphibious forces, we made our headquarters at an island about 150 or 200 miles south of Guadalcanal, called Espiritu Santos. There's where we would resupply and reprovision and stand by for calls to escort resupply ships going up to Guadalcanal. The ALHENA was one of them. I don't know what kind of supply she carried, whether it was food or ammunition or both. Two of us went along, two destroyers.

This was the second trip that I'd made with the ALHENA. The first time there was no incident at all. We just took her up and back. During the time that she was unloading at Guadalcanal, we'd get fire support calls from the various and sundry commands ashore.

I never will forget one where I was close to the shore up towards the north end of the island, answering call for firing ashore. My men were looking at the beach. They looked up on a hill and saw a man wigwagging at them, way up high in the hills. We were all pretty leery of Japanese at that time.

He was saying, "Send boat ashore." I wasn't going to send a boat ashore and get trapped by some Japanese. I didn't know what it was. We couldn't tell who it was. They were in Army drill, and in that uniform the Japs and Americans looked exactly the same when they were that far away. We didn't know who it was, and I wasn't going to take any chances.

I tried to figure out some way. I asked my signalman, "Isn't there some kind of a recognition system that we have?" No, we didn't. There's another incredible thing that was later corrected.

Then on a hunch our signalman wigwagged the question, "Who won the World Series in 19--?" and it came back correct. This seemed pretty good to us. So we sent a boat in and out came the famous Chesty Puller and his aide and a couple Marines.

Chesty Puller said, "I've got a whole group of my men up there in the hills." This was a great guy. He came up on the bridge and said, "I've got to get some men out of trouble. They are trapped up there. I doggone near lost my life getting down to the beach. Let me tell you where to shoot."

So he went up into control with my Gunnery Officer, and we just turned loose on this island. We just ploughed it with bullets, straight up and down the middle. Then we spread the fire power up two sides, and the Marines came down to the beach between. We sent for landing boats and they arrived in good time. We stayed there and supported them through this whole operation, until they got out of that trap and they all got back to their group again. This was a result of our fire power, and just happening to look up and see a lone signalman deep in the jungle.

This was a fortunate thing. Of course Chesty was duly thankful, and we became great and close friends.

After it was all over and while I was steaming slowly back to the landing area to let Chesty off, with his aides, he went down into my clean cabin with white tablecloth and had a great big hot steak dinner, took a hot shower, and cleaned up. The boys washed his clothes and dried them. We fixed him up with fresh underwear, gave him a bag of cookies and cakes and cigarettes and whatnot. Everything we could do to help in their rugged life ashore we did.

As he went over the side I said, "Chesty, glad we could help you out." He said, "Thank you very much. God, I wouldn't have your job for anything in the world." I said, "You mean to tell me you'd go back and go into that messy stuff over there and get yourself filthy and live on C rations. You've come to see the kind of life I lead out here and you prefer yours?" He said, "I sure do. When you get hit where are you? When I get hit I know where I am."

We were both in the right places. That was just one little incident. This was the first trip with the ALHENA. She unloaded and we took her back, and we had no incidents at all.

I don't remember the interval between this trip and the second trip with the ALHEAN, because it seems to me that there were several things that went on. I don't know how long it was or whether some of the outlying battles kept us so tense down there that we lost track of time.

So this trip with the ALHENA came as quite a burden to us. I remember that the crew was very tired. But it was all we had to do at that time, just to say, "This is war friends, and we've got to take the good with the bad. Let's not let ourselves get into any kind of a condition where we're going to criticize the powers that be. This is the beginning of trouble."

This critical attitude is typical of fighting forces under strain. We were getting tired. I hadn't realized how tired I was getting. Some times this is significant in the things that you do afterwards.

Q: Do I understand that you were being critical, that you were being asked to make so many trips up and back?

Smoot: Yes. This was the general thing that came from the crew and the younger officers — "When do we get a rest? When are we going down to Funafuti? When are we going to do this?"

"Well, we'll get our turn." So the morale began to be a problem. Some times a skipper particularly begins to worry whether or not he's going to get the best out of his men when the chips are down. When you go on a trip like this, you've got to be very sure that you don't make mistakes. One mistake — that's it. You don't get another chance in warfare, because it was getting kind of grim around there now.

However we took the LAHENA up and there was nothing untoward or suspicious or anything that happened on the way up as I remember. We went to Guadalcanal and discharged, and then were on our way back, if I remember this correctly, when things popped.

In fact I think that was one of the significant things about it out there. One of the reasons that it wasn't so dangerous becuase if whatever happened had of happened with her loaded we might have lost the ALHENA.

We were on the way back and had just cleared the channel, and were headed south outside of Guadalcanal to the open ocean. All of a sudden trouble started on the ALHENA. I didn't know what it was. We didn't see anything, we didn't hear anything. There wasn't any sound of an explosion, there wasn't any fire, there wasn't anything.

Finally we received a garbled message from the ALHENA that she'd been hit, torpedoed, and that it was definitely from a submarine.

The series of events that followed are not awfully important, but in the light of subsequent events and questions that were later asked of me, I tried to analyze as closely as I could what I did and why I did it at the time.

The first thing I did was to head right back towards the ALHENA, and got as close as I could to her. I'm sure that my idea there was to be sure that if she was going to blow or was in any danger of having a fire, we could be in better position to assist.

Secondly we weren't too far from reefs. The wind was in such a direction that if she couldn't use her engines she was going to drift and we were going to be in serious trouble. And I would like to take her in tow as soon as I could.

Now those are the things that I remember. This is what went through my mind. That's why I went back to her as fast as I could.

We were alone with her this time, we'd left the other destroyer at Guadalcanal. There wasn't another destroyer with me, I was alone with her.

And I was quite severely criticized for doing what I did, because my main objective at that time should have been to go after that submarine, if there was a sub. That should have been the thing to do - go get her, get that submarine, and sink it. Which I didn't do. I took action to save our own ship, justified or not, I did.

But I soon found out that the ALHENA was all right – she had power, she could make a little headway, and there was no fire. Her Captain signaled that all he wanted was to be sure that he had air cover. And he asked me to get a message off to the Task Force Commander that he was in trouble and wanted air support in case of a raid. And he wanted a tug to come up and tow her and get her in a safer location as soon as possible. He would probably be a prime target for both enemy air and submarine. Once the Japs have a cripple they send off the word where the crippled one is so they can finish her off.

That was my main objective – to see if she could get underway, then protect her, and then go after the submarine if possible.

Of course it was probably too late then, I don't know whether I ever would have gotten her anyway to start with. However that's not the right thing to say, because I might have been able to destroy that submarine, if there was one. As I say, if I had it would have been fine. Nevertheless my main concern was with the ALHENA.

It ended up that we finally took that ship in tow, because it took almost thirty-six hours to get a tug up there, and some more of our destroyers to help screen the ship because I couldn't defend her against anything. We just had the luck of the gods with us, because the Japanese decided not to follow up on that, and they never did send in anything else after her.

We got the ALHENA back with no further incident. The only significant part of it — they made a great todo out of it because the matter of war and the matter of principle was involved there. Perhaps I should have gone after the submarine immediately, I don't know.

Q: The citation for which you received the third Bronze Star Medal says that you drove off the attacking submarine and removed the wounded and contributed to the saving of the ship.

Smoot: I did remove some of the wounded. And I did contribute to saving the ship, because I took her in tow. I sent my machinist over there, who helped the people with some material that I had that they didn't have — welding equipment and whatnot that would help them. I did all that, true.

Did I drive off the submarine? Not consciously, I drove her off because I was there and because I dashed back just as fast as I could and circled the ALHENA.

It could be that the submarine, if there was one, just took flight. He didn't make a second follow-up attack. He had a cripple that he might have sunk with a follow-up attack, but he didn't. I never saw him, I never got a ping on him, I never located him. He never came back. And I got the ALHENA back safely.

They can word the citation any way they want. The facts remain that I didn't consciously drive off any submarine. I went back to protect the ALHENA, that's what I did.

I went back just as fast as I could, I circled her fast. And it's probably that action that sent the submarine skyhooting somewhere over the horizon to get out of the way.

Q: What's that word "skyhooting" that you're using?

Smoot: That's an old western cowboy word. You hoot along towards the skyline, chasing cattle.

Q: Do you recall any other incidents in connection with your duty down in Guadalcanal? Were you at that time pretty much through with the duty down there?

Smoot: That just about did it, as far as I was concerned. Time is vague down there.

I was getting pretty sick at this time, in pretty bad shape. I finally had to be carried off the ship. The doctors knew it. I had hemorrhoids so badly that I couldn't sit down or do anything.

Somewhere along this time, after the ALHENA incident, we had a couple of more cruises up there, none incidental, nothing happened. One was a large convoy we took up, there was nothing about that.

Then finally the MONSSEN was given a little rest and rec-reaction period down at the French island south of there - I forget what it was called.

It was down there that my Executive Officer went to the Task Force Commander and told him that he thought I was sufficiently bad physically that the medical authorities ought to take a look at me. Halsey was down there at the time, and Halsey's doctor came over. And I got off that ship that night.

They flew me home and I was in the hospital. I had lost over thirty pounds, I was down to skin and bones, had no appetite.

They were right, I should have left. But this was my ship, I had commissioned it. This was the only war the Navy had ever been in, as far as I was concerned, and I wanted to see it through.

But there comes a time when you're more harm to yourself and your crew than you are good. I think that was rapidly approaching with me. And if the Exec hadn't done it, I'm afraid I would have had to because I don't know whether I could have made another tour or not.

Q: Did you resent his going to the doctor?

Smoot: No, I didn't. He did it on his own. He was a fine young fellow, and I took it that he had only my best interest at heart, and perhaps the ship's best interest too. And he was probably right.

It turned out that he got Command of the ship by accident. The new skipper that had been ordered to it to relieve me was killed in an airplane crash on the way out there. So they didn't order another one. And he took command and took it into the big battle when the ship was lost in November at Guadalcanal.

Meanwhile I went back to the hospital. I was in the hospital about three months. They sent me all the way back to San Diego. My blood pressure was bad, I was in very bad shape. It took almost a year to come back.

Q: Was that one of the reasons why your next shore duty was in San Diego?

Smoot: Yes, that and propinquity. It was there, it was convenient.

The skipper of the Sound School at that time, a fellow named Burhans, had diabetes and didn't know it, or didn't do anything about it. He went to sea on the PORTLAND and killed himself on the PORTLAND.

He was a fine fellow, and I relieved him in Command of the Sound School. The reason was that I was there, I was available. I was practically well, but not well enough to go to sea.

Burhans wanted to go to sea in Command of a cruiser. So I got the Sound School and he went to sea. That's how I got that job.

And that was an interesting job because at the time the Sound School was down at the destroyer base. It was a motley group of ships and small offices and a terrible arrangement to try to run a Sound School. Admiral King sent one of his civil engineers out there to my staff. With him he sent three million dollars and said, "Find a place and build a Sound School."

So I went to the District Commandant. We had a place where the present Sound School is that was available right close to the Training Center, close to the water, in a very good location not far from the port entrance. It all looked pretty good, the land was leased, and the three million dollars set up a Sound School in no time at all.

Q; That must have been a source of satisfaction to you that you accomplished that.

Smoot: I thoroughly enjoyed the job. We built three large barracks. We built a technical building, and a sound maintenance building. There were about seven buildings we put up there in a period of a little over four months.

Meanwhile they started sending in the students faster than we could take care of them. So we used part of the Training Center for barracks until we could catch up with them. But we were really turning them out, because we had good teachers. We got wonderful instructors, and we were really turning out the sound boys then. We had the latest equipment, the best equipment. It was just thoroughly satisfactory.

They finally sent the Commander of the Training Command there too, an Admiral named Braisted. He came in and took my office, and became my boss.

I was promoted to Captain there, no exams or anything, just appointed while I had Command of this school.

Of course after it was all set up, ready to go, going fine, the organization was good, Braisted had come (he was more or less the overseer of the while thing), his flag had been hoisted, and I had done my job, so I sent a message to CinCPac and asked to go to sea. I wanted to go to sea. The war was getting on. Things were happening and I wanted to go back. I felt fine and I wanted to get another Command and go to sea.

Q: Is it part of your personality that once you've started something and it's going well that you want to go on and do something else?

Smoot: Sure, I want to do something else. Meet the challenge and let somebody else run it. Build it, get it going, but let somebody else run it.

But the letter never got past Braisted. He sent it back to me, torn in two, and said, "Admiral King has told me that all ASW assignments are frozen through the duration of the war. That was one of the conditions I got when I took this job. You are going to stay right here."

I took the letter and said, "Oh I can't sit still with this job Admiral. I've got to go to sea. Look what's happening down there. I just want to get out and shoot at Japs again. Besides this would ruin my career, I'd be nothing but a specialist ashore. I'm a line officer, I want to Command again."

"Sorry," he said, "very sorry, but that's the way it's going to be."

I took the letter back to my office and I sat down and I thought for a long long time. I took out a piece of paper and wrote in my own handwriting a letter to my good friend, Admiral Kaufman, who was then Commander Destroyers Pacific. I enclosed the letter that I had given to Braisted, and I enclosed it in the condition that it came back to me - torn up with his remarks on it, "Disapproved," just written across in big red pencil. I said, "Is this final? Is there any thing that you can do?"

About three weeks later I had orders to Command a squadron of destroyers. Braisted sent for me and said, "You went over my head, didn't you?" I said, "No, not exactly, I didn't go over your head. I just wrote to a friend, a personal letter to a friend, that's all."

He said, "Who was it?" And I said, "Well you know him very well. He's a classmate of yours." He said, "You wrote to Reggie Kaufman, didn't you?" I said, "Yes," and he said, "You went over my head."

I said, "He's not over your head, he's just a friend of mine. All I did was ask him if there was any thing he could do, that's all. Because I think by me staying here for the rest of the war, you wouldn't get any thing out of me and I wouldn't get anything out of the job."

He was awful mad at me, very mad with me. He gave me a very very mediocre, almost unsatisfactory, fitness report.

Q: Did he say why in the fitness report?

Smoot: Yes. He alluded to the fact that I got my job at sea against his recommendation and over his disapproval.

Q: In effect he was saying why he gave you less than outstanding when he explained that.

Smoot: Yes, that he did.

Then I had this series of Commands with Reggie Kaufman.

Miss Kitchen: You had a series of varied duties for the next six months, Admiral. Can you somewhat pull them together and tell me where you were and waht you did and why?

Admiral Smoot: Yes, it is sort of a confusing period, and confusing to me at the time.

My original orders sent me to Command of a destroyer squadron that was scattered all over the Pacific Ocean. As a matter of fact, at times there was a doubt whether it ever was an entity that could be identified as a squadron. Nevertheless it was on the books as a squadron, and that's the orders that I had, because he had to have some sort of orders to get me out to Pearl Harbor and get me started in the work that he wanted.

So when I got to Pearl finally and reported to him there was one of the destroyers, only one of the destroyers, of that squadron in Pearl Harbor at the time. The rest of them were scattered all over, under different commands and under different areas, doing different duties, and it didn't look like they'd ever be gotten back together again.

This was the time during the war when they were running the slot and when we were losing a lot of destroyers, so really their operations officers had themselves a job to keep any kind of an organization together at all. They did a marvelous job keeping enough destroyers on the front line, keeping them active and keeping them going and under fighting condition. It was really a rough period.

So this was a Command that Kaufman used more or less to get me out to his Staff to brief me, then find a job for me. That's what he really did, that's what it amounted to.

My benefactor just did me a great turn even though he didn't have a job for me. That's what it amounted to.

The first thing that came up was a simple bombardment. I had no sooner gotten to the ship Reggie had assigned me and settled down and unpacked my bags and was ready to do something, than he sent for me again, or his operations officer did, and said that they were forming a group of inter-island bombardment destroyers. And that they would be in groups of four destroyers, and I would have Command of one group, and that my Command was a specified Task Unit. And he named the ships, and told me to work out an operations schedule and get going. My assigned destroyers were all over the Pacific, but we proceeded to get them together.

I took off from Pearl Harbor with some task force, and acted as screen commander for the task force. I think we had just finished the operation at Kwajalein. It seems to me I remember that Kwajalein was finished. We already had Tarawa. So we were setting up forward area bases. These destroyers were going out to be as useful as they could in whatever job that we were required to do.

While we remained organizationally under the Destroyer Pacific Command all the time, after we got to Kwajaelein the area Commander wanted somebody to keep annoying the Japanese on the uncaptured islands, the ones that had been bypassed. These were about four groups of islands that were right around close there, consequently this was the job that I inherited.

We'd proceed to these bypassed islands and we'd shoot them up, daylight and dark and odd and sundry times, and they'd shoot at us too. Nothing very serious, because they didn't have much left to shoot with, nor were there many healthy Japs left. They didn't have any support and very little food, I guess. They led miserable lives, but we just made it more miserable for them by coming at all hours and keeping them awake shooting their place up and then going on to the next island. This I did for quite a while, maybe a couple of months.

Meanwhile my Command was changed from this that and the other thing, but it was still the same job. Until finally Kaufman came out to visit us in the forward area, at this time Kwajalein. He came aboard my ship and said, "Have you had enough of this now?" I said, "Well, you got anything better?"

He said, "Yes. We're going to take Guam. We've got Einewetok and that's all secured. We're setting up a forward base in Einewetok. I want to send all of the tenders that I've got and can spare to Einewetok."

"I'd like you to set up a destroyer base out there, all afloat. Don't get the idea of going ashore, I don't want you going ashore. Stay onboard ship, and set up a destroyer base at Einewetok. I will call you -- (then he sort of searched his mind). Have you got any idea?"

I said, "Well, what is it going to be? What's the job going to be?" He said, "You're going to be my representative really there." I said, "Well call it that - Destroyer Representative in Forward Area."

That was quite an interesting job, not very exciting. At one time I had six destroyer tenders, all anchored in Einewetok lagoon. They were busy constantly. The destroyers would go out to Guam, do bombardment duties and return to Einewetok. They'd all have troubles - they'd need new officers and men and repairs and supplies and upkeep and rest and recreation. And we gave it to them.

It was quite an interesting job, a hectic job, day and night, with never any sleep, going all the time, constantly.

We had one very interesting experience that perhaps the medicos might take up some day. As you know, one of the big problems that we had, and it developed badly as the war went on, were the homos aboard the ships and their activities. Where you don't tolerate the homos aboard ships, the general idea is to send them some place and put them in the brig. That's all we know to do, until they can be rehabilitated.

All the brigs on the six tenders were soon full with homosexuals. So I sent word back to Reggie, "Brigs are full and still coming in. What do?" He, very like him, sent back, "It's your problem. Your worry about it, I haven't any brigs."

It was getting so bad that I would put them on any ship that would go back to the States that I could, but most of the skippers didn't want any part of them. They had their own troubles. Their own brigs were filled. And they wanted an easy cruise back to Pearl. They didn't want to be bothered with a bunch of these wild ones.

I was standing up on the CASCADE, my flag ship, one morning looking around on the beach and and I saw them building an airport over there. "Oh boy," I said to myself, "I'd hate to be in that kind of a job. Isn't that awful over there, that awful dust."

The heat was normally around 110,115. They were sleeping in quonset huts at night that you could fry an egg on. How they got that job done I'll never know.

I was looking through my glasses and saw on one end of the field there a great big old tough dark - not colored, but awful dark - hefty Marine with a black snake whip. And he was using it, I mean literally using it. If the Congressmen could ever have found out about this - oh boy, what would have been happening. He was driving those men like animals - Seabees and everything in the world.

I got in my little boat and went over there. And who should I meet in charge of that place but an officer by the name of Bat Cruise, out of the class of '22.

I said, "What are you doing over here?" He said, "I'm trying to build an airport. My God I'm having trouble. I can't get anybody. They won't work for five minutes, they faint and pass out." I said, "Do you need men?" He said, "Do I need men."

I said, "I haven't any authority to give them to you. I suppose that if I do this by force I can be sent to jail. but I've got another six brigs over here that are crammed with screwball homosexuals. If you can use them, they're yours." He said, "How are you going to get them over here?"

I said, "It's no problem getting them over here. I'll put them in a motor sailor with a couple of good boatswain's mates. If they start jumping over, they can jump over, and good riddance. There are sharks all over the place, I don't care." You've got to be tough.

I look back on it now and shudder. But they went over there. They growled and hollered. A lot of them said, "Any place is better than this, living this damn brig."

They went over there and worked under this man, and strangely enough their homo tendencies disappeared. They did not want to do that any more. Furthermore they started working, and they got a little bit of pride in what they were doing. It turned out to be pretty good.

I reported the circumstances to my doctor. I went to the doctor and I said, "What's with this? Is there some psychological thing about this that's made men out of them, and they suddenly found out that their genes are turning in that direction, or have turned in that direction, or something?"

He said, "I'd sure like to know. But it's something that we might make a note of and keep for the record." Whether they kept it for the record or not, I don't know, but anyway that's the fact of the matter."

Those men were used gainfully, and I kept the brigs empty. When they came in I'd send them over there. For the next two or three weeks it just worked wonderfully.

Q: How many were sent over, do you recall?

Smoot: First it was a boatload. I had those little forty-foot personnel boats that would take about thirty men, and I suppose it was pretty near full, about twenty or twenty-five men. I had six ships, in the brigs there were about six in each. But I did not send every one of them, some of them had other problems - they had to have court martials.

The ones that I could send were sent just because they were homosexuals, or they claimed to be homosexuals because they wanted to get out of the war. They found out that was a way they could go home.

Q: Did this seem to be a rehabilitation for all of them?

Smoot: Yes.

Q: Do you have any records to the fact that this did square them away?

Smoot: I never did follow it up, because I turned it over to the doctor, and I don't know what he ever did.

It wasn't long after this that I left. The operation in the forward area was over, and Libby had come back with his divison from Guam. And I had orders to relieve Libby as Desron 56.

The main problem out there was personnel. We had liquor problems, people on board ship drinking. We had people going nuts. One colored boy jumped over the ship out at Guam one day with his suitcase and said he was going to swim to the mainland. He didn't want to stay with the Americans any more, he wanted to go join the Japs.

We were in all kinds of administrative problems when we were in the forward area with my headquarters on the CASCADE. The CASCADE was a big ship, and perfectly comfortable and wonderful, but an awfully easy way to fight the war. There wasn't any fighting close to me.

Admiral Kauffman sent a relief out for me some time in the early fall of '44.

Q: My records are that you were out there from March until October. Then you took over the NEWCOMB in 1944.

Smoot: I did, I took over Desron 56 in the NEWCOMB down in Manus in September or October of '44.

Q: So you were in the forward area going from one job to another and eventually being representative in the forward areas for this six months period. Then you said you relieved Captain Libby then.

Smoot: That's what it was, yes.

I flew down to Manus and relieved Captain Libby down there. Then I became ComDesron 56, the flag ship was the NEWCOMB.

Q: From the time you became Commanding Officer of Destroyer Squadron 56 with your flag on the NEWCOMB, I'd like to have you start with the beginning operation which I indicate as Leyte. How many ships were in your squadron? Do you recall the names of those ships?

Smoot: Yes, there were eight ships in the squadron. I used to know them all by heart. The NEWCOMB, the BRYANT, the ROSS, the R. F. LEARY - I can't remember the others.

Q: Out of those ships, there were only two that survived this period. Is that correct?

Smoot: Yes, we had casualties, we sure did.

Q; The NEWCOMB and the LEARY.

Smoot: The LEARY survived, yes. So did the BRYANT, but the NEWCOMB - no.

We had many casualties, but that was to be expected in the warfare that we went through.

The squadron was assembled down in Manus, when I relieved Captain Libby. They had quite an envious war record at the time. They had been in most of the major landings as support. The ships were configured for their accuracy of fire in support of landings.

They had the latest and most sophisticated equipment for support of landing operations that we were going to have to go through. And they were truly well trained and beautifully oranized under Libby, who was their original Squadron Commander.

So I took over a really magnificent machine, a wonderful machine already made for me. All I had to do was just give the word and we went. So I can't take too much credit for what happened later, or any of the things that happened later. It was just inherited in the equipment and the way the ships were trained and the way they were handled and maneuvered and their experience at the time that I took it over.

I was fortunate that I did get it at a critical time in the war and I witnessed an awful lot of very interesting things. And that was a period of very hectic wartime activity, tension and death, and one of the most terrible times of the war - the time that the desperate Japanese started using the kamikaze attacks. We went through all of that and saw it first hand.

Heroics there were, yes. Hysteria there was, yes. Everything that you can attribute to the human being I saw, and saw it good. And I witnessed death at it's worst circumstances, death that hurt. And death to the point where later you just sort of became completely inured to. It's just something that happens, like breathing. It wasn't pretty.

We assembled in Manus. The ships were trained down there in the coming operation. We had a few minor practice landings. We were briefed. Leyte was the objective.

My immediate boss was Admiral Oldendorf, who had Command of all of the old battleships of the Force. The whole Force itself was under Kinkaid. He was the Tactical Commander for the landing and Oldendorf had all the combat ships, other than the carriers and their supporting ships.

Oldendorf was a very thorough man, a very thorough and meticulous man, and one for whom I had the greatest admiration, because he left no stone unturned to be sure that all of his Commanding Officers were versed in the way he thought and how he thought and how he was going to do this operation. His foresight, and foreseeing circumstances that might develop, imbued you with the fact that he wanted you to take the initiative when you saw it occur. All he wanted to do was to be sure that you had his guidelines for what was going to happen.

You could put his guidelines down - very very simple. And that's to go after them, get them, and don't let any of them get away. That was his idea. So it makes it pretty simple when the idea is to go lick them, and do it in the best way you can and as fast as you can.

So I didn't have much trouble going back and briefing my skippers in what we were going to do. There wasn't much problem to it. All you had to do is tell them what kind of a guy is looking at you and the authority he's giving you. And that I'm passing that authority on, when we're in trouble let's give it all we've got. And history will never say anything that we can't be proud of.

The trip out to Leyte was uneventful. We had bad weather going out and got separated on occasion, but that's usual. We all prayed for good weather on the morning of the landing, and we had good weather on the morning of the landing, very good.

"Twas unopposed. We went in through the east gate, there wasn't a shot fired. We saw some reconnaissance planes. We never had anything hit us. Actually we had overcast and bad weather a couple of days ahead of time and went through a storm which probably held the reconnaisance planes back. And so they didn't have advance warning of our force movements.

The first casualty was from mines. One of my ships, the ROSS, got it right away by a mine. She was badly hurt; enough that she had to go back to Manus right away. She could maneuver and could get around, but she wasn't able to get into the fighting until months later.

The job of my particular squadron was towards the southern end of the beaches of Leyte just before you get to the Panaon Island, which is south of the passage. We had nine ships, so we must have started off with ten. I don't know who the other two were. They weren't part of my squadron, but they were assigned to me for this fire support mission. We lined ourselves up just about 2500 yards off the beach and went in with the group. Our speciality was accuracy for call fire. We supported the underwater demolition teams and their work in clearing the beaches to start with.

They could send back to us in the English language – "There's fire coming at us out of that yellow house behind the banyan tree, the upper right hand window." This was the way they'd tell us where we could aim.

We had this very sophisticated, highly maneuverable type of fire control with terrific fire power that we could lay in and just blow the stuffing out of these people. Consequently they didn't have any trouble ashore, very little trouble any place in the initial landings.

I think we completely caught the Japanese by surprise. There was something about it later that came up – that there had been a storm the night before, so they'd all gone back into their bivouacs. I think we sort of caught them by surprise. There wasn't anything that really developed for quite awhile. It was quite an easy and unopposed landing to start with.

We stayed on that line, shooting all that first day, until all of the supplies got ashore. Everything was taken in, and they were well lined up ashore. Then we retired that night.

I don't remember any untoward incident at all, or where we went that night. We may just have cruised up and down Panaon Island and through the strait. We didn't get in any trouble and nothing happened, as far as I know.

Then the next day we started getting worried about the coming battle. The Japanese were going to initiate their great opperation, whatever it was called. They were all in position and they were ready to go.

The next few days I don't remember very much except somewhere between the time of our landing and of our going down the straits after the Japanese in the battle of Surigao Strait there were two or three air attacks and the first kamikaze attacks on us there. One of my ships, the BRYANT, was skimmed, not badly hurt or taken out, but they lost a couple of men. It just sort of skimmed over the side, missed it, but it was a deliberate kamikaze, and the first one that we'd seen. These were isolated bomber attacks, not coordinated, very poorly coordinated.

And so the missions just went on, day after day, supporting the landings and resupply. We could keep track very well of where the battle was ashore because the communications were magnificent for these battle forces. When they were bogged down they'd call us and we'd go close to the beach for fire power support. Oh boy, they did like our fire power. They were hollering for us all the time, because it was good and it was accurate. It was terrific, powerful.

Q: That must have given you a sense of satisfaction to know you could deliver when they really needed it so bad.

Smoot: It was great, it was wonderful.

But the thing that I remember more than anything was that the communications were so wonderful compared to what I'd been in before. You knew just exactly how to get hold of your fire control center on the beach, and they knew how to get hold of you. Previous to Leyte it was just awful. Communication techniques had greatly improved.

And then the battle developed, the big battle of Surigao started developing. We could plot it's development because of excellent intelligence. We were all called over to Oldendorf's ship. I believe he was in the CALIFORNIA, I'm not sure.

Meanwhile the battleships were doing their shore bombardment. They used their big guns up around Tacloban, where the main force were. That was up towards the north. They were all up there, but the destroyers were mostly down around the southern end of the Island, helping the troops go in after the Japs.

We got the word that our intelligence had the Japanese plans lined up. In fact the Japanese were pretty naive in letting us know was much as they did about this. They talked too much, they said too much. And we broke it down pretty well. So we knew that there was going to be a three pronged attack. One was carriers from the north. One was the big heavy battleships coming through the San Bernadino Straits. The other was a strike force coming up through Suragao Straits.

We knew the constitution of each group. We knew what the enemy had, and what we had to face.

So Oldendorf said, "This will be a very simple operation. I will have four groups of destroyers. The destroyers will attack in order, on order.

"I will have one division of destroyers down the left hand side, one division down the right hand side. I will have one squadron linked up at each end of our battle line.

"All we will do during the period of the approach of the enemy is to cruise back and forth across the head of Surigao Strait. We'll just turn in our tracks and go back and forth and stay right in that line all the time. That's where we're going to stay. The theory of this battle is to cross the T.

"I will use my destroyers in torpedo attacks down the sides of the channel keeping out of the way of our fire. We'll fire constantly, and the destroyers will go in on my orders in succession by divisions firing their torpedoes at the approaching line of ships. And they will take such necessary steps as needed to protect themselves when necessary, but don't give themselves away if they don't have to.

"I'd like your plans in my hands by this afternoon by three o'clock."

This was say nine o'clock in the morning.

So we went back. My plans were already written up as most all the others were anyway. We knew what we were going to do, except we didn't know where we were going to be. So we had to orient our plans to where we were told to be. My squadron's position was on the eastern end of the battle line and some four to five thousand yards down the straits from the battle line.

Surigao Strait runs north and south. We were in the northeast area of the straits as originally disposed. This was our relative position to the battle line. Actually the battle line was disposed in line across the straits, and we were on their starboard bow while we were going east. Then when we would reverse course by ships turns we'd be on their port quarter. We'd just maintain that position as we cruised back and forth across the straits waiting the enemy's approach.

The other squadron would be at the other end of the battle line, like us disposed down strait toward the enemy's approach.

This was so that the Force Commander could control us by voice, and knew that he had us under control by voice and could dispatch us to the attack when he wished us to go. This was the only thing he was going to do - call us by code name to attack according to plan.

My code name was 'dummy two' at that time. When he said, "Dummy two attack," I knew what to do because I was going to do it the way I had told him I was going to do it.

Q: It must have given you a sense of security to know that he was so knowledgeable.

Smoot: It was simple, and he made it so. This is the way a battle should be. Don't complicate battles, they're bad enough as it is, you get enough complications.

So I stayed in that relative position. We didn't have much trouble. Once I think the TENNESSEE jammed a rudder and messed up the battle line for awhile, and we had to make a premature turn to keep the battle line from getting too mixed up, but he got back in control again. We had no problem at all during this tense waiting phase.

Further down the straits on both sides were the two divisions of DDs, who were going to make the first attack. They were probably two or three miles further down, closer to the enemy than we were, and closer to each shore — one toward the eastern shore of the straits, and the other toward the western shore.

So he had them fixed up in a nice sort of a funnel arrangement with the enemy coming right up the funnel. A division of destroyers, two squadrons of destroyers, and at the apex was our battle line to greet them. It was beautiful, a perfectly magnificent battle situation, just like out of a storybook.

Q: When it's done right it looks so easy.

Smoot: Oh boy, this was just exactly what they should have done at Savo Island, where they had the forces and everything to do it.

It was so beautifully done, and it worked. Everything worked just as it was supposed to work.

The only bad feature of it was the timing of my squadron's attack. Mine was the last of the three destroyer groups released in succession to launch torpedo attacks.

We listened to each groups verbal reports. We listened to when they launched their torpedoes. We listened to the conditions as they saw them at the time. So we were kept pretty well advised as to what was developing.

It was night, black as pitch, all the ships darkened. We relied on radar exclusively for maneuvering. If we'd been hit by torpedoes we'd never have know where they came from. The Japs had radar and saw what was coming too, they knew what was coming.

Meanwhile the battle line opened with their big guns. By the time my squadron was well down the straits on attack you could see the tracer bullets flying over our heads. It was quite a sight. It honestly looked like the Brooklyn Bridge at night - the tail lights of automobiles going across BRooklyn Bridge. There were so many bullets from our battle line producing this great big arching sight over our head. Bullets were rumbling over head. We could hear the shooting and then we'd see the bullets going down just like a streak in the sky.

We cranked up full speed right away just like I'd planned it, and went down the alley headed right straight for the lead Jap battleships. It took us a little bit away from land, more than I cared to, but I didn't want to upset the firing of the destroyer division that was ahead of me on the left. They were still firing, and they were down stream a little further than me. I didn't want to get too close to them. But by the same token I probably shouldn't have gotten so near the center of the strait. I got pretty close to the center of the strait.

My plan was to send my right hand squadron down the right hand side, the left hand squadron down the left hand side, and the middle division, which was mine, down the middle, cross the T, fire our torpedoes and get the devil out of there just as fast as we could. It's sort of like putting the battle line in a big funnel with a division of destroyers on both their bows and one on their head, dead ahead, with torpedoes coming at them from three directions. It's hard to miss that way.

It's a classic principle of the torpedo attack on a major battle line, and it's been written up for years and years; ever since torpedoes were invented - that if you can make that kind of attack you've achieved the ultimate in torpedo attack tactics. You leave your target with little to do in defense.

So we did that. But one of my ships, the ALBERT T. GRANT, in my division, (I had nine ships, divided up three each) the last one in my column, didn't get speed up fast enough, and she lagged way behind. I kept calling to her to catch up, but she got more and more behind.

I never did find out what was the matter because everything was happening so fast. But she obviously had engineering trouble and couldn't get speed up fast enough. We were going as fast as those destroyers could go - 35 knots. We were really tearing down there.

The LEARY was right astern of me, and kept beautiful position. But the GRANT got pretty far astern. By the time I let torpedoes go we were about eight thousand yards away from the enemy battle line. The GRANT didn't let her's go because she was too far behind. About that time we got word from the GRANT that she was being hit. We suspected she was being hit by our own battle line shells, and she was.

We found out later which of our own cruisers it was that had shifted fire and gotten onto the GRANT, locked onto her and really gave her the devil. She took about forty shells. This was the LOUISVILLE, I believe. This is what we figured from the color of the shell dye, and the direction from which it came.

The very studied results of the battle and the firing of the torpedoes, which were gone over and over and over for years and years and years afterward, studied at the War College and everything, indicates that perhaps we got two hits maybe, two torpedoes. But by that time the lead enemy battleship was in flames anyway, it was a mess and practically gone. The enemy cruiser had turned around and was speeding down the strait in flight.

The battle was practically over. And the TAsk Force Commander, Admiral Oldendorf, called all of his destroyers to assemble on him. He was going down the straits to knock off the cripples. Rendezvous was designated at a point on the west side of the channel. The destroyers were to assemble and act as screen and fire only when ordered. He wanted to keep control, didn't want us shooting at each other.

They had to stop firing on the battle line for about five minutes, when I reported that they were hitting one of my own ships, and that was the GRANT. They ceased fire for five minutes. Oldendorf's Chief of Staff gave me the devil for that later. He said, that I probably caused the battle lines failure to sink the enemy cruiser, because they had to stop firing for about five minutes.

I said, "Too bad, he shouldn't have fired at one of my destroyers." He said, "Well, I don't know what you were doing down there anyway." I said, "You approved my plan. You saw it. I gave it to you in writing. You approved it. If you didn't like it, then was the time to tell me, because I went exactly where I said I was going." That was Admiral Oldendorf's Chief of Staff. He and I never did get along.

Admiral Oldendorf just congratulated me. Oley never said anything, but his Chief of Staff gave me the devil.

So I got my destroyers together the best as I could. I ordered the LEARY to take the GRANT in tow and take her back out of the battle area. The LEARY never answered.

I found out afterwards why - he didn't want to answer. He didn't want to answer me because he wanted to go down and shoot some more. He didn't want to be called back. He knew what I was going to call him for, so he never answered.

I had to take my own flag ship and tow the GRANT out, but it didn't matter. I was sorry because I would have been in Command of the destroyers on the sweep down to clean up. But we never caught anything anyway. The one enemy ship that got away was already too far away, and planes got her the next morning. It didn't matter, but I wanted to go. If there was something to be done I wanted to do it.

So I had to take the GRANT in tow. Again we lashed alongside the ship and towed her back. Here's where I learned about doctoring. I was giving transfusions and learning how to give artificial respiration. Oh boy, the disaster on that ship was just terrible, shells from our own battle line killed about forty men. And later seven or eight of them died from wounds. There must have been a hundred of them wounded.

Q: Did they know it was their own shells?

Smoot: Yes. Her engine rooms were covered with blue dye. The Japanese didn't use dye.

Q: Can you describe the feeling aboard the ship?

Smoot: Bitter resentment.

I asked them, "Why didn't you keep up? What caused your trouble? The skipper of the GRANT never really did answer me. He said he had other problems and he wasn't worried about that.

That fellow, by himself, the skipper of the GRANT, personally went down into the engine room, in what looked like a sinking ship, in almost boiling water, and brought out eight men and saved their lives. He went down and pulled them out and kept them from drowning — the skipper himself.

I recommended him for the Medal of Honor, which he didn't get. I think he should have had a Medal of Honor. I don't remember his name — a big fellow, powerful man.

He never did explain to me why he got so far behind and I didn't see any reason to press the point. The deed was done, it was over. It was in his battle report, but I don't remember what it was.

Q: The NEWCOMB was given credit for sinking the Japanese battleship.

Smoot: That's a very generous statement. The thing that sank it was our combined efforts, I'm sure. I'm sure that we had at least one torpedo hit, there isn't any doubt about that. We're credited with one, and we may have had more. By the time we actually launched our torpedoes the ship was burning badly from our battle line fire power.

Our fire power from the battleships and the cruisers was just tremendous, frightful, devastating. This was the classic crossing of the T.

Q: I'm quoting from Morrison's book, he makes the statement that, "Although it had been damaged, the NEWCOMB's two torpedoes exploded in it and eight minutes later she sank." He also quotes you as saying that, and I read, "The most beautiful sight I ever witnessed - the arched flying of tracers in the darkness looked like a continuous stream of lighted railroad cars going over a hill."

Smoot: I'm sure I put that in my battle report, just like that. That's where he got that quote from.

It was a sight, the sight the like of which I've never seen before or since. I think we've fired our last classic crossing of the T - typical Navy battle.

So I took the GRANT in tow and took her back up to the area where all the tenders and supply ships were anchored, and she was made seaworthy and towed back to Manus. I think she was repaired and later got into the war again up in Okinawa.

We had one other very unfortunate thing happen about that battle, an unpleasant thing. I hate to make it a part of history, but that's the way it is.

After that night battle was over we got the word that the main Japanese battle line that had come through San Bernardino Strait was going to come through the east gate at Leyte, and was going to take us all on.

We were in no condition to meet this terribly big and effective force of the Japanese. They were much stronger than we, because we didn't have any armor piercing shells left. We'd fired them all.

As far as my destroyers were concerned I don't think we had more than a third of our torpedoes left, if that, less than that, probably a quarter of them left. We had been told not to fire all of our torpedoes, to fire a three quarter spread. So we had about a quarter of our torpedoes left.

We were hurried back up to the resupply area where all of the resupply ships were anchored, and told to refuel as fast as we could and to get as much ammunition aboard as we could.

I headed up to one that I was told to go to. It was a Liberty ship, I don't remember the name of it and it doesn't matter. But I went alongside, it was now dawn, just getting light, of the same morning. We'd been up all night, we'd been fighting all night long, we'd been through a devil of an ordeal, our boys were tired.

When I went alongside this Liberty ship there wasn't a soul in sight, except one dirty practically naked man lying on a mat on topside. So we blew our whistle.

That was the ship we were supposed to go alongside to get fuel and what ammunition and provisions he could give us. This was a regular U. S. supply ship, under contract, civilian owned.

Pretty soon an unkempt looking man, unshaven, long shabby beard, no clothes on, just a pair of shorts, came out on the upper bridge up there and said, "What in the hell do you want?"

I said, "We've been told to come alongside to get fuel. My whole division is trying to get fuel just as fast as we can. The Japs are coming in the east entrance, and we've got to get out there as fast as we can."

He said, "Well, we're not going to open any hatches until eight o'clock." I said, "Look, this is not union hours out here my friend." He said, "You can say what you want, we're not opening hatches until eight o'clock."

I said, "Well, you're going to open hatches because I'm going to send my crew aboard. If anybody tries to stop me I'm going to start shooting at you."

So I sent my crew aboard, they opened the hatches and rigged the hoses. We got the ammunition and the supplies. That fellow never said a word, and he didn't send a one of his men to help us until eight o'clock.

This was a Liberty ship — an American owned and American operated Liberty ship.

I wrote a letter about it. It went through military channels and finally got to the Maritime Commission. It's a matter of record with the Maritime Commission.

I don' know what they ever did, whether they ever made any issue of it or not. But this was not a very pretty picture for America's warfare machine. It's a terrible picture.

That's the only untoward incident that happened.

Anyway we were all lined up on the east entrance waiting for Admiral Kurita to come in and massacre us, because he could have, just one by one, because we didn't have much fighting power left.

That incredible incident of the two airplanes that flew over changed the whole course of the war.

That could have been disastrous. They could have set us back a couple of years. That could have been really disastrous.

Q: Do you want to amplify on that - about the two airplanes?

Smoot: It's a story that I heard years afterward.

It goes like this: Kurita and his battle force, which was a powerful battle force, were headed south down through the line of Kaiser-built flattops that were to the east of Leyte, and just massacring them one by one as they came down. We lost four destroyers in that attack that were out there, brave wonderful guys that went in the teeth of that power.

There was nothing to stop the Japs from coming through the east entrance to Leyte Gulf. He could have come in and just massacred our landing force, just taken his time.

We couldn't have stopped them, we never could have stopped them. We just didn't have the ammunition, the right kind of ammunition.

We look back on it now as one of the miracles of the war really that this happened.

The story that comes to us from Kurita's side, post war, is that they were all gloating over their great victory. And they were hearing about the trouble that their force was having down the Suragao Strait. They knew Oshima had lured Halsey and the big flattops way out of range.

Kurita was practically free to come in, clean up the landing force, and massacre all of our forces. He was well on his way, headed down our way, when he looked up and saw two or three of the kind of aircraft that only fly off of the big carriers.

They were used to seeing an awful lot of the kind of aircraft that fly off the little carriers. But it appeared it was a different kind of aircraft, and they identified them as the kind of planes that fly off the big carriers.

So he said, "Our ruse with Oshima apparently didn't work. Halsey has not been run off to the north. He's coming back down, has launched his planes, and they're headed over and have sighted us. We'd better get out of here."

And he turned around and went back.

The fact is he did see these different kind of planes. And if this is a true story, the planes that he saw were planes from one of Halsey's flattop divisions who had been ordered to go three hundred miles to the east of Leyte to refuel. This particular division didn't go north chasing after the phantom Jap carrier force with Halsey.

When our force was getting in so much trouble Kinkaid called for help. And this one group of Halsey's fleet turned around, launched his planes, and sent them over to Tacloban to refuel and help us out. Those were the planes Kurita saw. They really were part of Halsey's fleet.

Q: I never heard that story before about the two planes. I knew the stroy about Kurita thinking that he was going to get involved with large carriers, but I hadn't know of the affair of the two planes.

Smoot: This was as I heard it. He saw those planes that were going over to Tacloban from the one section Halsey left behind to refuel.

This is what we surmised. We can't help but say it because they did see those planes. They were the kind of planes that were launched from Halsey's force only. And they couldn't have been launched from Halsey's force because he was too far north. The Japs knew that, and so they began to doubt Halsey had really been lured away by Oshima's ghosts.

This is one of the quirks of fate that save us, otherwise I wouldn't be here talking to you. The whole course of the war would have been changed. It would have been disastrous.

I never knew what happened to Kurita. I haven't read that history at all. One time I heard he'd committed suicide, another time I heard he didn't. It doesn't matter anyway.

Nevertheless those are the little quirks of fate that influence the outcome of battles that you don't hear about.

I think, by the same token, that Halsey, as history gets older and older, (a revered and wonderful man, a truly great man), as times goes on, historians can severly criticize him for being lured off the way he was.

The Japs really didn't have enough air power to lure anyone. Our intelligence knew that there was very little left of the Japanese seagoing air force. We could have sent one divisions against Oshima and held the main part of his big fleet to guard the landing area.

If he had been where Admiral Spruance was at the battle of Midway, and Spruance had been where Halsey was at the battle of the Philippine Sea, the history of the war would have been entirely different.

In the battle at Guam, Saipan, and those places where Spruance wouldn't leave and go after them and we lost so many boys Halsey would have gone after them. But Spruance said, "My first job is to protect the beaches, and I'm not going any further." So he didn't. But Halsey would have gone after them.

He would have caught that fleet that night, and we wouldn't have had any more Japanese fleet. We'd have had a lot of our boys lost too, but Halsey would have gone after them.

Whereas if Spruance had been in Command down in Leyte instead of Halsey he would never have chased after Oshima and his phamtom force.

Of course there were a lot of little contingent operations that went on as we solidified our position at Leyte. One of them, an interesting one, was the Ormoc Resupply Echelon, so-called "Ormoc Resupply." This was a trip around the south of Panay, down through the Surigao Strait, and up the west side past Bohol to the Ormoc area on the west side of Leyte where the Army was really trying to get a foothole. Several of the Ormoc Resupply Echelons that went around really caught the devil from Japanese planes on the trip back. There were many many bad casualties and sinkings.

So it came my turn to run one of those Ormoc things. We went around, made the landing, resupplied, got back, never saw a plane. We didn't shoot a bullet, didn't have a thing happen to us, but I lost twenty pounds just worrying. I never sweated or went through so much in my life, because I had an awful lot of responsibility - a whole lot of resupplying and an awful lot of men and going over there with no air support, no nothing, not a thing.

Q: How lond a period did that that take?

Smoot: You'd start off late one night, and by the time daylight came you'd be over at Ormoc. You'd spend the whole day at Ormoc discharging supplies on the beach. While you were at Ormoc they would support you in the air if they had anything. The Army didn't have anything to support me on that trip, and the Navy wasn't close enough. So I didn't have anything, not a thing came, nothing. Then it took all day to do that unloading. You'd start back that night and it took all night to get back.

Q: You mean in thirty-six hours you lost twenty pounds?

Smoot: Well it seemed like it, yes. I never left the bridge, I never undressed, I never ate anything. I just stood up and paced the deck, giving orders, receiving orders, taking orders, listening to contingencies.

We had all kinds of phamtom things come. We had a midget submarine that came out after us, but he never did anything. It was just one of those little one or two man submarines. I think he must have had an accident and never got to us, but we definitely saw him on the surface.

We had motor torpedo boats come out from Bohol, but my destroyers drove them off. We didn't even have to shoot at them, they turned around and went back.

We'd stand all day long up on the bridge looking any moment for a whole flight of airplanes coming to get you. All we had was our own gun power to support us. We worried with all of these men and people.

Just the strain alone — by the time I got back there I was practically exhausted.

Q: You had your whole squadron?

Smoot: I didn't have the ROSS or the GRANT. I had destroyers from other outifts. I had plenty of destroyers and DEs. I had lots of support, but you can't defend yourself thoroughly against everything. I was responsible for them, and the most important thing was to get the stuff ashore as fast as we could. We didn't have any trouble, none at all. But I lost weight just worrying and sweating thru the ordeal of what could happen.

Then we made one trip up to the big island close to Manila. This was Mindoro, and we took that island around Christmas time with practically no resistance.

Finally some time later we went back to Manus for rest and recreation. Then we lined up for the Lingayen Gulf operation.

Q: You were there then for six weeks, two months?

Smoot: In Manus? No, not more than two weeks.

Q: The reason I was interested was because the Leyte operation was late October, early November.

Smoot: It was January some time that we went to Lingayen Gulf, because I remember the Mindoro operation was between Christmas and New Years.

Q: I was just trying to account for the operations between the end of October and early January. Was that Ormoc?

Smoot: That's Ormoc and Mindoro. We supported the thrust down the island to the south, one little foray down on Mindanao where they were planning later to make a separate landing. This was going to be done by the other fleet, not by us. Barbey's outfit was going to do this later. We went there to send some intelligence people ashore, so we had a little foray landing. I supported that. That was one trip I took.

It's hard to account for all that time. There're two months there in Letye. But it's mostly fire support power, trips to the Ormoc Resupply, and then this one foray down in Mindanao and the Mindoro operation.

Q: Then of course your travel time to and from Manus. But you were only there two weeks before you started out again for northern Luzon?

Smoot: Yes. I think we went right straight from Leyte to the Lingayen Gulf operations, so we didn't go back to Manus the second time.

We just had one trip back to Manus in the middle of the Leyte campaign just for resupplying, rest, and getting away from the firing for awhile. My division escorted a couple of tankers back. We were gone a total of two weeks, that's all. Then we went back to Leyte again.

Q: It was getting to be pretty constant pressure I would think.

Smoot: It was, it was quite a campaign.

By contrast the Lingayen Gulf operation wasn't. We were getting pretty old hat at it by this time. The operation moved so fast in Lingayen Gulf that really our fire support was only needed for just a couple of days.

We were harrassed an awful lot at night by the Japanese in Lingayen Gulf with motor torpedo boats. They weren't very effective. They didn't do any damage, except to supply ships. There were quite a few air attacks, and we were beginning to get more and more of these frightful kamikazes.

We had one little incident in Lingayen where one of them came at us, right at the NEWCOMB, hit our radar mast, took the radar mast off, skooted down our port side, and hit the water. And that's all the damage we sustained.

When we had a roll call of the men there was one man mising. Later after we searched the ship and everything we found his wristwatch lodged in one of the life rafts on the port side.

We knew his battle station was in 'battle one,' which was up on the flying bridge, as a lookout. With phones on he was supposed to look for surface and air targets. And he was missing, no sign of him anywhere on the ship, no sign of blood, no sign of anybody having gotten hit, nothing.

We withdrew that night as a group. We went north out of Lingayen Gulf, whole fleet did. We came in the next morning and had one devil of an attack on us. And that's the morning that one of the kamikazes hit the CALIFORNIA. It also hit a cruiser of ours, and we lost one of our Admirals, a Cruiser Division Commander. I can't think of his name, but I loved him. A wonderful man, he was killed in that raid.

We returned to our assigned station and started to patrol for call fire ashore. That's the main thing you do when you're not assigned any other mission. You just wait for "call fire." Army units ashore say, "We've got a place up here that's a hot spot. We can't break through. Let's have some Navy fire power." So we get the cordinates of it, start shooting, and then they spot us on. That's all you do. There's nothing to it, and we had gotten pretty good at it by this time.

When we got to our station there bobbing in the water was our lost man. He waved at us and said, "Will you take me aboard?" He had spent the whole night in that water bobbing around, with a lifejacket on. He was unhurt, unscathed, not a scratch on him.

Q: How did his wristwatch get caught?

Smoot: He didn't remember exactly, but he thought he took it off to save it, and he threw it. And then he dived overboard to avoid the kamikaze. He wanted to save his wristwatch, and he was in hopes that he could get back aboard again. When he saw us leaving he said he yelled like hell, but nobody listened. He though he was a goner, but he did not want to go ashore, and he didn't want to be seen by the Japs. But we ran into him the next morning. There he was unhurt, unscathed.

Lingaygen Gulf was pretty much of a cinch compared to Leyte. It didn't take very long. The Army moved rapidly here. They moved inland and call fire was over in just a few days, and for our support force that was it.

At the end of the Lingayen operations, we went to Majuro where we spent quite a long time relatively, reconditioning and resupplying in preparation for the Iwo Jima landing. That was the next thing that came up.

Interview # 3

Vice Admiral Roland N. Smoot, USN
Laguna Hills, California

by E. B. Kitchen
February 21, 1971

Miss Kitchen: Admiral, we had just finished the Lingayen Gulf and I'd like to have you pick up from there if you will, and give me a little bit of the people that you were with and who were under you and so on so that we can get that picture.

Admiral Smoot: The easiest way to describe it - first of all take the type command that I was attached to, this was under Reggie Kaufman, Commander Destroyers Pacific.

I was assigned to command a destroyer squadron, the number was 56. These particular destroyers had been trained over a period of many months in accuracy of close fire support for the UDTs, underwater demolition teams, for the various amphibious landings that we made throughout the Western Pacific in our attacks.

Assignment to a Desron like that is a rather loose designation only for chain of command and general administrative purposes. The fellow that makes out your fitness report is the Tactical Task Force Commander that you report to, and that of course some times changed daily. But for the most part, starting from the time that I went to Manus to join Desron 56 and relieved Admiral Libby, my Tactical Task Force chain of command was Admiral Olendorf who had the old battleships.

His command was really Commander of Battleships Pacific, but these were the old battleships. They were used primarily in gunfire support for the landings. They very seldom, if ever, went with any of the carriers because they weren't fast enough. So this was a fighting force to assist the landings, and destroyers got assigned to screen commands.

Some times I would be shifted from Olendorf's command just for a day or so to a screen command of a high speed resupply echelon who needed extra support because of the possibility of close attack.

So it was an ever-changing complicated Task Force Organization out there. If you ever tried to really lay it out in a consecutive type of command organization you'd lose yourself in a welter of change that went on all the time.

But for this purpose, and all the way through from the time I reported to Desron 56 and until I left it in Okinawa, where I was relieved by a classmate of mine who was assigned to command Desron 56, all through that time, my work was mostly in association with the landing forces - the support forces in all of the landings in the Western Pacific.

So the Task Force Commander changed and the tasks names changed, but Olendorf for the most part was my Commander. He was the man I really worked for all during all of these landings up to Iwo Jima. He was hurt in Majuro on a boat ride back from the beach, his boat hit a buoy and he sustained broken ribs, he was quite badly hurt.

Bert Rogers took over then from him, this was just before we went to Okinawa. So Bert Rogers was really in command when we went. My memory is kind of vague about this. It could have been when we went to Iwo Jima that Bert Rogers took over.

We were back in Jamuro refitting, refurbishing, and having a little rest and recreation after the Lingayen Gulf. As I remember we went from there to Iwo Jima, and it was before that when Olendorf was hurt.

Then I was under this one other boss, Bert Rogers. He took over the big battleships and became the Support Force Commander for all of the landings after Lingayen.

Q: Are you a Commander at this time?

Smoot: No, I am a Captain. I'm a four-stripe Captain. I was a four-stripe Captain when I left the Sound School. All the time during the war in the Pacific I was a Captain, until they made me a Commodore in Okinawa in May of 1945.

Q: Tell me the number of ships now, because you started with nine before Leyte and you lost some.

Smoot: There were nine ships to a squadron, three divisions, and each of the divisions had a division commander.

I had a double job – I was a Division Commander and a Squadron Commander. I had all nine of them. Then I had two other division commanders. They were full Commanders, real experienced destroyer people. So we started off with nine ships when I joined the division down at Manus.

In the first campaign, on the way into Leyte Gulf, we lost the ROSS to a mine, and she never got back in again during my tenure. She was repaired and worked later in the Pacific. She wasn't sunk or anything, and was repaired, but never got back to me.

Then we lost the GRANT. That was the night of the Surigao Strait battle. She was badly hit by our own shells. We knew that and could definitely determine later how it happened. We knew the ship that was firing because of the color of the dye.

Q: So you had lost two by this time.

Smoot: We had lost two, we were down to seven ships.

At times I had many more and some times less in the Tactical Force because we moved around so frequently for various jobs. But as an administrative command I now had seven ships.

From Lingayen we went back to Majuro for rest, and then we went to Iwo Jima. That's the way I remember it.

Q: Do you have the dates for Iwo Jima?

Smoot: It was in February '45.

Iwo Jima, as far as the support ships were concerned, was a relatively easy campaign. We were involved primarily in shore bombardment. We seldom had any attacks at all by air. There were a few sporadic attacks by single planes and usually at night - more harassment than real danger.

I'm talking about the support forces to which I was attached. Bert Rogers was now our Commander, and he was given the general assignment to support the Marine landing and the follow up assignment of bombardments. He in turn delegated them to his various squadron commanders, of whom he had two or three, and I was one of them.

I had seven ships now, but we were not involved in the big battle at Iwo Jima, because that was the Carrier Task Force's.

So we stayed there until the shore phase of the Iwo Jima campaign was considered secured. Then they left certain of the older destroyers there to support in loading and unloading the various transports that came up there. But the big battleships and the fast destroyers, of which my unit was part, went back to Majuro again to prepare for Okinawa.

I can't remember much about Iwo Jima except it was a tiring campaign, because the battle was going on night and day. The Japanese were dug in there and the Marines were really getting it on the beach. So call fire was constant all the time - not much sleep, but also not much real warfare for our destroyers.

I remember our work was fascinating to this extent - that we were right close up to the beach. We could see the advance of the Marines, we could watch them. And we could see so many terrible things which were awful to watch, in terms sudden death. I'll never forget this.

A crippled tank had gotten right close up to a Japanese bunker. I have no idea how many were involved in it or how many people were in the tank or anything, but here it was suddenly stopped. Although it continued to fire, out of the bunker came a whole bunch of Japanese with great big cans of gasoline, poured it over this tank and set it afire. So the boys inside were cremated. This was an awful thing to watch.

We could do very little about it. We could shoot at them, and we did whether we could get the Japanese or not, because they were pretty far over a hill. We could just barely see them in our glasses.

Call fire was the main thing. We were in position, and could see and watch, when the famous mountain was secured. We could see that, and actually saw the flag raised at Mt. Suribaci We could actually see that that morning - that battle up that mountain. We could watch the inch by inch progress of those brave Marines that went up there. That was a wicked battle.

Then when it was all secured, the battle then remained only for clearance of the Japanese caves and tremendous underground labyrinth of their defenses in the northern part of the island, which went on for several months or years I guess before they finally got them all.

We, as the support force for the landings, were secured. I don't think we were there more than two or three weeks.

Q: I think it ended about the 7th of March. At least there is the decoration and citation you received for your Gold Star in lieu of the Second Bronze Star Medal, and it gives the dates February 16th to March 7th.

Smoot: It wasn't really bad, in terms of being dangerous, in terms of being always under a strain, other than the normal business of being in battle, that of course was always a strain.

This was really the easiest landing that we, as a support force type, had. We weren't under air attack at all. A few stray Japanese planes would come down at night and worry us. They'd come down from the islands up to the north. They were just little reconnaissance planes, but that was all. We didn't have any air attack, just enough to have air alerts to keep us awake at night.

Q: You couldn't have been at Majuro very long, because you went back then to Okinawa in March.

3 Smoot - 161

Smoot: As I remember we arrived in Okinawa in April some time.

Q: I was getting my data on that Admiral from your Gold Star in lieu of a second Navy Cross. You received so many decorations

Smoot: That's because we were assigned to the task force. They cover the task force assignement in terms of when they give something like a Navy Cross, or a large combat type of citation, and they cover the whole period.

Actually it seems to me that we arrived in Okinawa, specifically Kerama Retta, in early April.

The approach phase of the Okinawa campaign was during the latter week in March, and the actual landings on Okinawa were on the first of April.

Then we started getting these tremendous kamikaze attacks around the 6th. I think the 6th was the first great big one. They were devastating, they were awful.

Q: I'm sure the whole thing is fresh in your mind, and I'd like to have you give me as much detail as you can.

Smoot: As far as the landings were concerned, they first landed at Kerama Retta, which is a group of islands to the south of the main island of Okinawa. They did this to provide a protected watershed for our support forces. It didn't take very long for the Marines to clean out the little islands around there and get that very well secured.

It formed a very fine sort of a protected area that gave us security for logistics.

Then in preparation for the main landing on the main island the battleships and the support destroyers would retire at night and get away from the islands, so that we could get a little bit of rest.

On the landing we all had our regular bombardment assignments, and we fired as long as we could. The Army and the Marines moved in very rapidly.

I remember that during the first few phases of it we had some midget submarine alerts, but they were easily taken care of. In my particular section of the front there I was providing fire support we didn't have any, but the boys up further north, towards the northern end, had a few midget subs that came out. Whether they ever got them or not I frankly don't know.

Q: What was your section?

Smoot: We were down towards the southern end of the island on the west side. It was the main landing front. My remaining six destroyers were almost in the middle of it.

We had specified fire support areas to shoot at and that lasted a very little while. It couldn't have lasted over an hour, because they moved in very rapidly. The Japanese took to the hills and went into the caves.

Then we were on call fire for the whole rest of the time, but we were always out there.

The battleships were patrolling a given area for support considerably off the beach, unless they were called in for heavy fire. Admiral Rogers, who had Command of the Support Force, would assign screen commanders for the day and the night. We had various errand duties and traded back and forth between task forces and assignments to bombardment.

Then we started getting call fire at night too, call fire particularly for lighting up the area.

In the meantime we really got a little bored for awhile, until early in the morning of the 6th. We heard from the carrier task forces and from intelligence that a large group of Japanese planes were heading for Okinawa. This was the first concerted attack by the kamikazes. It was a stinker, and we really weren't prepared to defend ourselves against such a ghoulish type of warfare.

Admiral Rogers concentrated his battleships in very close formation with a screen of destroyers around them. There must have been thirty or forty destroyers around him. We were moving fast and meneuvering on signals from him, to provide the most difficult target possible for these attacks.

Q: How far off shore were you at that time?

Smoot: Probably about fifteen or twenty miles. Out there where there was plenty of navigation room to maneuver, to use our guns, and to be sure that our bullets weren't going to strafe anybody on the beach - any friendly forces. We were in a clear area.

They came in on us. Oh boy, it just looked like millions of them. Of course it was fascinating. Really your heart was beating pretty fast when they were coming, because we could hear and listen in on all the air battles as they came through our magnificent fighter planes who took care of an awful lot of them.

But they didn't care. They came right in close to the water just ten to fifteen feet off the ocean. Then as they got close to a ship, they'd go up in the air and turn over on their back and dive right down onto the ship. Then you'd see all this great big billow of black smoke and explosions, if they happened to hit a vital place like a magazine of any kind. Then there was another ship with it's back broken, and many many lost sailors.

We got it the first time, the first one that came in on the NEWCOMB. We got three in about fifteen minutes. The first one hit us amidships. The second one came aft and hit us in about the same place, and wiped out the whole center of the ship. Both stacks were gone, one was leaning over. The engine room was just wiped out completely. There was a big fire back aft, which was beautifully controlled by the fire boys. But the ship was dead in the water. We didn't have any power. And we really didn't know how badly we were hurt, and whether we were going to sink or not. We didn't know whether our back was broken or what. But we'd been hit by two planes then.

Then while we were there burning, dead in the water, another ship had come up alongside us to help, we saw this other plane - a last straggler come in and head right for us.

What do you do during those last few minutes when you see this thing? Where is he going to hit and has he got a bomb? Is he going to get you?

The tendency for everybody was to spread away from the center of the ship, go as far as possible forward and aft. But I was on the bridge, I was on the port side of the bridge, and I just watched it. I couldn't go any place. Where could I go? I could jump in the water, but what good would that do. I wasn't too sure that I was going to live through this. In fact it looked to me like he was headed right for me.

I had my glasses up and I could see the Jap. He had a great big white scarf around his neck. At the last minute, I don't know how close he was to me, but I could see him raise his hands off the controls and push it forward. Then he put his hands up towards his head and gritted his teeth. He was that close that I could see.

What he did - he was headed right for the bridge, which would have been the end of all of us there because he did have a bomb. But our number one turret, which was completely without power, was trained around to the left. And the gunner in that turret by sight trained on that plane and fired just when that plane was probably not more than three hundred yards out. It was one of those influence type of shells that we had at that time.

By golly that thing went close enough under the right wing of the plane coming in to tip him up sideways, and it threw him aft away from the bridge. He skidded right over all the part of our ship that was gone from the previous attacks, which was hardly anything, it skidded right over top of that, into the ship next to us, killed a lot of people on that ship, skidded across the deck on that, and went into the ocean, and the bomb exploded when it hit the ocean and dashed in the side of the destroyer next to us. Of course the force of the explosion gave enough water pressure on her side to move the two ships together quite heavily, and there was a lot of damage done there.

It was questionable whether we were going to float or not, we just didn't know. Of course there were a lot of ships worse off than we were. So the tugs and repair forces that we could get together in a hurry and the destroyers that were not hurt were going to their aid and getting people out of the water. We just had to wait, and it seemed to me that we waited there until almost sunset before we were finally taken in tow and we made it to Kerama Retta. They towed us into Kerama Retta and it took us practically all night to get in there.

We no sooner got there than we got a message from the Task Force Commander to transfer my staff, if we were not hurt, (and I had reported that none of us were hurt) to the LEARY - another of my ships which was not hurt - and to prepare to join the battleships that were going to the north to meet the last Japanese battleships and the two remaining cruisers that were coming down to give battle to our forces in a suicide raid.

I learned something that I'll never forget as a result of that. I took the message and we transferred to the LEARY. There was no problem about that, that was perfectly all right. It was a normal procedure to transfer like that.

I took Command of the remaining ships that I had and went out and joined Bert Rogers. He put me in Command of the left flank attack group of destroyers.

This was a standard battle formation with a battle line of battleships and cruisers in the center, and the destroyers way out on either flank ahead and towards the oncoming enemy. I was on the left flank. I was told the position to take with respect to the flag ship. I knew the flag ship's speed and it's course.

It's a simple maneuvering board problem to get from where you are to where you want to be. We'd done it from the time we were in the Naval Academy. It's simple, it's just like kindergarten work.

None of my staff could work the maneuvering board. I couldn't work the maneuvering board. We were in shock and didn't realize it. All of us were in shock and none of us realized it. So I had to turn over the Command of the left flank destroyers.

I had to turn it over to my Division Commander, who had not been in the kamikaze battle. He was perfectly all right. He took us out in our prescribed position, and we headed north.

Then of course we were all ready for battle, condition one. Everyone wondering if we were going to see a real surface battle, the last one in history probably, when we got the word that Mitscher had taken care of the Japanese battleships and supporting ships.

Q: How long did it take you to get out of shock? I would have thought it would have been such a traumatic experience.

Smoot: I frankly don't know. I didn't even realize we were in shock at the time. We didn't have our doctor, he had been hurt. There wasn't a doctor on the LEARY. We needed so many doctors to take care of the injured. So we didn't know that we were in shock. I frankly don't remember.

I know that there was a great feeling of relief and relaxation when we got the word that we weren't going to have a battle. We'd had enough battle at this point. After we got the word that they weren't coming down we had a pretty good nights rest.

Bert Rogers kept the battleships in a very easy formation and we just formed a screen. I took Command of the screen then and we did all right.

My Chief of Staff was in deep shock. I saw him trying to put the maneuvring board on a bulkhead. He just put it against the bulkhead and let it drop, but he just didn't know what he was doing.

That was the first time I realized what excessive strain will do to the human mind, because I'd never been in shock before or since. I didn't know anything about it, but that was a very interesting experience. We didn't have any lasting effects from it, none of us, because we went right back the next day.

And the kamikaze attacks continued with increasing frequency and devastation. But this time they were concentrating more or less on the poor devils that were up in the lookout stations, Freddie Mooseburger's group of destroyers.

They seldom got down to the battleships again, but when they did they gave us the dickens. But they were getting less and less effective. The planes were slower and slower, and much easier to defend against. Also we knew better how to handle them as time went on.

But we lost a lot of ships to those terrific kamikaze attacks. And it wasn't the most pleasant thing in the world to see these things.

The Japs were scraping the bottom of the pool for pilots. They took anybody they could teach to fly a plane one way. Also their stock of flyable planes was fast approaching zero. They just didn't have anything, and finally went into night attacks and harassment maneuvers and that's all. But for about two or three weeks it was really tough going.

Q: Would it have been possible to have had the umbrella fighter planes over the fields from which these kamikazes took off?

Smoot: If we had had more carriers I'm sure it would have been perfectly feasible to have them over, but they took off from many many fields all over Japan.

They could have had the main ones covered, but we had so much support necessary for our own carriers that they had to take care of us first at the battle. They had call fire, they had lots of support. At that time I don't believe that we had much Army Air out there, which would have been their job, because we had no place for them to work from. So I'm sure that the carriers could not have done both. We had started bombarding Japan at this time, but where they took off from was little fields all over Japan and Formosa.

The best way to do was to have focal points on the line of approach, and have the destroyers and escorts in position so that they could give lots of advance warning, and also direct the fighters from the carriers to the points of contact. And this is what we did.

We had outlying destroyers way way out on the line of approach from Japan, who with their radars could give us lots of advance warnings about the approaches.

So the kamikazes themselves had to go through the screen of the carrier fighters to start with, and a lot of them were lost there. Then they had to go through the outer line of destroyers, and those were the boys who usually got the brunt of the first attack. Then the remainder of the kamikazes would come through and try to get the main battle force, which was us down at Okinawa.

It was this combination of defense against this unorthodox type of work that just through plain attrition wore out the planes and the pilots that Japan had to come against us. But while it was going, and at first when they had that elite corps of kamikazes who knew how to fly with good planes, there was almost hardly any defense against it at all. Those boys were going to get through one way or another, and they did. And we lost a lot of ships as a result.

My ship was one of them that was never any good again. It never came back to war at all. It was left in Kerama Retta, I stayed on the LEARY, and they kept a skeleton crew aboard her. I don't think she ever got back to the States, she was just a mess.

Q: The unit commendation speaks of seven enemy suicide planes attacking the NEWCOMB.

Smoot: I think seven or eight attacked us, but I was interested only in the ones that hit us. There were either three or four. I'm inclined to be a little bit conservative about it, I think there were three. I think that one of them missed us completely and one went in the water astern of us. But three was enough, one was enough. It just raised the devil.

If it was anywhere near you, you were either going to die from concussion or from the fire. But it so happened that these planes, the two that hit and really did the damage, hit aft, and I was on the bridge.

The bunting, all of the flags and the flag bag and the lanyards from which you hoist the flag, they were all on fire on the bridge. But that's all up forward. Midships was a mess.

People that saw us from a distance thought we were all goners. They didn't see how anybody could live.

Q: I want to mention the Bronze Star Medal, which you received from February '44 to May '45. That was the full period when you were in Command of several destroyer squadrons it speaks of, and then the Navy Unit Commendation.

Are we up now to your Command of Task Flotilla Four?

Smoot: We're getting close to it.

Actually from here on, as far as Okinawa was concerned, the main kamikaze threat was mostly over. The battle ashore was down to the point where they were trying to dig the Japanese out of caves.

Call fire for destroyers, particularly our group that was left, consisted of trying to hit specific spots in the hills at the entrance of caves. This was always very interesting, but as far as the unit command was concerned it didn't require much attention. We just answered the call fire and directed specific ships to the point we were told to go, and lie there until they told you to fire and when and where.

The field forces learned a lot of tricks about call fire at that time. When you're looking from shore out to sea and you see literally hundreds of ships of all kinds out there, and there is one destroyer that's firing for you you've got to locate her. And then you've got to locate her line of fire. Then you've got to locate your target with respect to the ship. So what they usually did was to ask you to fire a phosphorus shell at any given point that you could see close to the line of fire which they had given you. Then they'd spot you on from there, and you were in direct contact with the man ashore.

The most difficult problem of all was communications. Our communications at that time from ship to shore were very poor. It took a lot of learning and a lot of improvement of our communication system to get good, which we did before the Okinawa campaign was over.

We had little annoying attacks at night. Somehow or other a Japanese motor torpedo boat would get loose somewhere. We got most of those, but somewhere they'd get loose and come out and go all around the place. They never did any damage. They just annoyed us, kept us awake at night on occasions.

As long as it lasted and as terrific as the original battle was, im the opening part of it, it began to simmer down quite a bit. Then the Japanese would come down just two or three planes at a time and go over the airfields ashore and worry us.

It was about this time that we got the word that there were to be six senior squadron commanders of destroyers appointed to Commodore jobs and given the rank of Commodore with a broad stripe, one star, and they were to be called Screen Commanders. They were to be assigned in accordance with the Task Force Command's final objective.

This was when I got the word that I was to be relieved very soon. As a matter of fact my relief came within two or three weeks of securing Okinawa. I went ashore on Okinawa to take a plane to go back to Hawaii, and briefed again on my new job.

That was a very interesting experience because I hadn't been ashore on Okinawa. All I had done was shoot at her. By this time we had it secured sufficiently to build an airfield and set up control headquarters on the beach.

I remember Admiral Beauty Martin was ashore there and had a tent. I spent the night with him. During the night we had an alert, a Japanese plane came down, so we all jumped out of the tent and headed for our assigned air raid shelter. It was really a cave, a big one. This was their regular place to go for air attacks. But the trouble was you couldn't get in there because the goats had learned that this was a safe place to be too. This darn island was just covered with those stinking little measly goats. They'd go running for these caves to get out of the way of the coming attacks too. They didn't like the airplanes. They didn't like the bombing. They knew that they could get down there and be pretty safe. So we had to battle those goats more than anything else.

I just spent one night on Okinawa, and then flew out the next day to the Carrier Task Forces, where I received orders to proceed to Pearl Harbor and was granted thirty days leave.

Q: Tell me what kind of plane and how large a field was it to accomodate that type of plane.

Smoot: It was an amphibious plane. I actually took off from the water. I went to one of the little islands, and from there went back to Pearl, and then came home on leave.

And Missy complained that she had to spend eighty dollars to buy me some new uniforms, a broad stripe and a hat. Our home was in Coronado.

It seems to me that there ought to be more to tell about Okinawa than I've told. It was a tremendous campaign, wonderfully planned, but we were getting pretty battle wise by this time. Our landing equipment was better, our techniques were better, we were pretty battle wise.

The main thing about it was the human element. It was awfully tiring, particularly the unit commanders with their staffs, because there was never a moment that you could get more than a few hours sleep at a time. I think you lose a lot of efficiency that way - you don't think well, you do things on the spur of the moment.

Q: Who would relieve you if you were going to get a few hours sleep?

Smoot: My Chief of Staff. I wore out two of them – both with the same name, Harris, both of them reserve officers, both excellent officers.

The first Harris we still hear from. He's a fine fellow who lives back east in Johnson City, Tennessee. He's the head of a big lumber firm. He's a very fine fellow, very capable, and a good organizer and manager.

The second, another Harris, lives somewhere around Santa Barbara. He became nervous and tense very soon after reporting. I can't blame him at all. I think I would have been the same way, and so would anybody else. Coming from a shore job, just learning to be a naval officer, coming into the hottest stage of the war – he had a bad time, he really did, mentally and physically. He didn't last very long. He was detached after I left, and returned to the U. S. for rehabilitation.

I bring this out because I think that the main thing was fatigue, just plain fatigue that got many of us. Tension and fear was a way of life. It's a terrifying thing to watch human guided destruction come right at you, and the noise of the guns going constantly – it's really something.

My Chief of Staff and I spelled each other during periods of relative quiet. He could take over while I slept a few hours, and then I'd take over and he'd sleep a few hours. Then things would heat up again and we would all be at our stations.

This, as far as the Japanese, was really the climax. In terms of tension and danger Okinawa was the climax — and the beginning of the end for Japan.

The rest of it after that, when I became a unit commander and a Commodore, assigned as screen commander to a Fast Carrier Task Force, it was relatively easy for us in the support ships.

My staff was capable, excellent, and there were a lot of them. They assigned me one of those small high speed five-inch cruisers, like the SAN DIEGO as a flag ship. They were wonderful ships for that purpose. The Task Force Commander would put us right in the middle of the Task Force, carriers all around us. We were usually the guide for all maneuvers, so matters of station keeping also became simple.

All you had to worry about really was keeping your destroyers in place, run the resupply and refueling schedules, and be sure that you had your screen well placed for every phase of defense, and get your operations orders to the Task Force Commander in time. You spent a lot of time going from ship to ship. The Task Force Commander sent for you constantly, and we did this by breeches buoy. We had no helicopters then.

It was really a pleasure. I thoroughly enjoyed it, and what a contrast. From then on, until we landed in Japan, was really duck soup. I think I forgot to mention that my flag ship was in the USS SAN DIEGO.

Q: That's surprising that you could say any time in the war was not unpleasant.

Smoot: In comparison to the high tension of duty with the landing forces in our island-hopping campaign it was really pleasant duty.

Q: Leyte was that same experience, but was not as long in days and time lapsed as Okinawa.

Smoot: No, and we didn't have the great waves of kamikazes. We had some few kamikazes at Leyte. That's where it started. The BRYANT, of my unit, was damaged by a kamikaze at Leyte, but not badly, she stayed with us.

Yes, in terms of the length of the battle and the tension Okinawa was the climax.

Q: And the job as screen commander lasted five months.

Smoot: The period, during which I had this screen as a Commodore and was in the Fast Carrier Task Forces, was devoted primarily to planned attacks on the main islands of Japan. These were all organized, planned, and directed right from the Carrier Task Force flag ship.

As far as my duty as the screen was concerned, I had only to maintain an effective anti-submarine and anti-aircraft screen and schedule all refueling and other logistic supply schedules.

One interesting development came rather early in these attacks on the main islands of Japan. A Japanese fighter plane or bomber would follow the returning American Navy pilots in their planes back to the carrier group. He could get away with this at times, and not be spotted by our pilot or our ships radar. His objective was to crash land on a carrier deck in a kamikaze attack.

We got onto that very soon and established what we called "delousing stations." This was a group of two or three destroyers that we would station some twenty-five to thirty miles away from the Task Force in line with our own returning planes. All of our planes were ordered to circle over these ships. Of course the Japanese didn't know what to do and he would always be spotted. Then it just took one or two planes to get him and knock him out of the sky. Then our planes were vectored to the Task Force to land.

Q: You could even tell by sight that they were Japanese planes?

Smoot: Yes, by that system - his presence would be disclosed because he could not follow the coded orders of the destroyer task unit in the purposely complicated vector directions back to the Task Force.

So these delousing stations were among the innovations that were developed during the period of our attacks on Japan. It was the screen commander's responsibility to see that they were properly maintained and rotated. They had to be relieved on a regularly scheduled basis for logistic purposes.

Q: Are those the ships that were referred to as 'picket boats?"

Smoot: We had all kinds of names for them, "delousing stations" I thought was the best.

With Japan's obvious defeat getting closer we operated closer to the mainland and did actual bombardments. We'd send groups of bombarding ships, including cruisers, battleships, and destroyers, up close to the mainland and designated specific targets for bombardment. Some times they'd go right after a big steel factory or a center of municipal supply, - electrical and coal and gas supply centers where we could get them with guns close to the beach. All of this was becoming routine.

Some times my flag ship was included. But for the most part I stayed with my flag ship, the SAN DIEGO, right in the center of the Carrier Task Force.

Destroyers were coming and going all the time. We maintained anywhere between twenty and forty destroyers as a unit for this one Task Force.

I cannot remember the group commander that I worked for, I don't remember his name. I was with him all during those last few months before the downfall of Japan.

Then we withdrew and had a couple of weeks of pretty easy cruising.

Q: Were you given any forecast that something might happen on August 6th, when they did drop the atomic bomb? Were you given any alert to stay clear, that something was going to happen?

Smoot: No, not on my level. I knew something big and unusual was imminent because I was called over to the flag ship for a conference. They didn't actually say it was going to be a nuclear bomb, but they said that some spectacular thing was going to happen in Japan. We were to stay out and were not to have any airplanes in the air at all. We were going to withdraw pretty far to the east.

We were told that our withdrawal and inactivity was just for the purpose of a rest period. We were still going to attack again. But for the time being, we were just going to the high seas and resupply and have a couple weeks of pretty easy cruising, which we did.

Then of course it all broke in the press, and we all knew what it was. A couple of days before my own Task Group Commander told me what it was going to be, and told me not to mention it to anybody.

It really didn't impress me too much, because I didn't know what an atomic bomb was. We had had one in the United States at Alamogordo, but I had been out at sea all the time. I didn't get any dope on it.

The devastation of that thing, I didn't know what it was all about, nor that it would have such an impact on history. It didn't seem an awfully important thing to me at the time.

I was interested primarily in when Japan was going to give up. Germany had already given up. It was just a matter of days, it was due.

Then when the word did come, plans were fast and furious coming right from the President as what to do and how to do it.

I ended up in Command of a unit that was to assemble 10,000 enlisted men in transports, taken from our own combat ships. Each type was given a quota by grade and rating. They could start sparing people now because we didn't have to man the guns all the time, and we were not standing battle watches.

All of this was done at sea, underway - 10,000 enlisted men with their equipment, guns, and ammunition transferred to several trasnports that had been ordered to join us. And to do this all at sea, underway, was quite an operation.

The orders that were given at this time by Halsey himself, I think, were, "If you do see a Japanese plane approaching you and he looks like he's going to do something you don't like shoot him down as gently as possible."

The war was over and so there was no more combat theoretically. Nevertheless we weren't taking any chances. But anyway we didn't have any incidents.

All this had to be done at sea, underway. It was quite something to transfer 10,000 men at sea with their equipment, and put them aboard transports to land in Yokosuka on D-day. And to have a complete set of operation orders ready to give to my boss in a few days, who was then Admiral Badger, for his approval and to be passed on up to the Commander-in-Chief of the Pacific for his approval. I don't remember when I ever worked so continuously for so long a time.

However, as I said, I had a real talented staff by this time. These were top officers, they were number one. So the big thing was working against a deadline. We didn't have much time to sleep.

Q: Were you able to use your same staff in order to prepare the operation orders?

Smoot: I used my same staff and I could have anybody else I wanted. I needed an Assistant Operations Officer to help my Operations Officer write up his orders. So I just sent over to Badger, "If you've got somebody that you know is a good planner let me have him. I need him right now," and we got one. I did this for several jobs, and ended up with quite a talented staff.

Q: Did you stay on the SAN DIEGO?

Smoot: No, I transferred to a transport. I needed more room. And also they wanted me to be with the Marine General, who's name was Clement (he died later after the war) to coordinate the actual landing. There wasn't room for him and me on the SAN DIEGO, so we moved to a big transport that had plenty of room. I took my staff over there, and Clement took his staff. So we worked together very well. But all of this was done underway.

I don't think people realize what an operation that is to transfer 10,000 men and all their equipment at sea, never stopping, going night and day, ships moving all the time.

Q: How long did it take you to transfer that many men?

Smoot: It took a good two weeks. That doesn't mean that we transferred so many every day. It meant that some days were devoted to other exercises that we had to do. We had to tend to our logistic needs on schedule, and all that was done underway too.

It was a very interesting, but time consuming and very tiring operation getting this ready.

Q: How many thousands did you have to consider? We're talking now about a seagoing group becoming almost a naval district headquarters ashore starting from scratch.

Smoot: Yes, to start from scratch. Our objective was to set up the administrative headquarters ashore in Japan that would run what shore equipment we knew we could get hold of and use, to take over from Japan. So Yokosuka was a natural, because it was a big naval base with lots of room and lots of housing.

The landing was unopposed. Nevertheless we went ashore ashore armed to the teeth, and prepared to defend ourselves.

Q: How many went ashore to begin with - the initial landing group? Did the Marines go first?

Smoot: The Marines went first, they were the first to land.

We in the Navy were told not to land until we actually saw the Marines moving across our landing strip where we were going, which was a dock where I was to take my staff ashore. I already had the house that I was to go to and move into as the headquarters office of the senior officer present ashore. This was designated, and that was to be my job ashore.

We had to set up communications, run telephones that were fairly secure, establish headquarters for myself and Halsey, and for Admiral Badger and his staffs. All of this had to be done with the barest knowledge really of what facilities we could have and get.

We also were concerned as to whether their water was any good, whether we could drink the water. So we had to plan for setting up distilleries of our own. We had to take our own food ashore and plan for continued resupply.

Their bunks were little short ones. We couldn't sleep in them, our American boys couldn't. So we had to provide beds. We took all our beds ashore - cots, hammocks, anything we could get

All of this had to be done and planned for the 10,000 enlisted men that I had. Then the Marines had an equal number that they landed, I'm sure. So there were about 20,000 people ashore, all in one morning, all in Yokosuka.

We had no incidents at all. Meanwhile the battleships came in and anchored, and all of the small craft anchored up in the Bay close to Yokohama. And the Japanese freed the American prisoners of war.

On my trip when I was told to take my ship down to Yokosuka to get close in for the landing the prisoners had been freed and they were on the docks. To see American ships in there for the first time they just lost their heads. They just piled down on this little rickety dock as we went by.

I saw some of those prisoners fall in the water, and I'm afraid they drowned, because they just didn't have strength enough to get back up. It was a frightful sight to see.

We had boats in there as fast as we could and the prisoners, our own men, were taken back aboard the ships as we had room for them. We got hospital ships in there, we got transports, we got everything we could get in there, just as fast as we could.

Q: That was a dramatic experience, wasn't it.

Smoot: Oh, a terrific experience. I don't see why they had to turn them loose that way. It was fine to turn them loose, but they should have restrained them until we could properly care for them.

Q: Who was in charge?

Smoot: Nobody was ashore yet. The Japanese had turned them loose. There wasn't anybody in charge.

But as soon as we saw them on the dock immediately we sent boats in to get them as fast as we could, but they panicked in this one instance, and I saw them. The dock was just jammed, there were several hundred. They were in dark type of fatigues, loose fitting type of Japanese fatigue uniforms. I didn't get close enough to actually see them.

One of the other Commodores had that job of taking care of the prisoners. He was assigned to it. He was appointed from a screen commander to the rank of Commodore at the same time that I was.

We could see the American POWs crowding down on the dock, getting so excited and waving at us. They were jumping up and down. We knew they were completely out of control, and we could see people falling in the water. We didn't know at the time that they were weak of course, because we couldn't see in that detail. All we could tell was it was our men. We could also see that they were excited and completely out of control.

The Japanese should not have let them loose that way. They should have held them until we got there with ambulances to take care of them.

All they wanted to do was get out of that land and get aboard American ships any way they could. I guess if I were there I'd have been right with them.

But they were in awfully poor shape. They were weak and hungry. Although I've never had it confirmed to me I'm sure that some of those boys died that day, with freedom in sight. It was a terrible thing to see.

They had been released from a local prison around that area. Our ships were anchored all up and down along the waterfront, all the way from Tokyo down to Yokosuka. There were hundreds of ships.

As a matter of fact later on I was almost late for the surrender ceremony, because I didn't get the word until pretty late, and it was a long long trip out from Yokosuka to the MISSOURI that morning. She was clear up off Yokohama and that was a long trip. I got aboard just about ten minutes before the ceremony.

Q: I want to get to that in a minute. But I'd like to have you tell more about going ashore, and what happened, and what you found there, and whether there were any people to help you.

Smoot: When we got the word to land our part of the landing force, that the Marines had cleared everything and that there was no sign of any trickery, it just went smoothly as the dickens. It was just beautifully done. Everybody went ashore on time. We had planned it down to the minute.

I was given a certain dock that I was to go to, and I was told that I would be met there by the Japanese naval base commander who would have an English speaking interpreter. And he did, he was there when we went ashore.

I went ashore with an armed guard. The guard was armed, as we all were. We weren't taking any chances. No one knew what they - the Japs - might do. They were armed too - the Japanese. They had their side arms. I don't think they had any guns, there wasn't any sign of guns.

There was an Admiral of the Japanese navy and there was his aide, a Lieutenant Commander in the Japanese navy. There were about five or six different officers around him, and there was probably a company of Japanese enlisted men. They were all lined up in grim silence. The Japanese Admiral, through his interpreter, said, "I am at your service sir." I said, "I would like you to show me to these barracks. This is where our headquarters are to be." We had a map, which we showed him.

My aide and the Japanese Admiral's interpreter got together with it, and he took us right up to our designated set of barracks. They were clean and hadn't been damaged. That is, there was no sign of any of our bombing. I don't think we really went after anything much ashore at Yokosuka because the plan was to use Yokosuka when we landed.

Q: Had the Japanese done any damage, any sabotaging?

Smoot: No, they hadn't done anything. This building was in perfectly good shape, as was the officers club where Admiral Badger went - that was his headquarters, he was my boss.

That was the second place I went, as soon as I established my headquarters, which just took me a few minutes. Because all I wanted to do was leave my Chief of Staff there with all of my enlisted help to get the place set up for an office with typewriters, radio, telephone wires among our own various offices, get organized for logistic support, and take steps to insure our own comfort. We didn't know how long we would be there, so we had to set up housekeeping for a prolonged period.

In a few hours a messenger came for me and I proceeded to the Japanese officers club, Admiral Badger's designated headquarters, to attend informal pre-surrender ceremonies of the area conducted by Admiral Badger. He had a Vice Admiral - Japanese type - who was talking to him when I arrived. Apparently he found the same circumstances that I did. The Japanese Admiral was most cooperative, very prim and proper, but the place was ours, and he made it known that it was ours, and they were at our service, and anything we wanted all we had to do was ask.

Q: Were the Japanese disarmed? Did you require them to get rid of their arms?

Smoot: They had side arms only, no guns. Guns and ammunition were supposed to be placed in one location and turned over to us, and I guess they did.

I had a group of ordnance experts with my staff. In charge was a Marine Lieutenant Colonel, who took care of all of that, and he later said they had no problems at all. Most of the things were in caves, because they'd been living in caves for a long time.

We had no incidents at all. I was quite favorably surprised. As a matter of fact the next word I got was from Halsey - to please set up the officers club at Yokosuka for a party that night with all the fixings, including ladies. Where was I going to get the ladies? I got nurses, I got a whole lot of nurses off the hospital ship and invited them. Halsey came down and we toasted many victories and had a very pleasant evening that night.

Q; Was there liquor there?

Smoot: Liquor was there, our own.

Q: This now would be late August. Do you remember the dates? It was before the surrender ceremony.

Smoot: Yes, it was before the surrender ceremony. The surrender ceremony was the second of September. This was in late August. We were there for several days before the surrender ceremony.

I encountered remarkably few problems in setting up communications. This Japanese Admiral was at my service constantly and was most cooperative. In fact we became quite friendly before it was over. It's amazing how quick your enemies can become your friends when you stop shooting at each other. They saw that we were gentlemen. We weren't going to beat them. We weren't going to act like arrogant conquistadors at all. We were American military men and we had won a war, a long bad one. There was no sense in beating them to death now, they were cooperating. They soon got the word and were most cooperative to us. I was quite favorably surprised.

There wasn't any intermingling, we didn't have parties together, or things like that. They lived entirely in their own barracks, separate from us. But they were available to us all the time. As far as I know there was never anything overt or intended to be trickery of any kind whatsoever. All they wanted to do was be as cooperative as possible.

Q: When you saw those prisoners, was it difficult to treat them with a calm attitude?

Smoot: That part of it was very hard. When they had been your bitter enemies and done the things they had for four long years, you had a deep and abiding hate in your heart for them.

But I had made it very clear to my staff and the people aboard the ships that there was to be absolutely no incidents at all initiated by the American forces in any way. All that I wanted them to do, if they were attacked in any form whatsoever, was to defend themselves. But there was to be no evidence of hate or retribution. They had surrendered, and they were supposedly human beings, and we were to treat them that way.

It turned out that they did pretty much so. I can't recall a single serious incident.

I understand that there were incidents of minor consequence, where there was a question as to who was going to get what area for what purpose.

One such concerned an area where we had a communication outpost, where they planned to set up a signal station of their own. They didn't think we should take it, so the matter had to be referred to higher authority. It was all settled amicably, but there was a little unpleasantness there.

I learned a lot in an operation like that. I'd never had it before, and I don't suppose I'll ever have it again.

The human side of people comes to the surface when you stop shooting at each other, and comes to the surface very rapidly. We very shortly had quite a warm association, the group around us, within a month after I was there.

However the surrender ceremony on the MISSOURI was something else again. The Japanese that were involved in the surrender itself were just as cold and officious as they could be. There was nothing friendly about that morning whatsoever.

When the Japanese came up the gangplank they were in stiff full dress. They looked neither right nor left. They walked straight to the table, and stood at stiff attention, with never a smile, never a single gracious gesture.

MacArthur started talking, and gave about a five minute address. Then the Japanese replied. Signatures were affixed to the documents, and the Japanese turned on their heels and left. MacArthur followed immediately and that was it.

Q: How did you get your invitation?

Smoot: I got it by dispatch - by radio. It was delayed in getting to me. I was busy. I was on an outpost. I commandeered any boat that I could. Unfortunately I didn't get a very fast boat.

I arrived just before the Japanese officials. The only place that I could get to was up on a gun turret in back of the stand where most of the press was. And that wasn't a very good place to be, because the press were expert at elbowing you out. And I sure got elbowed, oh boy did I get elbowed. Any time I tried to move some place where I could see the ceremony I got elbowed by somebody with a camera. They're good at that. So I didn't see very much actually.

The pressure and the tension that we'd been under went away. We had many gatherings at the officers club at night, reminiscing, talking about old times, and about the war. And I saw many friends that I hadn't seen for a long long time.

In other words for the first time in four long years we were not a group of fighting men on board ship.

Now we were ashore. The war was over, and that old comradery started coming back again. This part I'll never forget. This was a wonderful feeling. Everybody was happy, and wanted to do anything they could, anyway they could, to get on with the business, and get set up whatever was needed, and get home.

Q: That was Port Director. Did you just continue on with the organization that you had set up as SOPA?

Smoot: Yes. Port Director included, among other things, the scheduling of the hospital ships and specially equipped transports to get our prisoners out of the prison camps that the Japanese told us about all through the islands, and of dispatching transports with landing forces to the various outlying areas of Japan were we'd take surrender. This included all of the by-passed islands that we hand't actually taken. We skipped a lot of islands. The Japanese were still there. The Emperor had ordered all of them to be prepared to surrender when the official American party arrived.

So there was a lot of scheduling of destroyers and cruisers to these various and sundry places. This was all done through the Port Director's office. I was under Admiral Halsey and his staff.

He was ashore mostly. He had a beautiful room in the officers club there, and so did Mick Carney, his Chief of Staff. I worked mostly with Mick Carney and Rollo Wilson, the operations officer on Halsey's staff. Rollo and I had a phone directly to each other. It was a private phone that we had strung ourselves. Rollo and Mick Carney were ashore in the same office building as Badger. Badger was my boss. So it was easy to get to them and see them all the time. Our offices were about a mile apart. My office was my sleeping quarters also.

I had no trouble handling any of the requirements of the Port Director of the shore establishment, as the senior officer present ashore. I imagine at one time I probably had fifty officers on my staff, and I needed them. We were handling so many details. But after we got settled down and it became more or less routine I think I got down to about fifteen or twenty officers. That was all I needed, and it worked fine.

I had one run in with General MacArthur's staff. That had to do with getting transport type ship over to Yokohama to pick up a group of American prisoners of war who were released, who had come from some place way up in the northern part of Japan, and who needed attention.

We soon raised a hospital ship somewhere north of Okinawa, and ordered her to proceed to Yokohama at fastest possible speed Immediately I got an enigmatic cancellation of those orders from a headquarters that was not Navy. The source was not familiar to my communication staff.

So I got my communicator to chase it back through the communications channel, and found out it came from MacArthur's headquarters. I also found out that he sent that hospital ship to the Philippines to get his wife and son and their furniture and bring them to Japan. And our poor released prisoners had to wait. My blood pressure reached the bursting point.

I don't think maybe you'd better print that, but this is true.

Q: And what happened to the prisoners?

Smoot: I got another transport later, but it took me two more days to get one. I just about blew the roof off of that place. I went storming up to Badger and we went over to see Mick Carney. He got on the phone and called somebody at the headquarters in Tokyo and talked to them. I heard most of it and the last thing I heard was, "That's the God damnest thing I ever heard." And that was Mick Carney. He slammed down the phone and said, "Go back and have a drink and calm your blood pressure. There's nothing we can do about it."

This is true – a whole hospital ship to bring Mrs. MacArthur and her son and their furniture to Japan. It took two weeks. There was a hospital ship completely out of use when we needed it so badly for our released prisoners.

Boy, how we needed them. We had lots of ships, but we needed every one we could get. The hospital ships were the ones we really needed because of the doctors aboard.

I can't think of very much more to tell you about that. Oh yes, there was one incident. I received a set of orders which gave me thirty days leave.

So I went up and saw Mick Carney, and said, "What are you giving me leave for? I just had leave. I had leave when I left Desron 56 in Okinawa, when I put on my broad stripe as Commodore and reported to Halsey as one of his task group commanders." Mick said, "Oh my gosh, I forgot about that. Why did you tell me?"

I said, "I told you because I know that Commodore Womble, who's working with me up there, has had no leave for about two years. He's been out here for a year and a half at least. If anybody gets leave he ought to get it." Mick said, "Well, okay. Womble will get it. And you stay here."

So he complimented me on letting him know, but he said, "I think you're a sucker though."

I became a very close friend of Mick Carney's.

I credit that little incident with a lot that happened to me later in importance of assignments and in work that was given to me that was good for me, and perhaps had to do consideraly with my making flag grade. Shows what little things sometimes shape our future.

I could have gone on and taken that leave, and they'd have found out about it later because Womble would have squawked, I'm sure. It was a lot better to have done it the way I did, and I think it helped.

It was maybe two weeks later that I got orders from the Bureau to go to Washington. I didn't want to go, and I sent a dispatch to that effect - that I was doing fine and wanted to finish my job in Japan. But it didn't work out that way. I was told politely to carry out my orders.

It turned out that that was fine, because the job that they sent me to in the Bureau was known as an "Admiral maker." I think that Mick Carney had a lot to do with it.

Q: So you actually were only on duty ashore about two months. You left in October, and reported to the Bureau on November of '45. So I'm sure that was a busy two months.

Smoot: It was. I saw a lot of Japan. We went all over every place, and saw a lot of the damages. I had a chance to fly down to Nagasaki and see where the bomb was dropped. I went dwon with Halsey's operation officer.

He and I and a group of planners flew all over the island to set up long range plans for the Navy's use of Japan as a Far East Station, because we knew we were going to have to administer Japan one way or another, and the Navy had to be in it. We had to have a shipyard, we had to have docks, we had to have places that we could operate from. So I saw a lot of Japan that I wouldn't otherwise have seen.

We also set up outlying communication centers, both radio and telephone, running lines by jeep and getting back into the back country.

Seeing some of the beautiful and unspoiled Japan was very interesting to me.

Q: Did the Japanese enlisted people ever work for you?

Smoot: Sure. We had a whole barracks of Japanese, commanded by a Rear Admiral and a staff. Any time we wanted something done they'd join right in. They drove all the cars because they knew the country. They were excellent.

I had my own Japanese driver for my personal jeep. I don't know when he ever slept, he was always available constantly.

Q: Did you ever have any fear, any incidents of any danger at all any place that you went in Japan?

Smoot: No, never did. I never had any fear at all.

We had one little unpleasant accident. One of the enlisted men, in moving a group of guns, dropped a gun and it went off and killed a Japanese civilian. It was in an outlying place where the Japanese hadn't accepted us yet completely. This gave them an opportunity to riot. They just blew the devil out of that outfit and just beat the hell out of them. There was a young Lieutenant, several Marines, and several sailors. They didn't kill anybody, but they were beat up. They were on their way some place to set up an outlying communications center. It was some of my men. This young Lieutenant was a reserve officer and just loved his job. He was a good telephone man, tops. That was his job. He was enthusiastic and capable.

It wasn't more than twenty or thirty miles from Yokosuka. It was out towards the Mt. Fuji somewhere, some outlying city out there that had to do with trains and train transportation. We wanted to have contact with them to control trains, more than the transportation, because we were using trains an awful lot going from north to south.

We were carrying loaded guns. I wasn't particularly in favor of it. I never did like it, and I wanted to get rid of them as soon as I could. But we were advised to do so, particularly on these outlying missions.

This poor Marine tripped and fell and his gun went off and it killed a young Japanese by pure accident. But they were worked up. They hadn't seen the Americans before, and they still resented us.

They weren't rescued, they made their own way back. Apparently the better judgement of some more elderly Japanese overcame this mob of kids. And they pulled them off of them and took them in their homes and cleaned them up, bandaged them and did what they could for them.

The young Lieutenant was not badly enough hurt, so he set up his own little communications center and sent a message to me. It finally got through. So we sent a group up there right away and brought them back in an ambulance and some jeeps. Several of them had broken bones, really badly hurt.

Q: That's an incident that I'd not heard.

Smoot: I don't think it's written up anywhere.

I wrote up to Badger, and he said, "We won't do anything about this. We'll drop it, because what are you going to gain by doing it? You're not going out and shoot those people. There's bound to be some incidents and this won't be the last one. There's high tension here. These people are defeated, and they've gone through an awful lot of things."

I was quite surprised at Badger, because he was a crusty guy. And I was quite surprised at his attitude, but he did it very wisely.

That was just the attitude that we had to take during that time in Japan - that this was a defeated nation. And they're people that we don't know. They are of entirely different backgrounds, entirely different type of education, entirely different character in every way. Their beliefs and way of life are so different from ours.

And we can't expect to come in here and lead our lives the way we'd lead them at home. We've got to be very flexible. We have got to understand. And we've got to treat them as gentlemen and as human beings, even though they were the beastly type of enemy that they were. We've got to treat them this way. We've got to live with them for a long long time.

Badger was smart enough at that time to realize it.

He said, "We're going to have to bring these islands back. They are in the worse state of decay of any place in the world. They are just beating the earth with no way to live, and we've got to bring them back. So what was our enemy must now be our patients.

"So let there be no incidents started by us at all, none. We'll lean over backwards to be subservient if necessary but don't start anything. Let them start it. Don't start anything."

I never had any trouble. I just acted like I always acted, and so did my staff.

This was the only incident that happened, and it was an accident. And it hit a time when there was high tension in a place that hand't been in contact before.

This was a lesson I learned - not to do anything without first clearing the way diplomatically. We had specially trained people for that purpose. They were trained for just this type of work, and I should have used them in advance of the technicians in this incident.

Q: You probably were lulled into a sense of security because you'd seen no trouble.

Smoot: That could be. But I was sort of brought to task a little bit for not using the talent I had on my staff.

Admiral Badger said, "Where was George?" I said, "George was up in Tokyo." He said, "Then you shouldn't have sent them out without George or one of his boys, because this was just what we brought them out for." But I had others I could have sent, and should have.

Q: Are there any other incidents that we want to discuss in this remaining two months time?

Smoot: No, the only thing was the shock at getting my orders. I was prepared to stay out there until we got settled. I'd like to have had Sal come out. I enjoyed it.

Q: You spoke of the British having a separate landing party?

Smoot: Yes, there was a British contingent. They had their own ships and they had their own landing force. They organized it their own way. It was coordinated with my landing force instructions and my orders, the orders that I had made up for my own staff.

It was coordinated on Badger's level, my boss' level, and the British landing force's level. They got together and coordinated which part of Yokosuka we would take and use as our headquarters and which part the British would take and use as their headquarters.

Q: Were there headquarters of any other allied powers? British and American were the only ones?

Smoot: Just British and American, that was all.

So the British had the section of their landing beach, which later turned out to encompass the hinterland further back from the area and included a great many of the caves in which the Japanese of Yokosuka and the Yokohama district had been living. Military and civilians - all of them had been living there.

Of course they had stashed all of their most expensive and personal belongings in caves, including great amounts of very fine china, old china, beautiful linens and silks. These had been stowed in some of these caves.

By the time I got to some of them and looked through them as part of my duties the treasures had been very roughly torn out of their storage places in some cases in the anxiety to get something that might be a little bit better. They were thrown on the floor and trampled, dishes were broken.

We barricaded the entries and posted sentries at each cave, but a lot of damage had already been done.

Q: Did it appear to be looting?

Smoot: Definitely so, and I'm sure it was mostly the British because they were there first. They went right to the caves and they didn't control the enlisted men at all. Some of the things they did ~~was~~ were just frightful.

I don't blame the British, because our boys probably would have done the same thing. But the British were there first.

The place where we landed was in the navy yard and the ship yard, and there weren't any caves there.

Q: You wouldn't have permitted it anyway, would you?

Smoot: I certainly wouldn't, if I had known it would happen, but I don't know that I would have thought of it.

Maybe the British didn't know about it until after they saw what was going on, and then they stopped it.

Because if you have a group of enlisted men that are in charge of a sergeant, and they go into a place like this under orders, and they are looking for something, you as an officer, unless you are there, have little control. You don't know what went on.

I say the British simply because it was in the British area. It could have been some of our boys that got in there, I don't know.

Anyway we closed the caves and there was no more looting, and there was no more souvenir taking at all, but there was an awful lot of it taken up to that time. This was within the first fifteen or twenty hours of the landing, just overnight. Then it was all stopped.

It was obvious that the caves required looking into to find out if anybody was hiding in there and clean them out. So the whole British landing force went up there. I would have too, I think, if I had had that area. It was just natural.

We had one other incident that was a little bit of trouble, but not very much. Of course wherever you've got Americans you've got a garbage dump. We had a garbage dump, and we had a big one. We contracted with the Japanese to take the garbage out daily and dump it at sea.

They would come in and get this big pile of trash and garbage that only Americans can pile up, they'd put it on the scows and take it out and dump it. We would pay them for this. It was a service that we paid for.

These were civilians. You couldn't tell after awhile because for the most part, except for the officers, they were all in fatigues. Everybody around the place was in fatigues. They didn't have much else left I guess.

One day as they were loading this garbage onto a scow there was a big explosion on the scow and several Japanese were killed.

What had happened was - some sailor, and I presume it was American, had taken a big box of unused ammunition, didn't know that it was unused, thought it was scrap stuff, hadn't opened it, and threw it on the garbage dump.

Apparently as the Japanese were loading it on the garbage scow it hit it just right to explode one of the shells, and it exploded all the other ones.

The Japanese informed me that they were not going to subject themselves to this possibility any more, that we'd have to take our own garbage out.

We changed their minds for them right away. We told them that this was an accident. My conversation with the Japanese was, "We'll be more careful in the future about this kind of thing, but don't give us that stuff about having to handle our own garbage. You will handle the garbage, you have a contract, you did it up to now, and this is your business and start right now or else." So they did, and we had no more trouble with that.

There was one part of my duty that was assigned as a special extra duty by Admiral Halsey, and that was to accept the surrender of all of the destroyers in Yokosuka, which I enjoyed doing.

It was an elaborate affair and set up with pomp and ceremony that only the Japanese can do, with everybody in full dress. It was done on one destroyer that was least damaged. Most of them were just hulks, half of them were on the bottom, because we really had bombed that place.

I went aboard with my staff. The Japanese officer in command and his division commander were there. They had the Japanese flag at full staff.

So when we exchanged pleasantries through interpreters I explained what I was there for and he said, "Yes, I have been so advised. Shall we get on with the ceremony?"

Through the interpreter he said, "When I haul down the Japanese flag, I would prefer to haul it down before the American flag is raised." I said, "That's perfectly all right. We'll raise the American flag. I'm in no hurry to raise the American flag. He said, "I just wanted to be sure about that."

We went through the ceremony and then he said, "We have been ordered to turn over all of the swords that the officers have to you. These are the swords." He had about ten swords lined up on a bench over at one side of the quarterdeck of this destroyer. I said, "Thank you very much. We'll take them."

He caught me by surprise by that. I hadn't been briefed about the swords. I didn't know, but I took them.

We doled those swords out very carefully. I had one myself.

The ceremony was all verbal - "In accordance with the edict issued by His Majesty Imperial (so and so) we acknowledge the defeat of Japan in the great war of the Pacific. (I can't remember the exact words, but this is like what he said.) We have been ordered to surrender the remainder of the fleet as it exists in Yokouska to the American authorities. Therefore I, as Rear Admiral so and so, Japanese navy, do hereby surrender these ships and their belongings to you the representative of the United States Navy."

I said, "In the name of the Commander-in-Chief of the Pacific Fleet, under whose orders I am operating, I accept the surrender of the remainder of the fleet in Yokosuka as directed by His Imperial Majesty, the Emperor of Japan. In so doing I accept as a token of the surrender the Japanese flag and the swords presented herewith."

So it's all a part of the record. I took the swords and the flag.

Q: Was there any visible emotion on his part?

Smoot: Yes, particularly in surrendering the swords. He did want his sword very much. He didn't want to give up that sword, because it was a samurai sword. I found out afterwards that some of these go back years and years and years.

This I think was a great mistake of the American Navy. We shouldn't have done this. We should have given those swords back right then, not kept them.

I kept mine for years. And then the order came out from the Navy Department to return the swords. It was a beautiful thing. And I hope that guy got it back, I really do.

Because as we learned later these all had great significance and background history to them. They were something like giving away half of your family.

We werent' briefed. Of course we hadn't received many surrenders from the Japanese. So we didn't know what to do.

I still have the flag. I was allowed to keep the flag.

Q: I would think that that should be with the Navy history collection in Annapolis or the Institute.

Smoot: I think they've got all the flags they want. This flag was not on the destroyer when it was disabled. This flag was raised for the occasion. So I didn't attach much real significance to it.

I asked Badger about that. I said, "How about these things?" He said, "You keep the flag, and dole out the swords. I've got a sword anyway. I got this Admiral's sword over here."

We all gave those swords back later, years later.

Q: I think Admiral Nimitz had something to do with initiating that.

Smoot: I'm sure he did.

Q: Your next job was one of some duration. It was over two years. You were sent back to the Bureau of Naval Personnel in Navy Headquarters. That was over in Arlington. What was the actual title of the job?

Smoot: It was called Director of Officer Distribution.

I relieved a young fellow out of the class of '22 named Converse in that duty, who undoubtedly would have been a real top notch Admiral. Unfortunately he had this high blood pressure condition which got worse, and he died at quite an early age.

Q: Why do you call it an "Admiral maker" job?

Smoot: I had never heard of it as an "Admiral maker" job until I got ordered to it. It was other people who had told me about it being an "Admiral maker" job. It was so called because of some five or six officers ahead of me who had had that job every one of them subsequently made Admiral.

Q: I thought that you meant that you had the control of assignments of officers so that you were able to guide their careers in assignments to point them toward promotion.

Smoot: That's a logical conclusion that you would draw, but that isn't the reason it was so called.

When you get ordered to duty like that from a sea job like I had, an important sea job and one that I had hoped that I could keep for awhile as a flag officer afloat, and get ordered to tha awful place in Washington in the headquarters where you have to go if they order you, it's a terrible come down. And I didn't want the job at all.

But I was told by people who knew at the time, including Halsey, "Don't be a sucker. This is an "Admiral maker" job, so you take it."

Q: Were you reverted to Captain?

Smoot: Yes, I reverted to Captain.

The Commodore job was made solely for wartime purposes. And we don't use the Commodore except in war.

I reverted to Captain, and that didn't bother me in the least. I recognized that the Commodore rank was temporary and it didn't draw any more pay. It just required me to change my uniforms and buy a special hat and a few things like that.

It's only devised for wartime purposes, because you have such large task forces that it's difficult to get an experienced four-stripe Captain who is senior to a lot of Captains who might come in under you. So in the frequent rotation of destroyer units in the task force the arriving unit commander is senior to the assigned task force screen commander. Continual rotation of that important force function was awkward and inefficient. So they activated the Commodore rank for screen commander only, that's all, to make a better administrative organization and better control in the task force line of command.

3 Smoot - 217

Q: Were you Deputy BuPers on this job?

Smoot: Not in this job, no.

This was a four-stripe Captain's job and designated "Director of Officers Distribution." That was under the old Bureau organization.

Q: You say that it called for greater human effort, more than any assignment that you'd had before, which is an astonishing comment considering what you'd done already. I want you to explain that.

Smoot: Yes, it did.

It's a little difficult to explain maybe. I have a technical mind, and always have had. I would like to have been an engineering officer, and probably would have made more money in industry if I had gone into some kind of engineering, which is beside the point. I didn't. I liked the Navy life, and it was very rewarding to me.

But up until this time my jobs had been at sea. I had command functions, whereby you have a capable staff and you have an objective. You have ships and you knw what they're built for. You train your men to accomplish their mission. You practice and exercise at sea for these kinds of things with the inevitable object in view - and that's war, to shoot and disable your enemy. This is the objective of the whole thing, no other objective to it. This is what we were trained to do.

I liked ships and I liked going to sea. I liked this technical side of learning to use the ships for their ability to destroy or deny the enemies forces. That's what you do. After all it's just a weapon platform that goes to sea. But the use of it, and the technicalities of its exploitation was fascinating to me.

So this is a shore job, after months of warfare where for the first time I am not using the experience of people to accomplish this wartime achievement and run ships. I'm using my own knowledge of the human being to pick out the kind of people to do these jobs, and specifically important people, people on the way up, people in the Captain's grade, the last non-flag grade in the Navy, who have gone through quite a screening process to reach this point in their careers.

You have thousands of Captains and you've got maybe hundreds of jobs that will make Admirals of them. Who are you going to send there? How do you pick them? I handled the Captains myself. How do you pick them, based upon what? What are the human factors involved in this kind of thing? You've got their families - for the first time you've gone into the hearts and home and minds of human beings.

One little incident to show you – my name was on the door. Officers from all over the Navy knew about me, they all knew about my position, but I didn't know all of them.

Lots of officers would come in my office and say, "Hi Roland, how are you? Good to see you again. And how's Sally?" And I wouldn't know him from Adam. I wouldn't know who he was. I hadn't seen him for a long time. And he probably wouldn't have known me really if he hadn't known he was coming after something.

So inevitably his next question would be, "Where are you going to send me?" When you don't know the name of the guy what are you going to do? By this time he's talked about Sally and the kids, and you feel ashamed to say, "Look Joe, what's your name? I don't know."

I had to do that once, and only once. But I never did it again, never again. The reason I didn't do it again was I got my secretaries busy, and I made a card file of all the Captains in the Navy, alphabetically. They put them in one cabinet file right alongside of what I called my "wailing chair."

So when they'd come in I'd have them sit down there, and I'd lean back. He'd inevitably get to, "Where are you going to send me?" And I'd say, "Reach in there and get your card, and I'll see what you've had, and I'll see what we've got planned for you." It was all alphabetical, so he'd get his own card and hand it to me.

Now I know who the guy is, now I can do something about it. So then I could send for his record and say, "Let's go over your record."

This is the next important thing - this record business, and the process of selection, and the process of assignments. Because assignments and selection go hand in hand.

Q: It's been so frightening to anyone in the Navy to see people who say they just didn't have the chance because they just didn't have the jobs.

Smoot: This is true.

So a man will stand in front of you and say, "Why didn't I get command of the MISSOURI? What's the matter with my record? I've got a good record. What's the matter with it? Why are you sending me to command a transport? That's the death knell. What are you doing that for?"

There's nothing wrong with his record. He has a good record. But if he'd sit there as I did, and read hundreds and hundreds of records he could arrive at his own relative standing. The records are good, but they can't be rated in isolation - only by comparison.

The reason I specify what a human thing it was to me was when I began to realize the tremendous amount of power that I had, it scared the hell out of me, it was really frightening.

So I had to be very sure. The Chiefs of Naval Personnel that I worked with were wonderful men, marvelous men. They all had been just marvelous.

The families and the human factors of directing people started to come into my life in a great big way. It's the biggest thing that I had experienced. There's nothing like it anywhere, nothing. This is the whole thing - when you use and manipulate people. People are the things that make everything go. And there's no other job in the world like it, nothing can compare with it.

You make mistakes. You're bound to make mistakes. You always do. Everybody makes mistakes. This kind of mistake though hurts so many people. It doesn't only hurt the person who the mistake was made on, but it hurts a lot of people below and above them. Because you've dislocated a system.

I didn't realize how mean some people can get - the letters that were sent to us anonymously, nasty telephone calls to Sal, frightful things, a bundle of human excrement placed on your front porch, all things like this. It was something.

I devised several systems to spread this responsibility because it shouldn't be in the hands of one man, it was not good. That system has been expanded more and more now. It relates not only to assignment, but it relates to the selection of officers for advancement and promotion.

You, as part of the officer personnel system, and particularly when you handle so many important assignments in the Captain area, the makers for flag grade, the people who are going to run our Navy, are called upon all the time, you as an individual, to brief the records for Selection Boards. You are called to talk to them about it. You tell them the significance of this kind and that kind of business.

It was through these efforts that this technical training also came into it, because I devised several technical things that made this simpler and made it more universally acceptable and understood, to categorize the human factors.

Q: Did you devise new fitness report forms?

Smoot: Sure. One of the new fitness reports that came out was after I went back there. As a matter of fact Converse had started it and it was excellent.

It got so that I could ruffle through a fitness report, and I could almost tell you by the curve of the check marks what kind of a guy he was and what kind of a job he would go to better. Would he be an aide type, would he be an operator, would he be an engineer or a technical man? Is he a leader? Is he strong? You can tell by the curve, it shapes itself right up.

I worked on this and worked on it hard with some success I guess, because it's still being used a great deal. Of course it's gone into computers, but they are really doing in computers the same thing that we devised.

The Navy was being drastically cut back with the end of the war. Naturally this reduced the need for personnel. That was another tremendous and traumatic experience.

Q; Did that come under your time there?

Smoot: It sure did, getting rid of all these people and what to do with what we had left.

Q: The ones that made the hump during wartime. Did you have to work on that? Do you want to expand on that, because that was a traumatic experience for so many people?

Smoot: That was an awful experience for so many. I don't think there's really much significance about it that you can explain in words.

We were given orders by the Congress to get down to a given number of ships and a given number of officer personnel in a certain time. So you just go through the list and find out those that will normally get out anyway because of time and grade —you count them off and process them for early separation.

It was heartrending to some of them. Reserve officers who wanted to make a career of the Navy - you just had to be hardboiled and get them out.

We some times had to leave ships right where they were. And they stayed there for months and months and just rotted because we didn't leave enough men aboard to run them.

Q: Weren't some people reverted to Commander from Captain, that was the selection board system?

Smoot: Yes. We had a special board for that purpose.

We had to develop the pyramid. There were some great inequities done in that too. We were badly top heavy in Captains. So in addition to separations there were reductions in grade to attain balanced officer structure for the greatly reduced Navy.

The class of '30 was on E group - they went back to Commander. We gave them the opportunity of retiring in the grade of Captain if they wished, or staying in, reverting to Commander and going through the test of the Selection Board. A lot of officers chose to retire, and because they had a combat citation they retired as Rear Admiral. Their classmates went back to Commander, and some of those did not make selection, didn't make Captain.

So here you've got an ersatz Admiral flying his two-star flag, but he's really a Commander.

It was a rewarding job, and I never worked at anything so hard in my life. The hours that I put in at that job were more than I did at sea ever, because I took it awfully seriously.

I went back later to the Bureau twice more.

Miss Kitchen: I was going to ask you, were you ever able to evaluate why you were selected for this job?

Admiral Smoot: No, often wondered.

My predecessor in the job, who was a class ahead of me, named Converse, I had only known casually. And I don't think he knew me at all. I'm sure it wasn't he alone that choose me as his relief.

In fact, from my experience in the job, I knew very well that he alone did not make the final decision in such assignments. But who picked me out from the welter of many officers, who were available and fully qualified I have no idea.

I don't remember who was the Chief of Naval Personnel at that time. I went through several Chiefs of Naval Personnel before I finished, and that's why I'm a little bit vague about it.

This particular job requires an officer who has a feeling for people and people's temperaments and abilities. To take a technical mind like mine and to try to orient it toward that kind of duty was quite a traumatic experience for me in the first place.

But anyway, it apparently worked, and at least it worked to the satisfaction of several Bureau Chiefs with whom I worked over several years in the Bureau.

It was during the very early months of my duty there that a circumstance developed whereby I was told about the four rules of life, which I have subsequently adopted, and which have guided my philosophy in dealing with people ever since.

Nobody exactly knows where these four rules of life came from. They have been attributed to the former Ambassador to Mexico, Dwight Morrow. They are very simple, and you get in trouble if you violate any one of them. Every time you get in trouble with the human being or a friend, you have violated one of these rules.

The four rules are: 1, don't take yourself too seriously; 2, don't take the other fellow too seriously; 3, don't let the other fellow know that you know he's an s.o.b.; and 4, don't ever get into a contest with a skunk.

Those are four very wonderful rules, and they merit serious consideration. If you ever violate any one of them you're in trouble. And I violated several right to start with in the Bureau.

I took myself too seriously, and I took the other people too seriously. I had the temerity to call another fellow an s.o.b. And I found myself in a contest with a skunk; I came out of it smelling very badly indeed. I should have used a different approach in the issue.

This job in the Bureau – I can see why it was called an "Admiral maker," because it was. At that time it was quite an important job. The responsibilities that rested on one individual's shoulders was entirely too much for a system as broad and comphrehensive as the Navy Department. And it didn't take very long to find that out. As time went on, following the war, the job functions were spread among many billets. Now it's more or less lost in the limbo of computerism and mechanical analysis.

And yet it can't all be run by electronics, because somewhere or other human warmth and understanding must be applied in the process of personnel administration. It's not to be seen and felt and heard and talked to, and you don't do it on machines, you do it by personal contact.

Q: I noted one item that you said — you speak of the four rules of life, and you relate one of your bad experiences to this man who was the best man at your wedding, when he didn't get a job that he wanted. Do you want to go on and amplify that?

Smoot: As I mentioned a moment ago this concerned one of my closest friends and best man at my wedding. He, like all close friends, in any type of personnel work will seek to use a friendly association to serve his own interests and personal ambition. It's very natural to do so — be it in the military or in private industry. It's called "influence peddling."

I know it, the Bureau knows it, everybody knows it. This was the thing to do. If you have a friend who can get you a good assignment — use him.

So this friend of mine used me. He wanted duty on the staff of Commander-in-Chief Pacific. There was only one job open in that staff at the time and he knew it, and he knew it was a good job for an ambitious Captain. And he was ambitious and capable.

There was only one hitch. The staff officer in charge of the department with the vacant billet did not want my friend. He wanted another Captain, and that was that. And that's what I should have told my friend. But I didn't, I didn't want to hurt his ego.

I made the mistake of saying, "Bob, you're not suited for that job. You're not a planner. You're not an operation officer at all. You're a personnel manager. You're the kind of man that should go to a district Commandant as Personnel Officer. Or you should go into the reserve business. You should really be a contact man, because you've got a warm understanding personality. You're not the kind of a man that sits down and plans and works things out."

This wasn't the thing to do. You don't tell a fellow what he isn't, you tell him what he is. You don't tell him why he can't have a job, you tell him why he can.

It took me a long time to learn this - this is what I mean.

In the letter that I wrote to him I told him several other things that I shouldn't have. And he sent that letter to the Chief of Naval Operations, who sent it to my boss in the Bureau of Personnel.

My boss sent for me and had a few things to say, like, "Don't ever do this again. Don't ever do anything like this again. All you do is get yourself in trouble and you lose a friend, and you're apt to get yourself kicked out too. Don't ever do it again. You take yourself too seriously."

And this is when I learned about the four rules, right then and there. He enumerated each one for me in order, and emphasized how badly I had violated their every concept.

Q: You said that the Deputy Chief of Naval Personnel had told you about those four rules?

Smoot: That is correct, Rear Admiral Tommy Sprague - a gentleman and a scholar.

Q: You also said early in our taping that you thought it was difficult to develop original thinking. At that time we both mentioned that this job was one that did help you develop original thinking. Do you still feel that way?

Smoot: You bet, it sure does.

Any job that has to do with the complicated facets of human relations develops human thinking. You can't be narrow minded. You have to think broadly. You've got to put yourself in people's places and in their minds if you can. You've got to stop thinking your way alone. You must try to think the way they think. It's a fascinating job. Anything to do with personnel is fascinating.

Q: You also took some extra-curricula work during this period, didn't you, over in Washington - a public speaking course?

Smoot: Oh yes, I did. I found it to be quite rewarding. I think one acquires confidence in human relations by making public appearances.

3 Smoot - 232

That job required personal confidence, and I had ambitions to make flag grade. So I figured I should be able to command a certain amount of presence that goes with the dignity of the office, and sought to learn some of the principles of public speaking. I also took some War College correspondence courses, too, at the time. I was busy.

Q: And so were you able to get yourself a good job out of that, after you did this?

Smoot: Yes, I did. I would have been pretty stupid if I hadn't. Out of that job I got command of a brand new cruiser called the NEWPORT NEWS. I had occasion to go to the shipyard where the NEWPORT NEWS was being built. It was nothing but a hulk. It's stacks weren't up, it's masts weren't up. It's bridge was partially completed. It was just an iron hulk at the shipyard down in Virginia.

My wife was standing alongside of me and I was looking at this mass of rusty steel. She said to me, "If you ever look at another woman like that I'll crown you queen of the may." I presume this demonstrates what 'command' means to a Navy man.

That was a wonderful, beautiful ship, and I thoroughly enjoyed watching it being built and put in commission. I ran it for a year.

But I don't think there was any single step in the ladder up to flag rank quite as important as that first job in the Bureau of Personnel as head of the detailers.

While I had the individual duty of detailing Captains, I had all of the other detailers under me. The Commanders and Lieutenant Commanders detailers particularly would bring their problems to me. We would have conferences every morning about the facets of detailing and some of the problems that came out of them. And we were able to combine all of the knowledge of all of these kids, and their experiences, and make a set of pretty good guidelines about it.

It was from those conferences and talking to these youngsters that we were able to get more out of the fitness report system. We were able to select the kind of people best suited for their jobs and do it faster. All of these reorganizations went through rather smoothly and easily during my period there. And it was a trying time - for our Navy was reducing to a peacetime status following a hectic wartime expansion.

We were getting rid of a lot of people. Some of the emotions that were expended upon me I could write a book about. Some time they'd come in my office with their whole family, and feeling ran pretty high.

You sure do see some things in human life when your future and the almighty dollar is right on the line at the moment.

Q: Didn't you find it interesting working with your staff? I'm sure they gave you the brightest.

Smoot: They were excellent. All of them were excellent, just tops; original thinkers, fast good minds; excellent.

Q: So you didn't mind the Bureau in the Washington duty as much as you thought you would?

Smoot: No, it was quite an education

We had an awful time finding a place to live. At the end of the war Washington was terribly crowded, but we finally found a lovely place to live. My children were at a critical age at that time, and Washington was quite important to them. We took them to all the favorite places. They had never been to Washington before, and at that age it was interesting to them.

Q: It's a wonderful opportunity if people took advantage of it.

Smoot: Oh great. The Smithsonian Institute - they went to everything, they didn't miss anything.

Q: We have skipped over the eight months when you were Chief of Staff while you were waiting for the NEWPORT NEWS to be commissioned.

Smoot: Yes. The NEWPORT NEWS was delayed for some reason or other, I've forgotten what it was. So I had to do something for about three months.

It so happened at that time that the Midshipmen's cruise was being organized, and I knew it. I had to get a lot of officers to go to sea with them and help them out. Rear Admiral Tex McClain was ordered as the Task Force Commander for the cruise. I knew Tex McClain very well, never did care for him, never will. But I figured it was a good opportunity to do the first type of staff duty that I'd ever done - staff duty at sea.

So this was a good opportunity to go to an operating staff at sea. I knew all about my prospective boss. I knew exactly what I was getting into, and I knew it wasn't going to be pleasant. It wasn't. It was probably one of the most unpleasant duties I've ever had.

Q; Did you go on the cruise?

Smoot: Yes, we went to the Med. We picked up the Midshipmen and conducted a regularly scheduled summer cruise to Europe and Guantanamo.

We had a perfectly delightful very close friend and classmate of mine who was the skipper of the task force flag ship, the MISSOURI. The task force command and staff were quartered aboard the MISSOURI. Jimmy Thatch was the MISSOURI's commanding officer.

There's no point of going into details of that unpleasant cruise. It's just one of those things you have in life, and one that I just look back on as sort of a nightmare. It covered three months, but it could drive a normal person nuts.

Q: You don't want to expand on that?

Smoot: I don't think there's much to be learned about it.

I asked for it. I wanted it. I wanted to try it out. I needed some kind of staff duty at sea, and this looked like a good deal for the interim period until my command was ready.

Q: You could probably just have gone out and watched them build the ship, couldn't you?

Smoot: No, I think the Bureau would have required me to do some thing more than that. So they would have put me on some board, they had lots of them, and I could have done just that. But I thought that this was something that I should have on my record, and it might teach me something. It did that for sure.

Q: Did it teach you anything?

Smoot: Yes, it taught me a lot. It taught me how to get along with very unusual people. It taught me an awful lot of patience. It taught me another facet of the human being.

And this fellow had it. I think he's dead now. He got out of the Navy in a huff, when he wasn't given a job that he wanted.

So I think it did me some good, but it was an unpleasant period.

He used me an awful lot in Europe in representing him at parties at night, diplomatic and official parties, where I could go in my capacity as his Chief of Staff. These parties would usually last until way late. In Europe you don't even sit down to dinner until ten o'clock, and they they go on and on and on until two or three o'clock.

I soon learned that my boss would set his alarm clock for five o'clock in the morning, and send for me. I would have to be fully dressed in uniform and go down and stand in his doorway while he was in bed. And he'd ask me about the whole evening. He had to find out everything about the whole evening, everything.

I tried once going down there in my pajamas, because I hadn't been in bed but for two hours, and he gave me hell for being in pajamas.

I have often wondered how a man of his explosive nature ever got to the grade of Admiral. At least he knew his own limitations. He attended very few of the social events. He was smart enough to know that he got too tight, didn't handle his liquor well. So he sent me in his place, and then he made my life miserable.

It was a lesson to me in the kind of people that sometimes get command, and then we discover a new personality. How important it is to know the personal side of people when you're responsible for their assignment to sensitive duties.

The poor guy – I saw him do a disgraceful thing one morning. He had asked the Commanding Officer of the MISSOURI if he could use the ship's band for a shipboard party – he had sense enough to know it wasn't his band – and the Commanding Officer declined. He indicated regret, but considered that the band had been overworked. They had been out on the rifle range and in parades ashore. He wanted them to get some rest before we arrived in Norfolk, where President Truman was scheduled to come aboard to present the ship with a set of wardroom silver.

The Admiral had a set of papers in his hand that he was reading from, and he wadded them up and threw them in the face of the Captain of the ship, then turned on his heels and walked off. This is the action of a flag officer in command of a U. S. Task Force.

So I say this was an unpleasant and terrible experience. I don't like to recall what I went through on this assignment.

Somewhere along the line somebody made a mistake, because that man was not flag officer material. I looked back in his fitness reports and studied and studied and studied the record to see if it disclosed these unfortunate characteristics. In retrospect we could see the indications, but not that this fellow was a martinet and a terrible tempered Mr. Bangs of the worst kind. Our revised systems would have disclosed these tendencies and he would not have been put in an important command or diplomatic mission of any kind.

The Bureau of Personnel has the prime responsibility of establishing a pyramid of qualified leaders - officers and enlisted. They are procured, trained, screened, graded, assigned, rotated, and, for one reason or another eliminated.

The Bureau of Personnel does this, nobody else. And a lot of it rests in the hands and the capabilities of a very few people. This is the weakness of the system.

Judgement - you can't mechanize it totally, you can't. You can't mechanize the complex human being totally. You can do a lot to mechanize it, but you can't mechanize it totally.

And that's why it's so important that you carefully carefully select the people that are in these detail jobs, very carefully. They must have a very humanitarian point of view.

We make mistakes, all of us do. And I think we succeed despite the people. And that's a great tribute to the human being. We're quite adaptable.

Q: Do you want to talk about the NEWPORT NEWS? You were only there twelve or fourteen months as Commanding Officer.

Smoot: There really isn't very much to talk about that assignment. It was a beautiful ship. We did the normal things you do in putting a ship in commission.

There are a lot of stories and incidents about the ship itself, and about the crew and officers, and the pleasure we had in the cruise - the delightful happy ship that it was - that in themselves would fill a book, but these are too numerous for this record.

Q: Let's do talk about that, and start with that next time.

Vice Admiral Roland N. Smoot, USN by E. B. Kitchen
Laguna Hills, California March 21, 1971

Miss Kitchen: As I recall you should have liked the duty aboard the USS NEWPORT NEWS as it's Commanding Officer because as you have said you detailed yourself to the job.

Admiral Smoot: Yes, insofar as I could detail myself. Of course major ship command also needs the approval of the Chief of the Bureau of Personnel.

Any ship like that also has the interest of the ultimate Division Commander, who would like to know who his skippers are. But there didn't seem to be any problem on the matter, as far as I was concerned, in that respect.

So when I heard about the building of the NEWPORT NEWS, down in Newport News Shipbuilding Company's shipyard, and what she was going to be - representing the most modern techniques of our new cruisers - I thought this was what I'd like to do when I left the Bureau. And so I detailed myself to it, and planned accordingly. And in planning accordingly you have the opportunity in the Bureau to pick your own crew to a great extent, that is the officers particularly and the leading enlisted men.

And it so happened that one of the senior officers who worked for me in the Bureau of Personnel at that time came to me and expressed an interest in coming as my Exec, and I didn't know him very well. I looked up his record and I made it a point to get to know him better, also his family. I was impressed with him, and we detailed him accordingly. This was nine or ten months before we were to put the ship in commission. His name was John Webster.

Q: Are you still a Captain?

Smoot: I'm still a Captain, yes. This was 1948 that all this planning was going on.

Being in the Bureau I was able to pick out some pretty outstanding people for the heads of departments based upon their records, and there wasn't a single one of them that I knew personally. I picked them out entirely from their records and the recommendations of the detailers themselves who helped me plan my crew.

Then from there on, the others that were ordered to the ship, were picked out by the Executive Officer, and the first Lieutenant, and the Gunnery Officer who were all on duty in and around Washington at one time or another and had the opportunity to come in and pick out their departments personnel.

This is an excellent way to collect the crew of your ship. So that everybody detailed to her not only wants what they're getting, but the people that are going want to go. So this starts you off really with three men on base and nobody out. You're really in good shape. It turned out that way. They were fine people, all of them.

Putting the ship in commission was not a new experience to me. I had put ships in commission before of course, but not a new one, not one with so many new and modern innovations. And so I was most interested in directing the development of the commissioning.

The Newport News Shipbuilding Company has been a very close friend of the Navy for years and years. They outdid themselves in making the arrangements. It was a beautiful commissioning and a beautiful service afterwards.

The City of Newport News collected nickels and dimes from the city's school children, and presented the ship with a magnificent set of silver, which I hope is still aboard because it's unique. It wasn't the fancy, oversized, and overdecorated kind that had been typical in the past. It was a modern plate type of silver, beautifully designed, and striking in it's simplicity. It served us well during the year that I was aboard, and I hope is continuing to do so.

Our shakedown cruise - I don't remember our itinerary - was not a very long cruise. We reported to the Atlantic Fleet in time and on schedule.

The commissioning of the ship itself was a beautiful thing done in Newport News Shipyard where Admiral Blandy, who was the Commander-in-Chief of the Atlantic Fleet at the time, was the principle speaker. It occurred in January, and normally you would think that we would have a terrible day, but we didn't. Like everything else that happened with that ship, we were lucky, and had a magnificent day for the commissioning.

I don't know how many thousands of people were there, but the ship was loaded and the dock was loaded. It was a totally inspiring thing to me of course, being the Commanding Officer of my first big ship. And she was a beautiful ship.

So then we followed the usual procedures of outfitting at the shipyard in Portsmouth, Virginia. This is required so that equipment of confidential and highly secret nature are installed under the custody of the Commanding Officer and his crew. You can't do this while under the custody of civilian shipbuilders. That's why there's always a period after commissioning when the ship has to go to a Navy shipyard.

Then the shakedown cruise and all the training period under the Training Command of the Atlantic Fleet was routine. Nothing unusual, except that we did have new guns that were automatically loaded. This was an eight inch cruiser, that's a big ship, with big guns. To load those big shells and powder automatically from magazines seven stories down without human hands touching them was quite a deal.

Q: Was this the first class of cruisers -

Smoot: The first of this class of cruisers, but not the first one of it's class commissioned. I believe the DES MOINES was the first one.

The DES MOINES had a lot of trouble with the automatic loading principles, and it had been pretty well worked out by the time I got my ship, so it worked fine.

Then of course there followed the usual routine of reporting to the Atlantic Fleet, and the Division Commander, (who was an old friend of mine) and the shakedown cruise off the Atlantic Coast where we did a lot of firing exercises under the Training Command of the Atlantic Fleet. Then we had the inevitable cruise down to Guantanamo, where we did most of the major part of our training and shakedown. And then final assignment to the Atlantic Fleet.

Our first cruise was a courtesy visit to Canada. I can't remember that there was anything startling on this occasion - many official calls and much partying.

The ship later went to the Med, but I wasn't aboard. She became the flag ship of the Mediterranean Fleet, and I'm sorry I missed that phase of her history.

But the significant part of the Command, as far as I was concerned, was experiencing the lonely position of the Commanding Officer of a big ship. You have your cabin to yourself. You eat by yourself. When you walk out of your cabin the orderly is standing out there and he yells, "Attention," and the bugler on deck blows the bugle and everybody stands up.

And so the wonderful informality of the smaller ship Command, which I loved, was gone. You're on a pinnacle as the Commanding Officer of a major combatant ship, and it's truly a lonely life.

I don't particularly care to eat alone, but you do a lot. But of course you can invite your officers in, and your crew, which I did on occasions, so that I didn't always have to eat alone in the evening.

I know of no other Command that is so totally completely at the apex, in terms of Navy habit and prestige, as the Commanding Officer of a big ship. There he is by himself in every respect - with total responsibility every moment he is aboard.

Q: How did that develop your character and personality?

Smoot: Maybe I can tell you of one occasion that its pertinent.

It didn't really change my character or personality at all. I have a tendency to be as humane as I possibly can. I'm not a disciplinarian. I never have been what's called a martinet, a tough leader.

And as one gets more responsibility, as I did throughout my career, I took the attitude that people under me, working for me, were going to do the best they could. They weren't going to go deliberately slack on their job and make it necessary for me to discipline them. It wasn't going to be a deliberate action on their part. And so if they did fall down on their job it was because they lacked the ability to do it, the basic ability, and hadn't been properly trained and hadn't been properly placed. If they're improperly placed then the thing to do is to have them ordered somewhere where they are more effective.

I had the occasion to do that with one officer on the ship. There's no need of mentioning his name, because he didn't last long in the Navy anyway. I had to have him relieved under conditions which were not too pleasant, because he felt it was ruining his career, as it truly was. But he had already ruined his career and didn't know it. He just wasn't capable of doing it.

As far as the development of character is concerned, you just had a bigger base to work on. You can't get as close to your men as you can in a small ship, so you have to rule through the echelon. And you have to make your position and your ability to command that ship felt through the echelon.

The only way you can do that is to have the confidence of the echelon immediately below you, and make a point in your Saturday inspections and other types of inspections to always spend a greater part of one Saturday with one individual group than you do with the rest of them. So that by the time a few months pass by you've really gotten around, they've gotten to know you, and you've gotten to know them better. You can get a little bit down off your pedestal on such occasions.

I had such an occasion one night when we were anchored in Guantanamo. The Master at Arms was using the telephone. It was about one o'clock in the morning. I was sound asleep and my telephone rang. In my scrambling around I reached over and picked up the receiver and said, "Hello."

The other end of the line said, "What in the world kind of an answer is that? Don't you know that on this ship when you answer a telephone call you give your name and station? And you do it promptly." And I said, "Yes sir, I sure know that. And I will tell you exactly who I am. This is the Commanding Officer speaking from his cabin." I can't repeat what went on at the other end, but it was very short and very quick. It was just two words, that's all, and then bang went the receiver.

I made a little note of that. Next morning I called the Executive Officer in, explained the incident, and said, "I haven't the slightest idea who that was, and don't particularly want to know. But I want him to know that he was absolutely right in what he did, because anybody that has been trained as our ship has been trained, right from the start, how to answer the telephone, by golly they should do it right, including the Commanding Officer." This made quite an impression.

It was a happy ship and I wanted it that way, but it was a tight ship too.

The crew knew that if they ever came before me at mast they were going to be punished. If there was any doubt about the guilt or non-guilt, then they were assigned a court. But usually by the time they went through the screening, to get to Captains mast, it wasn't whether they were guilty or not, it was how serious was the offense.

And I didn't go easy on the punishment. I leaned towards the maximum, particularly on withholding from liberty, which became awfully important to them.

So word got around - don't do anything wrong on this ship or you'll get it, there's no soft soap in that respect.

This is your instrument of control, right there at mast, on the men, discipline. That plus speaking to the crew and the different division on occasion, making a point to have dinner with them down in the mess on occasions and getting to know them. So you don't stand up there as a lone ogre who says "froggy" and they jump.

The objective is to let them know that you got command because you worked for it, and you worked hard, and you studied, and you were selected out of a lot of officers who wanted the job, but that you're still a human being and that you have human beings working for you. Gone are the days when you strap them to the mast and beat them with a black snake whip.

But there are other means of keeping discipline. One of the greatest means of keeping discipline is letting them know when they do something good they're rewarded, when they do something bad they get punished. It's as simple as that.

Q: And after your tour of duty on the NEWPORT NEWS you were relieved by whom?

Smoot: I can see him, but I can't remember his name. He was a big tall blonde, two or three classes below me. He didn't last very long, because a physical ailment developed. He got out of the Navy shortly after that.

The big ship command is the tops. The only thing I can say about it in resume is that it was too short for me. I would love to have had it for two or three years, because just about the time that I was relieved they began going places – foreign countries. The horizon was broadened and the duties were more complicated, and that's what I loved.

It was short. You learn to cope with loneliness, the loneliness of your position, the absolute pinnacle of a group of people who are right under you all the time, however you want to handle it. They are happy and unhappy, and they produce or not. And your ship is good or it's bad, depending upon the way that you run it.

There's no two Commanding Officers the same. No two run it the same way. And it shows the versatility of our system, and it's all right, it's very good.

Q: And of course so many men want the command, there are so many eligible at that point, that they can't leave you with a command more than a short time.

Smoot: This is the whole reason. I don't know if it's a good idea or not. This remains to be seen. So far I think it's proved to be pretty good.

It isn't absolutely necessary that you have a big ship command to become a flag officer, there are other things that you can do, but it does help. At that time it was very important, it was almost a necessity.

I think that that covers the NEWPORT NEWS very well. It was another command, a more important command, a beautiful command, a delightful command, and taught me this sense of being alone and the great responsibility that's on your shoulders.

Q: From there you went as Aide and Chief of Staff to Commander Cruisers Atlantic Fleet.

Smoot: I was asked for by the then Commander of the Battleships Cruisers Atlantic (that was the title), Vice Admiral Hoke Smith, with headquarters in Norfolk. This was later changed, but at that time it was more or less, in spite of the name, a shore going job. He had all of his staff ashore.

This was the first personal type of assignment that I had, where I was specifically asked for. And it was the first personal type of a job I had where you are Chief of Staff and Aide to a flag officer.

Hoke Smith was an enigmatic character, a capable officer, but very enigmatic. I'm not one to talk or judge him at all, it isn't my business to do so, only insofar as it affected me. I found it very difficult to work for him, because he wanted to do everything himself - this was the trouble.

So what I ended up bing was more or less of a steward to the rest of the officers. They were under my stewardship to be sure, because he did ask all the questions through me - about how all the various heads of departments on the staff were getting along.

This was all right, except that I didn't function in command decisions as a Chief of Staff should. And by the same token I don't think that the Fleet Gunnery Officer or the various Division Commanders particularly cared to have their lines of communication so limited. They'd like to talk to the Admiral directly, but he made it hard to do so.

But this was the way he ran it, so that's the way it was. I was the spokesman for the staff, a very difficult thing to do.

Hoke Smith either liked you thoroughly or he didn't, and he apparently liked me. There was a great social affiliation there - he loved parties and he loved card games. He gave a lot of parties, and gave them well. But he entertained people he liked and never seemed disposed to include the whole staff in anything. So there was very little cohesion there, except insofar as I could accomplish it at my level.

I had regular meetings with the staff. I tried to make it a daily affair. It really got boring. And there really wasn't much to do until one day very early in the morning we got word that the MISSOURI went aground.

This is a story that I could write a book about myself, and probably should some day.

CinCLant designated Commander Cruisers Battleships Atlantic Fleet to be the Task Force Commander to get the MISSOURI off the beach. I don't know how much should be told here.

Q: I think your part in it, and what you knew of it should be told here.

Smoot: Okay, I'll just go through the whole thing, and try to condense it. It's a book in itself.

Q: In the thought "this is your biography" the stories of the whole thing may not need to come in, but what you knew and what you did and what you saw I think would be pertinent to your biography.

Smoot: I'll limit it to that, if I can.

I was the Chief of Staff, and as such really held the same position under Admiral Smith on this special Task Force as I did on the administrative staff of Commander Battleships Cruisers.

We left a skeleton staff at headquarters ashore to run the Commander Battleships Cruisers routine duties. We moved the major part of the staff, the senior officers (including me), aboard the MISSOURI and lived aboard her for the whole time that it took to get her off – some three or four weeks, as I remember.

Basically we had a report to make. We had to keep meticulous records of everything we did daily. We had to recruit civilian help from all over. We had a lot of publicity. The Press came right aboard. We probably had pretty close to 10,000 letters written to us telling us how to get her off the beach from all over the world.

So with the Press, with the public interest of the thing, with the fact that it was President Truman's ship, named for his home state, and the fact that it went aground under the circumstances which it did, made it a great national public relations job more than anything else. For the first time I really got close to public relations and what it meant.

Why did it go aground? It went aground because the Commanding Officer made a mistake.

How did it go aground? It went aground going at fifteen knots and it planed itself up on the beach and rested there with the weight equivalent to the R.C.A. Building in New York.

That's where it was sitting – down on the sandy bottom of Norfolk Bay, some half to three-quarters of a mile north of the regular ship's channel.

It lifted itself about fifteen feet above its normal floating depth in the water, but on an even keel. It was on hard sand with no rock underneath it. It defied the pulling power of every tug we could get together in Norfolk for a couple of days. It was thus evident that we had a real problem facing us. So we recruited experts in the matter.

Q: Wasn't there difficulty keeping it upright at the same time?

Smoot: No. The bottom of the MISSOURI, and it's type, is as flat as this floor under us. It has no external keel. It was resting squarely upright.

And there was very very little damage done when we finally got it off. There was one old anchor buried in the sand that scraped the side of the ship and ripped about a twenty to twenty-five foot hole in the false bottom and flooded a couple of the side tanks. And that's really all that happened to that ship. It was amazing how little damage was done.

But to get it off constituted some three or four weeks work. The general plan was to burrow thru the sand under the ship with every type of underwater device we could get; to soften the sand, and hope the ships own weight would break it down. We dredged a channel around the ship and a channel astern of it to deep water, so that when it did start breaking the sand underneath it and it floated we could tow it out. This was all a matter of dredging.

So we got dredges from wherever we could, and dredged a big channel all the way around the ship, and a big channel out to deep water in the Norfolk channel itself.

Then we used divers with high pressure air lances who would get down underneath the ship and would soften the sand by running these lances underneath the ship.

Q: Lance – what does that mean?

Smoot: It blows water at very high pressure into the sand and just washes it out.

And gradually with all this going on from the ship we washed the sand out from under it and she settled lower and lower until we finally got her to float.

In the meantime we had tugs and anchors out and kept a strain on the ship at all times, so that if there ever was a break in the sand we would know it – she would start moving right away.

This is essence is a very brief resume of what actually happened.

Q: Now your part in it –

Smoot: The organization of the crew, the assignment of the jobs, the constant consultation with the Commander of the Task Force, and with the experts that we got aboard, and ocean salvage – most of it was Navy. We have wonderful Navy salvage people. A lot of them are civilians, but they're hired by the Navy, but they know their jobs. The Bureau of Ships was invaluable in the aid that they provided to us, experts that were already hired by the Navy.

So it wasn't an awfully expensive job. There wasn't an awful lot of money involved in it.

All it did was break up schedules of ships, but it was pretty good practice for those ships that were assigned to that kind of duty because this was for real.

We had excellent public relations people aboard to handle the Press. Not only the Press, but important people, V.I.P.s, came to visit us to see what was going on.

The handling of letters and phone calls and telegrams - this was all done by our own staff. Every letter was answered, every single one. Most of them could be answered with a word, "Thank you for your interest. The matter will be looked into and we'll see if we can get it."

We got some queer ones too. For instance - the essence of one letter was: "I can tell you how get the MISSOURI off the beach. Get somebody who knows about false teeth, they know all about suction."

Another one was, "Take a whole lot of fans and put them on barges at the entrance of the Bay and blow water into the Bay and float it off."

Those were the kind of letters that we got. We got an awful lot of them.

Q: Did you get any that had any intelligent suggestions?

Smoot: I suppose we did, but in most of those cases we had already taken the action and wrote them to that effect. We thanked everybody and told them that their suggestion was received, and that we had already taken that type of action, or that it will be looked into to see if we can use it and see if it's practicable.

We had a unit that did nothing but handle correspondence. When there was ever a question about propriety of the reply, there was a Captain who was the head of it, he would always come to me and we'd go up and talk with Hoke Smith, and then we'd get in our public relations officer. It took a lot of time.

I'll tell you there wasn't much sleep in that crowd for three weeks. I was never so tired in my life.

There were some sad things too. The Commanding Officer himself, who was responsible for putting it on the beach, was understandably very low mentally, and at one time tried to commit suicide. His name was William D. Brown, and he was a very capable officer.

To me his assignment was a mistake in the first place. And I think it's pertinent to bring this up with my experience as a detailer in the Bureau of Personnel.

Brown was a flamboyant capable smart submarine officer. He'd spent most of his life in submarines. (He was two classes behind me, I think he was the class of '25.) Bill had spent most of his Navy life in small ships.

Now this is an art in itself, small ships is an art all by itself. You have an informal command in small ships, particularly in submarines, very informal command. There's not so much formality in the things that you do.

Frequently the skipper himself takes the deck, and he does all the navigating, unless he has particular confidence in his Exec and his Navigator and other officers. Unless he's training them under certain conditions he usually always brings the ship in and takes it out of port himself, and he does it by eye.

You just go over and you look at the chart. The ship is small and it handles well, and you know where to go. So you keep your small ship in the channel - from buoy to buoy - mostly by eye. You know your ship and your channel, and you just navigate from buoy to buoy.

But not so on big ships. I learned this very very soon on big ships when I had command of the NEWPORT NEWS.

You have a Navigator for a purpose, and your Navigator is a real busy fellow in navigating a ship channel. He plots every minute where your ship is by known and fixed navigational aids, every minute on the minute. So that if anything ever happens and you have a grounding, there isn't a minute that you can't say to yourself later on, and prove to the court, "There's where we were at 9:31½, right there. There's the marks. There's the chart. And it shows it right there. There it is."

And he didn't do this. He was the Commanding Officer. His Navigator was back in the chart house doing the things a Navigator does, but the Captain didn't pay any attention to the Navigator. he didn't ask the Navigator anything.

He just gave the orders directly to the helm, to the people on the speed indicators, what speed he wanted. He was coming out of the shipyard at Norfolk, and he had to make a right turn to go out of the channel to sea and have a short shakedown cruise out at sea, after the engines had been overhauled. And this was his first time aboard, first time on a big ship.

He was the boss, and he did it. He gave every order. He was up there looking through his glasses, as he did on submarines. And there's an awful lot of buoys right up there where you make the turn, a lot of buoys. There are fishing buoys, there were buoys that marked a certain area that we went through to have our degaussing gear checked, there are the anchorage buoys, there are the mooring buoys, there are all kinds of buoys up there, and there are the channel buoys.

But unless you know exactly where you are the many buoys can confuse you - you get in trouble. And the ship doesn't go exactly the way you steer it, and the way you think it's going. The wind and tide and everything else affects it, and you have a fraction of a movement depending upon that. Ships also "crab" in course changes.

So you've got to know where you are, within just a few feet, constantly when you're in narrow channels with a ship this big. And Bill Brown didn't do that.

So when he made his turn to the right, he saw what he thought were the main channel buoys.

Q: Did anyone say anything to him about that?

Smoot: Yes, the Navigator said, - you're turning too soon, or too late, or whatever it was.

He didn't ask the Navigator for the course. He said, "I see the buoys that I'm heading for." He saw two buoys all right. They were the buoys that were the entrance to a small fishing channel going up the Bay. He headed right straight for them at fifteen knots. And he hit the sand, and lifted that ship to the weight of the R.C.A. Building, because he didn't use the navigational procedures that are there to be used, and did not use his Navigator.

He was court martialed for that, was found guilty, was appropriately sentenced and retired from the Navy in understandable dejection and disgrace.

Q: You spoke of this being wrong detailing.

Smoot: Yes. He was an eminently capable officer, but I think that he should have been assigned to a staff job on big ships before getting command of one. He should have had some duty on big ships for awhile just to get the feel of them. But he came to the MISSOURI when the ship was in the yard. He didn't even have a chance to go out with the former skipper. He went directly from small ships to the biggest ship in the Navy too soon, without some interim training.

You've got to get that feeling of the very vast difference between small ship's handling and big ship's handling. You don't handle them the same. You don't do things the same with them.

I'm not trying to castigate Bill in any way at all. This was the way he was trained and this was the way he was going to do it. He was the Commanding Officer, and by golly he was going to do it his way. That's the way all Commanding Officers did.

If he had been detailed, even like I was to a Midshipmen's cruise, on a big ship or a task force commander on a big ship he would have gotten the experience he needed. I had three month with the task force commander on battleships, the MISSOURI itself as a matter of fact. And I learned a lot in those three months. I learned how different they are from small ships, very very different. And I think Bill should have had the same opportunity.

Q: Where were you at the time the MISSOURI broke loose, do you recall? What time of day was it, or night?

Smoot: I was on the bridge. It was early in the morning.

We were pretty sure it was going to break that morning, and so we planned our big effort for the morning high tide. We knew that we were going to have high tide at a certain time, and we planned to put all strain on it then.

We had done it the day before and it didn't go. Our divers went down and said, "There's one ledge down there that's really holding it. I think we can go through tonight and in about ten to twelve hours we'll do it.

So we put all strain on it the next morning, and she broke very nicely, sort of easy and with grace. Once she started moving, you could feel her go down, the sand went out from under her and pretty soon she was afloat. It was quite a day.

Q: Were the public relations still on board?

Smoot: Everybody was still on board.

Then of course we went back to the shipyard. Admiral Page Smith became the new Commanding Officer. (He later became the Commander-in-Chief Atlantic, four-star Admiral.)

I don't know where Page was, he had another job, I've forgotten what job he had. He was immediately called by Admiral Smith, who said he wanted him for the new C.O. So Page called the Bureau and they talked it over with the Commander-in-Chief Atlantic. So Page took command.

Q: Was he aboard at the time it broke loose? Who took it to the shipyard?

Smoot: No. We did, Admiral Hoke Smith and his staff. The task force that was aboard took it to the shipyard.

We had the Navigator of the MISSOURI aboard, and he did the navigating when we went back to the shipyard. But it was actually being conned by one of the professional Norfolk pilots — as is usual when tugs are involved.

It was still the responsibility of Hoke Smith to keep it afloat. But he had little to say, because the pilots were aboard and they were maneuvring it by whistle signals and towing it with many tugs. So there wasn't any problem getting it to the yard.

There are a lot of personal things that I could tell you about events that happened, but I don't think they serve the purpose in this. Such as the occasion when Bill tried to commit suicide, and the trouble ashore Mrs. Smoot had with the wives and their nervous breakdowns. It was a tremendously traumatic affair.

Q: Could you sketch that briefly - the wives of the staff?

Smoot: Particularly the wife of the Commanding Officer, who was a very nervous type of woman. Mrs. Smoot spent an awful lot of time with her, otherwise I think she would have taken an overdose of sleeping pills many times.

Then the Navigator's wife - a fine looking young girl -. felt that he was responsible. There wasn't much communication and they didn't see each other for three weeks. None of the officers wives saw their husbands.

In fact I didn't see my wife. We lived aboard that ship. There was no leave for anybody. No going ashore for a moment, which was right, the way it should be. I didn't have any objection to that.

There was the morale factor of the wives ashore, who were without true knowledge of what was going on. There were so many rumors and stories written that blew the thing up sky high, way more than it should be in terms of the people that were responsible and thepossibilities of court martials and ruined careers and everything.

If you were the wife of an officer who was responsible for it, you're awful nervous and particularly if you can't do your part to comfort him or do whatever a wife does.

And I have to give my wife a big up for the things that she did, because Mrs. Hoke Smith isn't that particular type of a woman. She doesn't communicate too well. So it was Mrs. Smoot's business, and she did it, and did a whale of a job. I was mighty proud of her.

Q: That's an interesting footnote that probably isn't written in the books or reports anywhere. It would be a facet that probably wouldn't come out any other way. I think that's interesting.

So in your seven months in that job you had almost one month out in the salvage job.

Smoot: Yes, involved with that. And the rest of it was really office work. I didn't particularly care for it actually.

Then Holloway came aboard (he relieved Smith). He immediately took the staff to sea. He streamlined the staff as it should be. It wasn't a shore going job after all, it was Commander Cruisers Battleships Atlantic Fleet, and it should be at sea. And I was very pleased to get to sea, but I wasn't there very long. I think I was with Holloway not more than a couple of months when I was ordered back to Washington.

Q: Can we describe going back to Washington, and your job then was Assistant Chief Naval Personnel for Personnel Control?

Smoot: Yes, this was the echelon above the detailers in Bu Pers. In being the echelon above the detailers you inherit enlisted and officer procurement, detailing, training, and career planning. There are so many facets to the job I can hardly remember. This was a broader type of job and a very worthwhile one to me. I thoroughly enjoyed it.

Q: You were there for quite a while, the longest time you'd been any place.

Smoot: Three years. It's hard to conceive that I was there for three years, but it went like lightning. I was busy, really busy.

I think I went through three Chiefs of Bureau of Personnel, as I remember. I started with Roper. I know DuBose was the last one. I can't remember the other one.

Q: Do you have any particular episodes or anecdotes or personnel relations or development of your own during that period that you want to comment on?

Smoot: No, I don't have any generalities that are particularly significant.

Q: When did you become Admiral? That was during this period?

Smoot: 1950, when I reported for this assignment. That was a flag officer's job.

The selection to Admiral was, of course, a big thrill. The system provides for given year groups being considered. You start off with 900 odd people in a class, and you end up with about eighteen of them selected to Admiral. That's quite a competitive system. To be chosen is a great feather in your hat. I, of course, was very happy about it to say the least. It's a traumatic experience.

I've sat on selections boards and I know how they're run. This was another function of the billet of the Personnel Control - the setting up of the selection boards, choosing people to be members and overseeing the procedures.

So when my turn came to sit on a selection board I leanred again another facet of this complicated system of the Navy of the advancement up the pyramid. Basically the fitness report system itself is, I think, sound. I don't know of a better system. As an organization gets bigger and bigger and bigger however, you can't have the number of experienced people that are needed to properly career and intelligently assign the outstanding potential officer from the time he's a kid all the way up to flag grade. Somewhere mistakes are going to be made, whether it's going to be made in the Bureau in the assignment process or by the man himself who is trying to better his career chances or by his commanding officers. It's an awfully complicated thing.

But in general, I do have to say this conviction: the officer who makes flag grade rates being a flag officer. Admittedly there are probably some officers who don't make flag grade who for some little reason, some funny little reason some where along the line, missed something, and probably could do just as good a job in a flag grade as the contemporary who was selected when he was passed over. There's no doubt about that. It is not an infallible system, as practiced in my time.

In reading say 500 fitness reports, and I've done this hundreds of times, you get so you can go through them in just a few hours. You can just flip through pages and immediately divide people into about three main classes right away.

You'll isolate the bottom fifteen to twenty percent right away. Similarly there's no doubt about the top ten to fifteen percent. And that remaining middle sixty-five percent - that is the area, these are the officers where career assignment and advancement becomes real tough.

When the Navy started getting bigger and bigger we had to go to some kind of a computer system to assit in career planning. That was just beginning to be installed when I left there. I had made representations to each Chief of Bureau for whom I worked that we were fast approaching the need for mechanical assistance.

We already had enlisted detailing and selection broadly disseminated, and to a great extent mechanically assisted. I think the system was initially started by Holloway himself. It was his idea when he was the "Deputy Chief for Plans" in the Bureau of Personnel. He started it for enlisted men, and now it's practically all computerized.

This was an interesting hard-working job. And I don't think I could have done the job that was expected of me if I hadn't had previous experience in the Bureau. I don't think anybody could take on the upper echelons of running the Bureau without having previous personnel experience.

Q: Did you have the pressure on you personally, as you did when you had the Officer Detail?

Smoot: Oh yes. Any responsible assignment in the Bureau of Personnel calls for long hours and much frustration.

Q: Individuals coming and asking you to do them a favor?

Smoot: Very definitely, sure.

Q: I thought maybe the echelon above you might have been somewhat removed from this.

Smoot: No, you get it in any echelon. Your friends are going to call on you. No matter what assignment in the Bureau you have, your friends will seek you out for personal favors.

Quite frequently the Chief of Naval Personnel comes to detailers with a letter in his hand and says, "See what you can do about this." This is just human relations.

Q: It shouldn't be a handicap because you do know someone.

Smoot: No, it certainly shouldn't. But it had it's effect I'm sure in certain cases.

Of course I made it my business as I went up the ladder to be guided by the theory that says - if you're going any place you've got to be known in the E-ring of the Pentagon. No matter what job you take, ultimately you've got to be known in the E-ring of the Pentagon.

I'm skipping ahead now several years; in my next job ashore I asked for such an assignment in preference to being assigned as Superintendent of the P. G. School.

That's about all I can say about this Personnel Control job. It was a routine job, hard job, tough job, very little sleep, a job that requires experience, and a rewarding job in that you're still handling people. And if you like to handle people it's rewarding, and I did.

Q: You didn't have any bad experience like you had before when you wrote someone a letter of explanation of why he didn't get a job he wanted and he took it to the CNO?

Smoot: I had had my lesson on that, and learned the hard way.

Q: You then went to Commander Cruiser Division Three, which would seem the next logical step having been a Cruiser Commander.

Smoot: This was perfectly logical detailing. And being in the Bureau I picked it out myself and went there with the approval of the Chief of Naval Personnel and with the approval of the Chief of Naval Operations, who has to approve these jobs.

Q: Where was Cruiser Division Three?

Smoot: In Japan, working out in Japanese waters. I believe I relieved Tyree.

Q: During that time I understand the name was changed, but the job stayed the same?

Smoot: The job stayed the same, it was just a reorganization within the Pacific Fleet. Also there were different cruisers that were assigned during my tenure. I think before I was through with that year's job, I'd been on three different flag ships. The unit commander moves around, but this was usual with Pacific Fleet operations.

Once you get out there and have the designation the flag officer job and staff usually end up in a designated task force, and you have specific ships assigned. It's a multiple command job at sea. That's a fairly routine type of job.

At that time the unit I was to command was in Japan, and as I remember it I joined them in Sasebo. We didn't have the relieving ceremony there, because I wanted to go to sea with them for awhile and operate with them and see what the previous Division Commander did and how he did it. He also wanted to go up to Tokyo, and to be relieved on the way up there, so he'd be in Tokyo and take a plane back home. He had orders to some place in the U. S., and that's what he wanted to do rather than beat his own way from Sasebo to Tokyo and then go home.

And so it turned out to be a nice comfortable three day cruise up the Japanese chain of islands with three ships in the Division. And we did all kinds of exercises: shooting, task force maneuvers, night raids, and it was fun. I quite enjoyed it. We had three cruisers and three destroyers with us on that little foray and it was both enjoyable and educational. I thoroughly enjoyed it, I love the function of command.

Halfway up the coast we had a relieving ceremony aboard the flag ship. We got all the ships around us and hauled down his flag and hoisted mine, and went through the rituals of re-life. So then I had the other day and a half to operate the task force and take it into Yokosuka.

The war in Korea was mostly over by that time. There wasn't much going on. There wasn't any reason to go to Korea any more as a show of force. So we were doing "boy scouts' dates at various liberty ports in Japan.

They sent my Division to every port that they could get into. Nagoya, Yokohama, Sasebo, Kobe - we made them all. I sent my Public Relations Officer on ahead to get in touch with whatever Navy authorities were there, or if not, the local Mayor of the town, and sent my greetings. But he already knew because CincPac had cleared all these amenities ahead of time.

But I wanted the local authorities to know by personal letter, to give them the courtesy, and request permission to come and see them and make an offical call on them, and I was always greeted. And it was quite an interesting job. I thoroughly enjoyed it.

It was my first contact with foreign governors, and other civilian officials. I wasn't very good at it at first, but it was interesting.

I don't think I learned too much, other than broadening myself in international relations - I did that. I certainly did that.

Q: Did you notice a difference between then and the Japan you went into when it had just been conquered?

Smoot: Oh yes. They were very glad to have us, and most enthusiastic about doing everything they could for the sailors. This was the beginning of that period when the Fleet was welcome wherever it went, because we brought money and we brought trade. They had recovered remarkably by this time, and they loved having us there. They still weren't able to stand on their own.

So it was rewarding in that respect. I learned a new field of dealing with foreigners; international relations. Again I was dealing with people, an important facet of my life and care It's always been an interesting thing to me, because fundamentally I think I'm a technician.

Q: You have said that before, I noted that comment. However it seems to me that every job you had you broadened your own relationships, and it's always been with people.

Smoot: Yes, it has, it's been most interesting.

In general it's really the basis of everything. You can't do anything without people anywhere. You've got to live with them, and you've got to either follow them or lead them. And you do both throughout your career. The degree to which you do one or the other determines your road to success or failure in any endeavor.

The tour of duty as Division Commander turns out really to be a series of assignments of task force commands. I think I moved to at least three ships, and I never knew what the next job was going to be. I ended up going back across the Pacific to home waters with a stopover in Pearl Harbor for a few days, and then went on to San Francisco.

We did some public relations work in San Francisco. I don't remember what the occasion was, but anyway we called on the Mayor there. Then to Oakland, and finally ended up in our own port at Long Beach. There I guess I was relieved.

Q: I think you went to another job while you were in Long Beach - Commander Mine Force. How did that happen?

Smoot: I asked for that job. That's the type command that is a natural step up after a multiple command at sea. I was still a pretty junior flag officer. This Mine Force interested me, being again a multiple ship type of command, but also a tactical command. Headquarters were in Long Beach - an area I like and know well.

We didn't have personal quarters at that time. There were government quarters for senior officers on shore duty there. The Base Commander had quarters. He was a Captain, and really served under me in terms of providing service to the Fleet.

We had our office on the Naval Base at the Mine Station there. But the Mine Force Commanders through my time, and two Commanders after me, lived out in Long Beach in public quarters, not in Navy quarters.

Now they have combined the Mine Force job with the Base Command. Commander Mine Force Pacific is also the Base Commander, and the Commander of the Naval Station also. He has a Chief of Staff for his Mine Force, and a second Chief of Staff for the Base, another Chief of Staff for the Station - each with three separate staffs - a cumbersome and inefficient use of personnel.

I was only there for about a year, that's all. I took one flying trip to the far west, where part of the Mine Force was stationed in Sasebo, to be sure that I got around to my command and everybody saw me and knew who I was.

There isn't very much that I can say about that, except getting my type command behind me at an early age. There was nothing much that I learned that I didn't already know from the multiple command that I had with cruisers.

We had technical problems. We were developing some new small wine sweepers. The Bureau of Ships had decided on a contract with Packard Engineering to put in some small high speed engines that were supposed to be very endurable. They were so darned endurable that we couldn't get them started. That was the only thing, but that was a technical problem which was corrected by sending them all back and having them redone at the contractor's expense. In the meantime the small coastal mine sweepers were practically immobilized.

In general I quite enjoyed it. I went to sea often with them and watched their maneuvers and their mine sweeping. We had routine exercises that we set up ourselves. We had very capable young Commanding Officers and Division Commanders. There were a great number of multiple commands in the force.

They were a lively sociable group of people. Mrs. Smoot and I were on the go constantly, socially.

But this was another good public relations job, and it turned out to be right rewarding.

Q: It was basically all training?

Smoot: All training. Type command is training, that's the main thing that it is.

Q: There weren't any real mines to sweep in those days anyway.

Smoot: No. I think we can drop that with that.

It gets to the point where in your flag grade you're detailing yourself and careering yourself, to be sure you get broad experiences as much as you can. That's why in some respects it's good and in some respects it isn't. It gets your broad command behind you, but it also doesn't give you an opportunity to really get to know what you're doing and put into effect any of your own ideas and see how they work out. You can put them into effect, but then the next guy comes along and by the time they start taking effect he gets the credit for it.

The tour is so short, it isn't good. I don't know what can be done about it, if it's policy to establish a broad base of that type of duties for a flag officer before he really gets important. You haven't got much time in the flag grade to get through all of it with a unit command, a division command, your shore duties, and all that. You just don't have enough time.

I was a flag officer from 1950 through '62. That's twelve years. You take one tour in the Bureau out of that, that's three years. There's nine left to you. A unit command - there's another year gone. A type command - another year gone. You're up to five years now. Then another shore duty - probably three years, and you're down to two years.

Q: How long was it before you mave Vice Admiral?

Smoot: When I went to Taiwan, 1958.

Q: Before that you had then had your duty in the E-ring of the Pentagon?

Smoot: Then I had my duty in the E-ring, where you get to be known, just as close to the Secretary's office as you can get.

Q: You were going to expand on that I think.

Smoot: The philosophy of it, yes.

I was offered the job of Commanding Officer of the Postgraduate School in Monterey – a lush good wonderful job.

Admiral Holloway called my up from Washington and said, "I've got just the thing for you. It's just right down your alley. You're technical, you're good in personnel, you're fine in morale and running the thing, you've had lots of experience. Here's the top job of the whole outfit – Commanding Officer of the P. G. School."

And I said, "Jimmy, I don't want it." He didn't even answer he was so taken aback. Here was the plum of a shore duty job coming up and I said, "No, I don't want it, because I want to make three stars, and I'm not going to make three stars there.

The only way I'm going to make three stars is to come to Washington and get to be known in the Pentagon. If I'm not any good and can't make three stars, that's where I'm going to be found out. But I'm not going to make it as Commanding Officer of the P. G. School."

He said, "I have to admit you're right. But you're giving up a real wonderful job. It's quite a plum." And I was, I had an awful lot of second thoughts on that.

Q: This time your progression had been so perfect along the line to being three-stars —

Smoot: I didn't want to give up then. And it turned out all right I think, although there was an occasion later on when I had second thoughts about it. But that's beside the point and really isn't significant.

Q: Will you tell me about that later?

Smoot: Yes.

Q: I think we ought to specifically indicate what the job in the E-ring of the Pentagon was however.

Smoot: I went there as Assistant Chief of Naval Operations for personnel.

Q: And who was the CNO then?

Smoot: When I first went there it was Mick Carney.

Q: Who was the Secretary at that time?

Smoot: Thomas.

Q: You spoke of having a job that would get you close to both of those two people.

Smoot: Yes.

Q: You were in that job for how long, about three years?

Smoot: I think that the combination of that job plus the "Deputy CNO for Administration" was three years. I think I was in the personnel job for about two years.

This latter job is a numbers game. It's intimately involved with the annual budget. It relates to the future: where is the Navy going, how many people do we need, in what grade; how many officers do we need, in what grade; how do we go about getting them, how many do we need to get every year, how many are we going to lose every year? This is the technique of keeping the Navy staffed with people, that's what it is, coming in from the bottom and going out from the top, both officers and men. And to do nine-tenths of it is statistical, that's what it amounts to.

So that if some emergency occurs and the Chief of Naval Operations determines that we must expand and take some ships out of mothballs, for instance, where are we going to get the people to man them. So you are also involved very closely and deeply with the reserves, because this is the source for sudden expansion. And what kind of people - you need to know who they are, where they are, what their training is. So that by pressing a button you call them to active duty, and you must get the right men in the right billets. Or if there is no emergency you must plan for replacements in all categories required by normal attrition.

In essence that's what this job is. The reason I enjoyed it, in the first place because it was technical, and I was there during the period when we were trying to mechanize as much of the personnel game as we possibly could. We were just beginning to catch up with the times. We had developed such a big Navy that we were becoming inefficient in administration. If we continued Washington would be bigger than the Fleet. So we had to mechanize, and fast.

We were able to call together a considerable amount of talent from the industry and from colleges to help us do this.

There were great advances going on just about this time in mechanized control of people in industry. They had gotten to the point where organizations, like General Electric, could not handle administration by personal control, they had to handle it through machines. And we began mechanizing at that time.

So it was close work, long hours. The Pentagon type of duty is from eight o'clock in the morning until eight o'clock at night almost every day. This is the way it is. I don't know why it should be, but it got to the point that if your office light wasn't on at night people wondered if you were sick at home. There's so much paper work. Then there's so much phone work, there's an awful lot of people calling. And there are innumerable conferences.

The Vice Chief of Naval Operations, who was Don Felt at that time, was a great believer in using every bit of talent in his officers that he had in CNO. He administered through committees.

One of the committees I was on was the Budget Committee — budget and finance, which was an interesting thing for me because I still don't understand budgets and finance. But the justification of the personnel part of the budget became my pigeon while I was there (under the Deputy Chief of Operations for Personnel). So I would coordinate with him on all the justifications of personnel, and we had to have the figures right at our hand for it.

This is as well as I can describe this billet. It was a technical job, and basically dealt in numbers.

For the first time I was not running my job on the basis of the "warm body." I was now a technician and a statistician and a small cog in a great big wheel. But I also learned the way the Pentagon ran — why we had to have the number of assistant secretaries we had, what the Secretary's job was, what the Chief of Naval Operations' job was, what the Deputies jobs were.

The D.C.N.O. (PERS) couldn't always attend the CNO conferences, and so I attended in his place. We had a conference every single morning with first Admiral Carney and then Admiral Burke.

My boss was the DCNO (Personnel) who at that time was Vice Admiral Holloway. Holloway's job was basically Chief of the Bureau of Personnel. His office was in Arlington Annex. He came to the Pentagon usually for the morning conferences, but even when he did I always attended also because he wanted me to be there for continuity. There's where the daily plans developed — from these morning conferences. There's where we went into the intelligence room and listened to our expert briefers on daily developments throughout the world.

I was fortunate in this particular job to be given the security clearances that allowed me to attend these high level intelligence breifings.

I found out what made the Navy run then, and I got to be known, and I made it a point to be known.

I also took a refresher course at that time in speech making. I went over to Georgetown and took another three weeks course in speech making, which I enjoyed.

I don't think that there's very much more I can say about this job. I don't think that it broadened me, or that it improved my general ability to be a good naval officer. It certainly taught me some new techniques. It took me away from the thing that I liked best, and that was working on the warm body end of personnel.

Most of our technicians were people who pounded machines. They came out with great long strips with thousands of figures, and the interpretations of these strips on various and sundry big cardboard displays. So that when the Secretary wanted to know something we didn't have to go through long technical dialogue. Simple diagrams, showing trends, were the tools of our trade.

This is what the Secretary liked, this is what CNO liked, this is what everybody liked. They liked to see comparisons with last year, with next year, and how. So you have to portray these matters on charts. The development of those charts was mostly my job in matters of personnel.

Q: Did you have to go to any of the hearings on the Hill?

Smoot: Oh yes, every year in the Budget hearing.

This was an interesting thing to go up there, because the personnel budget, outside of shipbuilding itself, for the most part was the biggest slice of the Navy budget. We had a budget in those days of around three billion dollars, because pay comes out of that.

There's a lot of details in "Budgetry." I don't know how to read one of those complicated budget forms and I never intend to learn, although I served on the Budget Committee I did not learn, because I could hire CPAs by the dozen if I needed them to interprest now the forms for me and put them in terms that I understood.

It was a simple matter to go before the Military Affairs Committee on the Hill, and the Finance Committee, because for so many years we had a certain way that demonstrated how we used our money and basically those never changed. You have so many people that you pay so many dollars to, you have so many stations that you have to keep up that require so many dollars.

The thing that they were interested in were changes. With our system they could spot them immediately. In fact it was our business to see that changes showed up with emphasis. If last year a particular cost center in the budget was a hundred and ten million dollars, why is it a hundred and seventy-five million dollars this year? You had to be sure that you knew why.

I found that these so-called horrifying experiences before the committees were not horrifying at all, they were quite educational. And in general there was a very close association of comradery and understanding which grew with the years.

Q: Is that possibly because you were well prepared?

Smoot: For year after year we were well prepared. I think you're quite right, yes.

For the most part I just remember one incident. I'm trying to think of the Chairman of that Finance Committee that we used to go before. He was a Congressman from up around Santa Barbara and he was a famous Congressman, awfully nice fellow. He was supposed to be awfully tough, but I didn't find him tough at all.

One of the things in which I had a particular close interest, and one that always seemed to end up in my lap, was the matter of "Contingency Funds."

Contingency funds can be a multitude of sins, and it can throw a red flag in front of anybody when they say "contingency" because when you come right down to it it's how many parties you can give on it. Of course they must be official and be obligations. That's what it amounts to. And boy, we had to be awful careful with that.

Q: You're not serious — how many parties you can give. You mean emergencies to take care of?

Smoot: No, parties. An awful lot of contingency fund goes to Task and Type Commanders because they've got to return obligations in terms of large dinner parties, large social gatherings, cocktail parties, and other social events. They haven't got the money to pay for those things personally. When you're going to have a large party two or three times a month, it's going to cost you plenty. You can't pay for that out of your pay, so you have contingency funds.

Any major Type Commander has a contingency fund, and he's responsible for accounting for every nickel of that contingency fund. If he spends five dollars of it in buying somebody a drink, he's got to account for it.

I had a contingency fund out on Taiwan, and it was a big one. These Chinese entertained us. We had a great big home out there, and we had to entertain them in return. You can't always "take" and not "give," even Congressmen recognize that.

When I had command of the Cruiser Divison we'd go to many places in Japan. The Japanese officials would entertain me ashore; I'd entertain them on board ship. While it isn't awfully expensive, it was a lot more than I could afford out of my allowance for my normal one meal a day in my cabin, when you'd have twenty or twenty-five people in and you'd give them a real fancy dinner. Or if you took them ashore you gave them cocktail parties to return in kind what they gave you. You can't serve it aboard ship. If you go ashore you can't get that for nothing.

So there are contingency funds, and these are the things that this particular Congressman watched. When I'd start he'd say, "Now Admiral, I know you people have to return your obligations, but we don't want to go whole hog on these things. We want to be sure that you have enough, but not too much. Now you tell me why you need this particular amount here to this particular item. What's happened out there?"

"Well Mr. Congressman, so and so. I've got it detailed here exactly. If you'll take the figures from last year as we have them here you will see that this place is growing by leaps and bounds." Maybe it was Alamogardo, New Mexico, or some place like that. "Whereas last year this fellow had a staff of some fifteen or twenty, he's got three hundred there now. This is the important part of it."

I just cite that as an example of some of the work that we had to do before the committees, and even though you're handling tremendous amounts of money the most important thing about it was annual changes. They were the things that had to be justified, which is true of anything.

That's about all that I can remember of that particular job. The time came when, I don't know particularly why, it's never been clear to me, the Deputy Chief of Naval Operations for Administration was suddenly detached. I never did find out why. It was probably a personal thing with him, but I was called up one day by Admiral Felt, the Vice Chief, and he said that he was going to change me to the "Deputy job."

At that time the Deputy was a three-star job - "Deputy CNO for Administration." But Don made it very clear that it would not be a three-star job for me.

The VCNO was planning on some major changes in the setup of CNO, and Administration was going to be down graded. So he asked me, "Do you want it, or don't you?"

I said, "What happens to me if I don't?" He said, "Well, you can stay right there where you are." I said, "What do you recommend?" He said, "I recommend you take it."

So I took the job. I found it to be really less interesting than the job I left.

What the Deputy Chief of Naval Operations for Administration was, was really a catch all for all the nits and lice that you couldn't actually ascribe to military type of work. This was the firing and hiring of civilian personnel. This was the administration of the maintenance funds for the building itself or the part of the building that you occupy. This was the job for the purchase of furniture in offices. It supervises the staffing of secretaries and assistant secretaries - that is typing secretaries, administrative people, file clerks, and people like that. It has to do with all the civilian personnel in the Navy's part of the Pentagon. It was administration for CNO, not Navy wide.

It was less demanding. I was quite disappointed about it. But there was a major change at that time in the personnel organization. They down graded the job of the Assistant Chief of Naval Operations for Personnel Control to a Captain's job. That was why they were really looking for another job for me for another year, that's what it was.

Fortunately about that time the fellow that had the job that I went into left, for what reason I don't know. I really don't know why he left, but he left sort of under a cloud, and very shortly afterwards retired and left the Navy completely. I don't know why that happened.

I relieved him, took over the job, and spent one year in it, and found it to be rather dull and just an office type of a job which was not inspiring at all.

The only thing about it was that I still did have the opportunity of attending the CNO conferences, and also the Secretary's conferences. So I kept myself informed, and made it a point to comment whether I was invited to or not when I had a chance, because I wanted to be heard from.

So I think that probably helped when I was called up to the CNO's office one morning after I'd been to work about fifteen or twenty minutes, and wondered what I had done now.

Arleigh said, "How would you like to go to Taiwan?" I said, "I would like to go any place that's got a three-star job with it." And he said, "That's what it would be." So that's the way that happened, it was as simple as that.

Q: Is that true of the selection of all three-star Admirals — that there is a job, and they are put in it, and then they become a Vice Admiral?

Smoot: That's it, yes. That's an appointed job. It's not really a Navy wide selection for advancement. It's a promotion as far as money is concerned. It also gives you another star, and a certain amount of prestige.

But take the case of Admiral McCormick, who was a Rear Admiral. He went to Chief of Staff for some job with CincPac with three-stars, became a Deputy CNO with four-stars, and then went to a district job with two-stars. He ended up his career as District Commandant as two-stars.

So it's an appointed rank for the job. It does give you prestige. When you retire you retire with the pay of the highest job you held. So it is a great advantage to you.

So with three-stars in an isolated job like that, no matter what it was, of course I'd take it. At that moment it looked like the only thing I could get. I was in hopes that I could probably get another seagoing job - like BatCruPac, or maybe Chief of Staff to Commander Pacific, or something like that that had three-stars. But it wasn't in the cards, so I took Taiwan.

Q: You said at one time you may have regretted not going to Monterey - was that at this time?

Smoot: Yes, right there, when they told me to take the job as Administrator.

I thought – oh boy, that's the end, I've really blown it for some reason, I don't know why. I thought that would be the end because it was definitely a demotion, no doubt about it. Going from one job which kept me right up on the front step all the time with the possibility of maybe relieving the Chief of Naval Personnel if he left, and then to go to a job that was really housekeeping. Really I was awfully disappointed.

Arleigh offered no explanation for it at all, he never did. But whatever it was apparently it did not close the door on the future.

The Taiwan assignment was great. I was the first non-aviator to be assigned to the Taiwan job. It had always been an aviator's job before.

I found out afterwards that CNO called in Admiral Stump, who was CinCPac at that time, and Admiral Stump objected to my assignment, but only mildly. He said he would rather have an aviator. Arleigh said, "Why? There's no point in having an aviator. I don't see any reason for it. It's an island and a non-aviator can handle the job as well as anybody else."

I had known Stump, and I think that he saw that Arleigh really wanted to do something for me. That's the way I got Taiwan.

Q: Before you go into the detail of the United States Taiwan Defense Command, I want to mention the fact that that job was four years, and you saw a great deal of activity during that time. You were also awarded the Distinguished Service Medal. So I hope you will describe the detail of that command.

Smoot: It was without a doubt quite a way to end a career — one of the most fascinating and different types of job that I'd ever had.

Basically there's historical background to the job that form the subject of speeches I have given on various and sundry speech circuits in Los Angeles for the first four years after I came back from Taiwan. It stems from the fact that President Chiang Kai-skek, a great and wonderful man, was let down by the United States at a time when he probably could have made quite a showing for himself on the mainland against Mao Tse-tung's communist forces.

And so he escaped to Taiwan with some 50,000 of his followers. Somehow or other through quite a wonderful hegira, which should be told some day, he got to Taiwan and there he set up his government in exile.

For what reason has never been quite clear to me the State Department realized that maybe here was the opportunity to set up an important bastion in the forward area, and right on the door step of communist China, and so give President Chiang the prestige he deserved, ambassadorial recognition, and establish a military advisory group for him, and also a senior command on the island.

I wasn't the first, I was about the third. The first command that went there in this capacity was the Commander of the Seventh Fleet. He sort of used that as his headquarters rather than Japan. This gave the Gimo military backing, and ultimately a seat in the U. N.

The military title of my job was "Commander Taiwan Defense Command." It stems from a treaty that we have with President Chiang's government.

The treaty says in essence that the United States will assist President Chiang and his military forces in the defense of Taiwan against any aggressor. These are just very short terse explanations of a very complicated treaty. And as far as the offshore islands are concerned (they don't call them offshore islands, but associated islands) that the United States would assist the President and his military forces in the defense of these islands provided the assault against them was a threat against Taiwan itself.

So a status of focres agreement was set up and the Taiwan Defense Command was organized ashore. It has a rather large staff made up of all three services. Traditionally the command had always been Navy, because it is an island and that sort of puts it in an area of military defense in terms of a Navy rather than an Army or Air Force.

It's a typical type of a study in defense that has always been a big problem with the Joint Chiefs of Staff - who's going to command this and who's going to command that in these outlying stations. An island - it's natural that it comes under the Navy. A big shore going bastion is the Army. When there is a territory it's the Air Force. They have these pretty well worked out.

I was it's third or fourth Commander. The staff is made up of all the services. The Air Force has had the Chief of Staff job - he's a Major General. The staff is about 120 to 125 men equally divided among the services. It's a typical military staff with divisions of operations and plans and communications and logistics and intelligence and all it's personnel and all the standard things.

It's located right in Taipei in a large independent building that at one time was used by their congress. It was used as a sort of major meeting place with the President. It was a good building with plenty of room, more room than we really needed. It was turned over to the military and we staffed it and ran it. We ran the building, paid for it, paid for maintenance, bought the furniture, and set it up. It's a little 'pentagon' out there.

What does it do? What's the reason for it? What does a staff like that do that has no combat forces at all assigned to it?

The status of forces agreement does say that in the event of emergency the Commander of the Taiwan Defense Command can call upon the three services for such forces as he needs, depending upon the circumstances.

There's only been one incident when we had to call upon our military forces; it happened when I was there.

This is an oversimplification of the thing of course, because if you wanted the reason for the Taiwan Defense Command laid out in black and white I think they'd have an awful time describing it.

But it does give President Chiang prestige. And they felt that perhaps this might be a means of maintaining a bastion of strength and prestige in the forward area that represented a defense against communism and maybe even a constant threat against communism, because it was there. And it recognized that this is the one facet of Chinese hierarchy and background that is on our side, and we will not recognize the mainland regime because it's communism. And so ergo - here is the center of Chinese culture and we will stay with this.

When we went out there the reception we got was fantastic, just simply fantastic. Nothing like it I'd ever seen. We were immediately herded right up to the VIP guest house.

I traveled by Navy plane all the way from Washington. Mrs. Smoot went with me. Arleigh Burke gave us a plane, and it took us all the way out. We stopped on the West Coast for a day or two to see our children, and then took the same plane and went all the way.

I had to stop in Honolulu for a conference with Admiral Felt, who was then CinCPac, to be briefed. I was wearing three-stars now.

We went to Guam and then Japan. In Japan we left the big four engine plane. The officer that I was relieving, Admiral Doyle, came to Japan in the small Taiwan Defense Command's personal plane. We went to Taiwan in that plane.

When we circled the field I never saw so many people in one place in my life. They had half the Army out there, the Marines, and the Navy, and all the high brass, everybody except the President and his wife - they weren't there. But the President's son was there, and the President of the Chinese Congress which they call their Executive Yuan. The personal Aide to the President was there. The Chief of the Army, the Chief of the Navy, and Chief of the Air Force were all there with their contingents. What a reception!

It took us an hour and a half to get out of that place. I was wearing whites. All the wives were there too. They were all lined up. Their receptions were beautifully done. There were stands put specially for the occasion.

On my right was the Minister of Defense, Minister Yu Tai Wei whom I got to know so well. (He was such a wonderful man, one of the most brilliantly educated men I've ever met anywhere.) I was in the middle, and then the Chief of the General Staff, General Wang Shu Min was on my left.

We had the firing of the seventeen guns, the band passed in review, and the Armed Forces passed in review. Boy oh boy, what a thing!

The reviewing stand was built just for this purpose. It was covered over with all the flags, the American flag behind the Chinese flag, beautifully done. The red carpet, the whole thing, was there.

We walked from the plane right straight to this place. Mrs. Smoot and all of the ladies were seated behind us on this special stand. It took about an hour and a half - the whole ceremony with everything that went on, passing in review and whatnot. I made inspection by foot all on red carpet. They roll out the red carpet. When they say "red carpet" it is something. It's just magnificent.

This went on for four years. There wasn't anything they did that wasn't elaborately done, done to the kings taste, done beautifully.

We were immediately sent up to the President's guest house, where we had about three rooms, four boys, and Sal's private maid

For four years we were in the hands of people, people, people, people, people.

We stayed at that guest house about five days. Sal was called by Madame who said, "We have a place where we think you will like to live."

We went to a little private dinner that first evening with Madame and the President. A big reception was planned for the next day.

It was a big reception given by Minister Yu Tai Wei at what corresponds to Blair House in Washington, a big center where all of their major receptions were given. The President and his wife did not come to that reception, that was all military. The American Ambassador came, and all of the other Ambassadors from all of the other countries that were there. It was a big reception. We stood in line there with a red carpet another hour and a half.

The first few days were sort of hazy - just one thing after another, just one party after another, one great big whirl. And I thought that it was going to kill both of us, but we learned to cope with it because it went on for four years.

Then finally we got to bed that night quite late after the reception and the dinner.

The next day I went up to meet my officers and my predecessor. We planned for the relieving ceremony, which was about two days later.

Meanwhile Sal was called by Madame and said, "We'd like to take you up and show you where we think you'd like to live," and she took her up there.

Meanwhile I was going with the Minister of Defense making calls on the various Chinese command that they had established.

Our future home was about a hundred feet long in front and about seventy feet wide. It had seven bedrooms, three or four baths, a living room that would house this whole area. I'd never seen such a big thing, it was magnificent.

The place looked down two thousand feet below over the whole city of Taipei. The Generalissimo lived just above us, about two or three blocks, up the hill from us in Yang Ming Shan.

We could see that what we were in for was quite above and beyond anything that we'd had. We ended up with a total of twenty-two servants. We had servants and servants.

Of course this included eight gurrds. There were guards around that place constantly. Never without a guard at both gates. At the front gate and back gate there was always a guard.

There were three drivers. There was a house amah, a laundry amah. There was the downstairs boy and the upstairs boy. A boy that took care of the ashes only - all his job was to take the ashes out of the fire places, which was the only heating we had. All cooking was done in a coal fired stove downstairs. Then there were three gardeners. All together there were twenty-two.

This is the way we lived for four years, a manner in which we'd like to become accustomed.

Q: When we got to this point Mrs. Smoot came downstairs, and I asked her if she hadn't found it difficult to go from this life of constant care back to the level of living that those of us in the United States are accustomed to, and she said, "No. One of the reasons was that you always felt that your phones were bugged, and all the rooms were bugged.

Smoot: Yes, we were definitely bugged out there. I think all of the head military people were bugged.

We would have them cleaned up every once in awhile by the American Security Force. They'd come in and electronically clean them up, but the Chinese would put them back again.

It was sort of a friendly bugging and understanding. We looked at it as something that wasn't definitely designed to spy on us in this respect, it was to seek casual information. They dont' particularly think that that was bad. They weren't very expert at it, because we were always able to trace it down and find out where it was.

I'm sure that the Ambassador was bugged. I'm sure that the Chief of MAG was bugged.

In our case it was the telephones - all of them were bugged. At that time we had to go through a central board. We didn't have dial phones. We'd lift up the phone to make a call and we could hear breathing on the phone, and it wasn't the operator. He must have had asthma. It didn't bother us at all.

If we were imprudent enough to talk about classified matters any place except in the most secure places, of which there were very few, then we deserved being heard. And we deserved having our secrets passed to them.

On the other hand if we did want to talk about something that was intimate or personal it was far better to take it for granted that there were methods of listening to us when we were in our home and at other places, in our automobiles and in our office, so we would write notes to each other.

The military, of course, had three or four places that were absolutely secure. One was at our headquarters designated for our morning conferences and other top secret conferences that we had to have. Those places were impossible to bug, and we knew it. Besides they were sterilized electronically on regular schedules. They were used for very special high level policy meetings. The Ambassador had one, I had one, Chief of MAG had one, and the head of the Air Force out there had one.

American Air Force had one because he was running a very highly top secret program that I was privy to, of course. And I was always at his meetings when we planned these things.

Each of us had a special place that we knew was clean.

This whole experience out in Taiwan - it's really difficult to know where to start or where to stop, or what really to give to an essay like this in terms of what are the highlights. It's almost impossible to separate your personal feelings from the military feelings and from the country's feelings.

When I say "country" - I mean their country, because we learned to love them very much. We made very close friends out there. They are really truly warm-hearted lovely people. They are so different from the other orientals that we met.

The Chinese live a life very much like ours - they would be insulted if we said that. They would think that we live a life like theirs, because they're five thousand years older than we are.

Q: What is the place of the woman, for example ---

Smoot: She's very important. As a matter of fact on the mainland when they used to have plural wives, before they became Christians, which a lot of them are now, the number one wife was the most important person in the house including her husband. When he came home he was just another one of the household.

The children are very important, and they're deeply loved by the Chinese parents. Their homes are warm, loving homes. They're pleasant to go into. It isn't a cold type of oriental atmosphere that you would suspect at all, it is not, it's anything but that.

I think that their dinners, even their formal dinners, are the most delightful type of dinners anywhere in the world. They have fun at the dinner table. They sit down to have fun, not only to enjoy their food, but to have fun. They have all these games they play at the dinner table, and they get loud and noisy.

The hostess expects that her dinner talbe is going to be a mess when they get through. The food is put in the center and it's passed to you from center. There's a lazy susan in the center. Food is passed to you, usually by your hostess, who some times has to reach clear over the whole width of the table. She uses her serving chopsticks, and passed food to you from the center, and it dribbles all the way to your plate. The mark of a very successful dinner in China is a very dirty table cloth.

It also is a very noisy party. The noise of the games they play at the table, they get serious about them, but it's all in fun. They laugh loudy and often.

I don't know of any party I'd rather go to than a good group of about fourteen Chinese at a dinner party where the ladies and the men are there together. I don't know of anybody that has more fun.

Q: So your professional life and your social life were completely interwined.

Smoot: They were, yes.

They had great respect for us. They had great respect for all the military out there. But the respect was not only engendered by the position that you held, but you became a fast friend or not with them. And it began to show very well whether they liked you or not, or whether you showed that you liked them.

Their entertaining is mostly in their own homes, except when they have big parties. Then when the big parties are thrown they're usually three or four hundred people. But they entertain close friends in their own homes.

The President entertains in his own home almost exclusively, but he's got two very large beautiful homes. One home up on Yang Ming Shan can probably seat only about fifty or sixty guests. The home down in the city of Taipei, or on the outskirts of Taipei, can probably seat about two hundred people.

The Chinese are most gracious, delightful hosts and hostesses. They are warm, friendly, and easy going. To enter their living room you feel like you're part of them, part of their lives. They make it a point to be most hospitable, Madame particularly. The President, of course, has to talk to you through an interpreter.

But on the other hand Mrs. Smoot and I have been in their home when we were the only guests. On these occasions I've heard the President speak English very well.

As a matter of fact their biggest dog, Baron, only understands English. So the Gimo has to speak to Baron in English.

The dogs join us at the table too. There are two of them -- one a beautiful big Saint Bernard, and the other is a little mutt, both just as important to them as their children.

We got to know those two people very well and admire them, and we still hear from them. They're very dear friends of ours.

As for the military work itself I found that it was not too confining nor was it too complicated. If I were to define what I actually did it would be the most difficult thing in the world. I can't describe the things that took most of my time, becuase they were very highly classified and I can't talk about them. It had to do with intelligence matters over on the mainland. It also had to do with intelligence matters of our own host and what their plans are.

Everyone understands that the Gimo's whole reason for being, and that of all of the people that came over with him, the 50,000 or so, is to go back to the mainland and to rule it and defeat communism there. And the fact that he's been able to maintain this facade, this ambition, in the eyes of his own people for these twenty odd years, and to keep this objective live and in front of his own people, and still maintain their confidence and be their ruler, is a tribute to a great man. And he is a great man.

You might ask - what kind of government it is. I think most people would think it's a monarchy, and a very strong strict monarchy. I don't call it a monarchy. It's true that there's no doubt about his being the boss, the reins of control are in his hands and he's a strong man. And he's been able to maintain control for many many years.

If you had to describe it - I'd call it a benevolent oligarchy, because he does use the brains of his people. He calls them in for conferences and makes his decision after listening to them. And they are not arbitrary decisions. He's willing to listen, and does listen.

He has engendered a great deal of criticism because all of the important positions of the government, and for that matter the positions in the country's economy, the banking side, and the major positions in industry, are held by mainland Chinese people who came over with him. There are many well qualified and smart native Taiwanese people who object to this quite strenuously, and probably quite rightfully so.

Whether this still goes on since I've left, or not, I don't know. I can't believe that it does, because in the years that I've been gone Taiwan has burgeoned into a tremendously active and highly capable manufacturing country.

They have terrible smog. Some times I couldn't even see the land down below where we lived, just dirty black smog.

They are continually trying to develop new industries today, and some of their works are very good.

We were taken all over the island. There wasn't an industry at the time that we were there that we didn't visit and watch the whole process of how they did it - including glass makeing, weaving, iron ore industry, cement block industry, oil industry. You name it, and we saw it all.

Q: You were saying it was difficult to describe what kept you busy because of the fact that so much of it was classified, but you did mention intelligence. Are there any other phases of the work that you can mention?

Smoot: Of course we were always prepared for an emergency.

The offshore islands are a symbol to them. The offshore islands don't amount to a thing except a symbol. They are probably the most highly developed and defended pieces of real estate in the world today, magnificently defended.

Diplomatically and militarilly any incident that could occur or develop that might give them the opportunity to make a move to "return to the mainland," and in so doing have the assistance and backing of the United States, would be welcomed with great enthusiasm.

So one of the biggest jobs we had to do was to keep them from being too overt in their military actions around the offshore islands, where many many battles developed between their air force and the Chinese communist air force, and between their navy and the Chinese communist navy. One of the most serious of these incidents occured right after I arrived in Taiwan.

I arrived in Taiwan the first of July, 1958. About three weeks after I had gotten there we were at a big dinner party at Government House. I don't remember who our host was, it was one of the heads of the government. All of the important people of Taiwan were there, as well as all of our own top military brass.

I was approached by the President's aide, who grew to be one of our very close friends. He's a contemporary of ours, maybe a little younger than I. He's in Washington now. His name is S. K. Hu. If there was any one Chinese in the military in TAiwan that I saw more than anybody else it was S. K. Hu, because he had direct access to me and direct access to the President without going through channels. That's the way it was with him - a wonderful man, and very successful Chinese.

He came to me at the dinner party and spoke over my shoulder and said, "Admiral, I'm going to have to report to the Chairman of the Joint Chiefs, General Wong, and to you, and to the President, that the communists have opened an intensive bombardment on the offshore islands. They began about such and such an hour (and he named the hour) and already they have fired over a hundred thousand shells. This is considered an emergency that's going to require some help."

Needless to say the dinner party broke up, and I hardly saw Mrs. Smoot for the next six weeks. The bombardment was intensive and generally directed against military installations and resupply operations.

This surprise situation was exactly what the Chinese would like to have used to involve the United States in a military asction against the communists directly. We had to refresh our memories frequently on the specifics of our mutual defense treaty.

The treaty provides that if any attack on the "offshore islands" endangers Taiwan itself we will assist in their defense. Otherwise we can only help in terms of advice and logistic support, no directly military support.

It was a hard thing to say, and I had to say it to the President, until I got word otherwise. And that would probably not come through me, it would come through the Ambassador. I had to tell the President that we could not be directly involved militarily in this affair. We could and did take over military defense of Taiwan itself, thus releasing his own military forces to defend and resupply the offshore islands. This was a deep blow to them.

But it soon became apparent to all of us what the United States position was going to be.

We were going to have to prove to the Gimo and his military, and to the people of Taiwan, and to the world at large, that Taiwan could continue indefinitely to resupply the besieged offshore islands. They could continue to do so even if the Chinese communists continued this bombardment at the intense level which we were experiencing at the outset of the attack.

How were we going to do it? That was the military problem. We devised methods of doing it. There is always a counter to every type of warfare. You can't blanket a whole island with shells. You always leave some place where you can get in, and we got in.

We had to keep up the morale of the Chinese people that were out there. We had to be sure that communications were always open, that provisions could get there, and that they could maintain themselves, and that they wouldn't suffer any real serious casualties in great numbers. Naturally there were going to be casualties, but for the most part there were very few.

This was their job. And as for the U. S. support - we took over the military defense of Taiwan completely.

So to take over the defense of Taiwan required increased military forces. So certain elements of the Seventh Fleet reported to me. I also called in the 11th Marines from Japan - this was the 11th Marine Air Wing Detachment - a tremendous group of wonderful people who can take up their airfield and move it where it is needed and be ready to go in a week. They are remarkable. And I called on the Fifth Air Force for what help they could give me with logistic planes and other things from down in the Philippines.

I got everything I wanted, but everything was for the defense of Taiwan itself, not the offshore islands. We served as escort for their convoys, but we wouldn't let our ships or planes shoot at the mainland.

The Chinese wanted to bomb the mainland, using their own planes and their bombs. Their objective was to silence all those guns - a very logical quest. Why not silence those guns?

We put this development to Washington, because I honestly couldn't answer it.

The reply - in essence was: "No, don't let them do it. Don't tell them 'no,' but just tell them you're not going to support them if they do, because this is just what they're waiting for - to develop some kind of big hassle over the mainland, and then we've got to go to their help." This was right of course, and we proceeded accordingly.

We developed a study which proved to them that, for every-one of those guns that they might silence by the type of bombing they had available, they'd probably lose almost a squadron of planes. This of course was too big a price to pay, and they were convinced of the proposals in feasibility.

These were the kinds of things that went on and on, and we had to be patient. Back of it all we knew, and I am sure that the majority of the Nationalist Chinese military planners knew, that the communists couldn't keep that concentrated bombardment up indefinitely - it's too expensive.

Consider a continual artillery bombardment of several thousand shells a day - this depletes your arsenal pretty soon. And this is what it did, so that sometime in October, after about three months of bombardment, the communists announced that they thought they had punished their deserters enough. So they were going to resort to their peculiar system of firing on every odd day of the month, which they still do.

They still fire a few propaganda shells on every odd day of the month. It doesn't bother anybody. Very seldom do casualties result. They were mostly propaganda shells anyway.

The school children would run out after school and go searching all through the fields looking for the shells and the pieces of shrapnel. The government would give them the equivalent of an American nickel for every piece of steel that they turned in.

The bombardment incident greeted me very early in my tour in Taiwan and educated me the hard way, and without much preparation in the fields of diplomacy and touchy tactical and strategic situations.

But I think aside from the guidance that I got from our own CNO, and from my own immediate boss, Commander-in-Chief of the Pacific, the greatest assistance that I got was from China's grand and wonderful Minister of Defense Yu Tai Wei.

I think if I were to build a pyramid of people of whom I think most highly he would be near the top, and I include anybody that I've ever known. I think the man is fabulous. He was the Defense Minister at that time, and continued during the whole four years that I was there.

Tiger Wong was the Chairman of the Joint Chiefs. They have another name for it, it isn't quite the same, but it means the same thing. He was the head of all the military and reported directly to the President.

Tiger Wong is still my closest Chinese friend. Minister Yu Tai Wei was a gentleman to admire, but not one with whom you develop warm friendship. The man was simply fabulous, but as an individual person he wasn't as warm as the Tiger. He was aloof, but a great and wonderful man, and a wonderful thinker.

Those weeks were quite a strain. I lost about fifteen pounds, and was hardly ever home. I could hardly ever leave my office until after twelve o'clock at night, because that was when we could have direct correspondence to the States. The time difference in Washington made it more convenient for me to communicate after twelve o'clock at night. It was morning in Washington then, and CNO and his staff were at work, so I could give them the latest status reports directly.

Also at night we had to write up the daily resume, which had to be designed for the Press media and other non-military authorities, including our own American Ambassador. It had to be a precisely worded resume of the day's operations - what we had done, and what the outlook for tomorrow was, and what we were going to do. All this took time, and I had to oversee every bit of it. We developed two daily resumes - one for the Press and one for CNO.

I had a wonderful staff who worked long hard hours. So it was a strain, but it was interesting. And then just like that it was over.

Q: Is it conceivable that a wrong decision on your part could have started an international conflagration?

Smoot: No doubt about it, yes. If I had, without guidance and counsel, taken action to turn our own Air Force loose over the mainland to silence those guns we would have the makings of an international conflagration.

Q: You had the authority to do it.

Smoot: Not exactly, because at that time it didn't look like the threat to the offshore islands was sufficiently great to be a threat to Taiwan. If I had decided that it was a threat to Taiwan itself, and that the way to meet it and to get it over with was to go ahead and bomb the mainland using U. S. forces that would have been the spark plug which could have started a real international conflict.

Q: Did you find it an extremely difficult relationship with the Generalissimo over your decisions?

Smoot: Some times, yes. He's a military man himself, a good one, but he's smart enough to know that the provisions of the treaty were pretty clear. He knew enough to know that he could not bully anybody into breaking that down, even though I was just fresh there. He's too much of a gentleman to try that.

Q: Did he ever try to put pressure on you?

Smoot: Oh yes, frequently, almost daily.

But when he gets a direct "no" he knows how to take it. He understands that it's a military decision, and there's nothing personal involved.

It didn't affect our personal relations in the least. In fact I think it cemented it. I think he respected me more for standing up for our position, although he was deeply disappointed in the American decision. This was his chance to return to the mainland, and this is his whole reason for being.

This is the thing that I think the American people don't understand - this "return to the mainland" objective of the Gimo. I think it's one of the most important things that I learned out there. The Gimo looks at it as being inevitable, that ultimately he will - and that we will help him.

We look at it, and most of the world looks at it, as a stupid foolish fancy, that he hasn't got a chance of doing it. There's a story that I can tell about it that takes an awful lot of the foolishness out of it.

The story started one very beautiful Taiwan day when I was called by the President's oldest son, Chiang Ching-Kuo, a great and fine man. At that time he was a three-star General in the Gimo's army and he heded up an organization called the "Special Forces."

Ching-kuo called me one morning on the phone and said, (this was long after the emergency was over, a year and a half later) "Would you take a trip with me?" I said, "Sure. Where are we going?" He said, "I prefer not to tell you where we're going. I understand that you can't leave the island, and that if you do leave the island you have to have the approval of your boss in the Pacific, but we're not going to leave the island. We're going to stay on the island, but we are going in my plane. I prefer that you take your Chinese aide who can interpret for you."

My Chinese aide was a fabulous young Lieutenant Colonel in the Chinese air force, who could be my adopted son today. He was just the grandest young kid, but he was killed in an air accident two years after I left.

"Take your Chinese aide and be prepared to stay overnight!" It sounded intriguing to me. We were going on a fishing trip, or what were we going to do? It sounded good, taking the Chinese aide. "Uniform?" "Yes, I prefer you be in uniform." "Okay."

So we set out in his plane, and had three or four rounds of simply fabulous noisy Chinese bridge on the plane. (I'm bringing this in because it has a significant point later.) There were all kinds of friendly arguments and a wonderful lunch. His Chinese hostesses entertained us with the Chinese aboriginal dances during the flight.

I never looked at the territory, and didn't know where we were going, and didn't care. That was two hours of the fastest flight I've ever been in, all done purposely. The same thing on the way back – they didn't want me to know where I went, thus the distractions.

We landed in a place, I don't know where it was. The only thing that I could say is that it's somewhere in the middle of the island of Taiwan. That's all I could say. I'd never been there before, I've never been there since. And I don't know of any American that has. Maybe they have, I don't know.

I reported this. It's all in intelligence back in Washington. It's unclassified, so it's all right.

We landed in this perfectly beautiful spot that looked like a great big extinct volcano. The first thing that I could see was a field of a great number of tents. They seemed to stretch out for acres and acres. There was a nice little airfield with a short runway that we landed on.

Then we went through the Chinese ceremony of my arrival, and took a review of a regiment of well trained troops. Then we went and had dinner. Then we played more bridge, drank a lot of saki, and sang. And we were entertained again by an aboriginal group and then we went to bed. Don't know yet where I am.

Before we went to bed I said, "How long are we going to be here, Ching-kuo?" He said, "We'll be home probably for lunch tomorrow. I want you to see something tomorrow morning."

So we got up the next morning and had breakfast. We all got in jeeps and went to a big level field adjacent to where all these tents were, and I was treated to a beautiful review of troops. We trooped in line in a jeep with the flags flying, and that was done just magnificently.

When that was over I was introduced to a two-star General who wore a peculiar type of insignia on his uniform. This was the "special forces" insignia. He said, "Come with me," in pretty good English.

He took me to a tent and he said, "This man's name is so and so. (I can't remember his name.) He comes from a little mainland town called Pu Li. We just happen to have a map here of where Pu Li is."

Pu Li is across the Taiwan Straits above the Canton River deep in the Haaka Valley, one of the most isolated areas of southern China. As a matter of fact I think it was written about by Mitchner in "Hawaii," this Haaka Valley. That's where some of the Chinese that went to Hawaii came from.

Pu Li was up the Haaka Valley. "This man's mother is still living there. His father was there, but we think he's dead now, he was killed. His sisters and uncles and aunts are there, they're all living there. All the men in this tent either came from Pu Li, or they have friends of family in Pu Li."

"All of these twenty men that are in this one tent have been trained to perfection in the art of guerrilla warfare, and they have some of the nastiest and most horrible instruments you've ever seen. They are clever, and they are motivated. They're quick and they're strong. They are to be dropped in Pu Li some night."

"There's three to four hundred of these tents, and three to four hundred of these little villages up the Haaka Valley — all with relatives, all with families. These men know the towns, they know where the bank is. They know where the stores are, they know all about them — these people do."

"The Gimo wants to drop these people — five thousand of them — up the Haaka Valley some night, maybe two or three nights."

"They go up there night after night in these low flying planes and come back. They don't drop their people. They just go up there to show that they can do it, and they don't even get fired at some times. They hardly ever get chased."

That's what the Gimo wants to do. What would happen with five thousand of those trained guerrillas on the loose in this isolated part of the mainland?

What would happen is up the Haaka Valley they'd have people that were devils at night and in the dark who could kill, disrupt, disturb all of the surrounding communist area. And during daylight they could disappear with the people that lived there because they came from there. They know all the people, they could just disappear.

They would be the type of guerrillas exactly like those that Ho Chi Minh uses in South Vietnam.

What does the Gimo want? He wants us to support him in crossing the Straits, and to help him support a beachhead on one of the isolated beaches across the Taiwan Straits on the mainland for about a week while he makes this landing. Then he says, "You're on your own," he doesn't care. That's all he wants, and that's his return to the mainland.

Well who knows, who knows whether that might work or not? I think it might.

Q: You're saying that's why his dream is not such fantasy?

Smoot: That's true. He's a military man, he knows what he's doing. He knows that he's not going over there and make a frontal landing on the mainland of China and defeat Mao Tse-tung and all his forces, he knows that. But he's got a plan, and it's a good one.

I was taken on this trip probably to see a part of his major plan, not to talk about it, not to analyze it at all. I was taken on a special trip for a special purpose.

On the way back we again were entertained on the plane with a noisy loud bridge game, fun, and lots of food and saki.

I never saw where I'd gone and didn't care. And I don't know yet where I was and don't care.

I reported it to the Chief of Naval Operations and he said, "Okay, they've got a special place down there. We can't tell them that they can't do that, but if he ever asks for any support tell him - no, we can't support him."

Well they asked for support many times, and I told them, "No," and they said, "Why?"

It got so that before the time was over there that the United States was letting them drop up to about twelve to twenty men at a time on the mainland, and they did. These were called harrassing forces for sabotage. You've read in the paper where they blew up some railroad tracks.

They'd go over where they had a bunch of guns annoying the offshore island, and they'd sneak in at night. They've got little midget submarines, and they take twenty or thirty men over there and put them ashore. They go up and cut the throats of all the gun crews and just leave them there, and then they disappear. The communists wonder why their guns aren't firing, and investigation finds all their crew with their throats cut.

It's harrassing, and a horrible thing to say, but this is their way of doing things. This we let them do, but we won't support them in any of these things.

We didn't give them submarines, and don't recognize that they have any submarines. Why I don't know, it's stupid I think.

But the Gimo is not a foolish man, and he is not going to try to return to the mainland in big force, and he's not going to involve the United States and embarrass us and him in anything like that.

He keeps the confidence of his people because he is a great and wonderful leader. Now what's going to happen to him - he's eighty some years old. What's going to happen to him - he's going to die some day, and in the not too distant future.

When he does I think that Ching-kuo is going to take over - his son, the one I went on this trip with. I think Ching-kuo will command the respect and admiration of the military that's there. They like him now, he's a good man. He has the respect of the "money people," the overseas Chinese, the military men of China, and the industrial people of China. Not exactly like his father does, but very much so.

He doesn't have international prestige. He's not known internationally, and he may never be. He has a Russian wife, who is a perfectly delightful lady, and a non-communist just as much as you and I. She's a White Russian, a perfectly lovely lady.

I think that eventually Taiwan is probably going to be a source of embarrassment to the United States. They're going to wonder why we're still supporting it. I think this will happen just as soon as they try to approve a two China seat in the United Nations. I think that when that occurs we will find that the Gimo or the Gimo's son, whoever is running it at that time, will have no part of it and they'll completely withdraw. If they withdraw from the United Nations, we've got to withdraw our support from Taiwan. Then they're on their own, and that's it.

Q: Did you find each day as your tour came to an end wearing or tiring because of the constant requesting?

Smoot: No, I didn't. There were no two days alike. If I got tired of anything it was the social life. The social life was terrific.

We had one little problem about the social life and that was this - every time that an important person came to Taiwan (we had people like Eisenhower and Johnson, you name them and we had them) there were three major parties that were given. One was by the President, one was by the senior U. S. military man, and one was by the Ambassador. I was the senior U. S. military man.

Usually you could plan on a two day visit by a very important person like Eisenhower or Johnson. He'd arrive one morning, spend that night, that night, and the next day and the next night, and then go. So you had two dinner parties and a luncheon, maybe two luncheons.

The Gimo would never tell you what he was going to do, that was beneath his dignity. It's nobody's busines what he is going to do in terms of entertainment.

Like the time that President Eisenhower was there - he was there for two nights. We were pretty sure that the Ambassador would take one night and Gimo would take the other night, and I'd have a luncheon. So I was pretty well set up, it looked like it was fine for me. I sent all my invitations out for a luncheon on a given day. That was the only luncheon he was going to be available for, and that made it pretty easy for me.

The Ambassador sent his invitations out for a dinner on one of the two nights available - he had to do that. Frequently it was wrong.

What happened? The Gimo decided he was going to give the luncheon. So I had to take one of those dinners.

This would happen at the last minutes, so we had to be very versatile. This was always the case, but interesting.

There as never an uninteresting moment, ever, It was always interesting.

Other than these special events our daily life was a series of social engagements. We had plenty of help doing it because Mrs. Smoot had an aide and I had two aides, and we had our drivers. We had so much help around the place that all we had to do was be careful that the calendar didn't make mistakes.

There was no part of the island that we weren't eventually taken to, and taken to in great style, and thoroughly enjoyed.

My birthday was always an occasion for some great and wonderful festival that took us to some remote and beautiful outlying place - they had a lot of them - and the same way with Mrs. Smoot.

The relationships with our friends got warmer and warmer as time wnnt on. There're so many things that I could tell you about it, about the personal side of it.

I had office hours and kept office hours, just like the Chinese kept office hours.

I was granted the distinct honor of being asked by the President to attend his cabinet meetings once a month, which I did. I sat in on his cabinet meetings, and I'm sure that I sat in on them when they were open cabinet meetings, but this was more than had been asked of anybody before. I felt flattered about that and found it interesting.

Militarilly the Gimo was never demanding about any particular thing as far as more help, more this, more that, was concerned. He took the attitude to make do with what he could because he had some wonderful men and some wonderful help and assistance, and he was doing fine. So he was not hard to get along with at all.

Social life was tremendous, both among our own people and among the Chinese, and among the foreigners that were there. There were many many Ambassadors from many countries. It was difficult to budget our time.

Tiring, yes, but both Mrs. Smoot and I were in good health fortunately and we made it our businees to stay in good health. We had good doctors out there. As far as the food itself - we had American food.

Our Ambassador was a career Ambassador. He had had twenty-five years duty in China in one kind of a political job or another and came to Taiwan as his first Ambassadorship. He married late in life, had always been a bachelor, a professional newspaper woman.

I'm not going to belittle him at all, I have no right to. I guess he was a wonderful man and did his job well, but he and I did not get along very well because I'm a hawk and he was a dove. I believed firmly in the business that if you're going to do something, do it to win. He seemed to have the attitude that if you're going to do something, do it to compromise. I got sick and tired of that.

Furthermore in my first conference with the American Ambassador he said, "Now you're going to find that the best way for you to do is to try to live like a Chinese." I said, "Not me. I'm not going to live like a Chinese. I'm an American and I'm proud of it. When the Chinese come to my house they're coming to an American home and they're going to have American food."

And furthermore the Chinese loved it. Their finest meal was to come to the Smoots for a roast beef dinner. They ate at our house and loved it. We did right in that.

As I look back on it, the Ambassador was the only annoying thing that I had in my four years in Taiwan. He left under sort of a veil of something or other, I never did find out what it was, but he left very suddenly about three months before I left.

Q: The one event you don't want to miss is having been made "honorary citizens."

Smoot: Oh yes, we were made honorary citizens. I was coming up to that because this was another thing that annoyed the Ambassador. He felt that if anybody should have been made an honorary citizen he should have.

Mrs. Smoot and I were invited before the legislative Yuan to a beautiful and lovely ceremony which was attended by all the dignataries of Taiwan. We were officially designated Honorary Citizens of Taiwan, and we still have the certificates that they gave us. So if we want to we can go out there and live and pay their taxes and live the way they do today as citizens of Taiwan.

It was very flattering. I have to give Sal, my wife, an awful lot of credit for that because she was downright beloved by the Chinese. They were just crazy about her. I think that more than anything else she was probably as great an ambassador as has ever been out there. She still hears from them. They are still crazy about her, nothing like her has ever hit Taiwan. So I have to give her credit for that. I think she's responsible for that almost completely.

Then there's one final thing I think that I want to tell you about - this was our departure.

Our departure was indefinite for two or three years. But each time my tour of duty came up to end, which would normally have been two years, and then three years, and then four years, the Gimo called me up and gave me perfectly explicit instructions that I was to stay another year. This went on each year as the time came for me to go.

Finally after four years, fof personal reasons I really wanted to go. So I went to him and told him that I had told the Chief of Naval Operations that I wanted to be relieved in April or May of 1962. The personal reasons involved the very desperate illness of my mother, and also a professional future in civilian life that was quite important to me.

Besides I felt that we had done our part out there, and from then on anything that I did was going to be almost repetitive and maybe downhill even. It's always been a proclivity of mine that if you're going to have to move anyway, get out while you're on top. Always leave them laughing - this is the same thing, and it's true. Far better that I leave when they still wanted me to stay than for them to want me to go.

So I made up my mind that we were going to leave in 1962, and told the Gimo and the Ambassador. The CNO agreed and arranged to have a relief sent out for me. My relief was to arrive the first part of May.

We were officially harrassed for about three weeks in the delicate neglectful way that the Chinese can do, and that can hurt. Now they admitted openly that we were going to leave.

They made this admission openly by inviting us to an insignificant, poorly done Chinese farewell party given by a third or fourth class officer in one of the legislative Yuans, an unimportant officer that we hardly knew, with guests that were totally unknown to us and absolutely of no importance whatsoever. This was publicized as our farewell party.

Supposedly this was the beginning of our farewell parties. We didn't really know what was going on, we didn't understand.

I went back and talked to my Chief of Staff and said, "Do you know these people? Have you ever been in their homes? Do you know anything about them?" No, he didn't know them. I said, "Well, find out about them. I want to know why this is listed by protocol as one of the official going away parties."

It didn't take long to find out that this was the peculiar Chinese way of letting know that they're unhappy with you and that you're gone against their will. And so for a period of three weeks we were given the real silent treatment - no phone calls, no nothing, no invitations, not one thing.

It turned out fine because we were able to pay off some of our obligations to our own military, and we were also entertained by them. We had quite a good time.

Then one day, and I don't remember how imminent our departure was, but it was still about a month away, Madame called Sally. She said, "I hope you realize that the treatment you've gotten was deliberate. This is our method of telling you - we love you and we don't want you to go."

Sal said, "It's a devil of a way to do it, it's hurt us deeply." She said, "Yes, we meant it to hurt you. We want you to know, and we don't want you to ever forget. Now we realize why you must go, since your mother is involved and the matron of the house is very important. Now we'll turn on the warmth again." And everything was all right from then on.

We had to be poured aboard the plane. It've never had anything like it in my life, and will never again. We were exhausted physically and emotionally.

It ended with a great big ceremony at the Gimo's, where he decorated me with the highest Chinese medal. The Commander-in-Chief Pacific was there, Admiral Felt, and he decorated me with the Distinguished Service Medal.

The departure was a tearjerker. Sal help up very good until all the amahs came down (the household servants), with little gifts of flowers, and then she broke down.

A big U. S. Navy plane was turned over to us to take us to Hong Kong where we boarded the SS CLEVELAND, and had a perfectly wonderful trip to San Francisco via Japan.

I can't think of any better way to leave the service, nor could I have had a more rewarding job. We gained a wealth of friends and experiences from those wonderful people out there that can never be replaced by anything. It was a great character builder, and we gained a wealth of intimate friends that we'll never forget and still hear from.

Q: I know that you were awarded the Military Order by the government of Portugal.

Smoot: That was on a Midshipmen's cruise that I was assigned to in the capacity of Chief of Staff to the Task Force Commander.

One of the visits that we made was in Portugal. We arranged to visit Salazar, the Premier of Portugal. He invited us to the castle, a perfectly beautiful trip. While we were there he just kissed us both on each cheek and hung this medal around our necks, just for being there.

It's the oldest military order in the world — called the Order of Aviz. In reading over the Portuguese language of the commission that comes with it, it indicates that if we ever go to live in Portugal that we shall be given lodging, food, and transportation for a period until we are settled in our own home

Of course the commission with these provisions was written some eight hundred years ago. It's possible that the lodging may be a tent, and the food may be bread and wine, and the transportation may be a donkey.

Q: And you did retire on June 1, 1962, and where did you go?

Smoot: Yes. We came back on the CLEVELAND and had a perfectly lovely trip. The master of the CLEVELAND flew my flag and gave me complete run of the bridge. In fact I used to go up there and work some of their night navigational problems and take sights and thoroughly enjoyed it.

The first night that I was aboard I had an experience — I didn't realize what was the matter. We went down to our perfectly lovely cabin and I was tired. We had had a terrific sendoff in Hong Kong by all those people who came over there to see us off and all the friends that we had made in Hong Kong. We'd had a real rough week over there, so we were awfully tired.

We went to bed in a very comfortable cabin that they had assigned us on the CLEVELAND. It was a beautiful ship and a beautiful cabin. I lay down and was wide awake, I could not go to sleep. I was tense. I got up, I paced the floor. I put my clothes on, walked out, came back, and tired to go to bed again.

I finally realized what was the matter - I'm on a ship and I haven't anything to do with it. I've got to know what we're doing.

So I took the privilege that the Captain gave me and I went up on the bridge. I read the night orders, which he told me I could do. I looked at the PPI. I saw the projected navigational track. I talked to the officer of the deck, went out on the wing of the bridge, looked at the sea and the sky. I said, good night to the officer of the deck, and went down to our cabin and went to sleep.

That's what I'd been doing for forty years. I had to know that the night orders were okay and that this ship was in good hands for the night, or I couldn't go to sleep. So I did that every night on the trip, then I'd go down and immediately go to sleep.

Technical retirement was in San Francisco, but we settled in Los Angeles. I had previously met Mr. Henry Salvatori, a very wealthy and influential man in the Los Angeles area in the industrial field. When I had Command of the Mine Force Pacific several years before, we did a lot of entertaining of important guests returning normal obligations. Mr. Salvatori was one of those guests. I liked him and he seemd to like us. He told me, "Whenever you get out of the Navy, if you want to do something for awhile, come see me," so I did.

I went to him and he made me the president of a little company of about four hundred men located in Inglewood. I worked down there for Henry for about four years.

Then I retired completely for the first time in Laguna Hills. We love it down here.

I'm a member of the Board of Directors of this mutual type of organization that we have. We don't own our home. What we do is buy a share in a mutual, and for that share in a mutual we have the privilege of occupying a place of our choice under certain rules and regulations, which is called the "Occupancy Agreement." Theoretically in forty years we will own this place. None of us are going to live that long, and so our equity is what we could get for it by selling. It has greatly advanced in it's value now, almost ten times what we paid for it.

We thoroughly enjoy it. I've just been told that I am to be the president of this corporation for next year.

Q: I think it's interesting, because I'm president of the Board of Directors of the cooperative in the housing in which I live.

Smoot: You know what it's all about then. We administer the funds completely.

Q: So do we, and it's a big job, and I'm sure they're very fortunate to have you. My people think they're fortunate to have me, and I hope they're right.

Smoot: I hope they're right too about me. I sometimes think they've made a mistake, because I'm not a business man fundamentally.

Q: I wanted to make one comment so that anyone who reads this tape or the manuscript can picture the surroundings in which you live.

You have beautiful beautiful objects of art from the Orient. Plus you have behind me some shelves of mahogany that display many items that you have done with your own hands. Each one is an object of art and holds another beautiful item in it. Also you are an expert in clock repairing, and you're an excellent carver. What other talents do you have that we haven't mentioned?

Smoot: I bought my wife some pearls while we were in Japan. They were lovely pearls, but one of the strands broke some two months after we bought them. So I took them down to the jeweler in Taiwan and said, "String them." And he said, "We can't string them. You have to take them back over to Hong Kong to string them."

So the next time I went to Hong Kong I went to our jewelers. I went in the back room and said, "Now fix these pearls for me, and while you're doing it I'm going to stay right here and see how you're doing it. Then I want you to give me some lessons on some things that happen, and then I want to buy plenty of equipment so that I can string pearls myself." So I learned how to string pearls properly.

I should have been some kind of a mechanic rather than a naval officer. I'm a technician. I love to do things with my hands.

As far as the carving is concerned, I carved these things because we had a whole drawer full of jade pieces that had been given to us, perfectly beautiful little pieces of carved jade. So what do you do with little pieces of carved jade - put them in a drawer and nobody sees them. So I got the idea of mounting them in wood.

I got a special kind of very hard wood in China. I don't know what the name of it is, it's sort of like our maple except it doesn't have any eyes in it. It's very hard, very close grain, white wood.

The fascinating part about it was that while I am a carpenter at heart, I love to do carpentry work and have done an awful lot of carpentry, I have never done this small fine delicate type of work. The thing that makes it possible is the use of Chinese tools.

For instance there isn't a saw made in America that could saw these little holes that are required in some of the things.

They make their own saws out of piano wire. They just take a piece of piano wire and an old broken file, put the piano wire on a stone and chip it. They take a piece of split bamboo and make a bow out of it with the piano wire, and they chip it very neatly and very easily, and then turn it over a little bit and chip it some more. The first thing you know you've got one of the finest saws in the world made of piano wire. It's excellent for very close fine work.

Q: The things he is describing are maybe two or three inches high and the holes are a quarter of an inch.

Smoot: Some of them are just little bitty things - an eighth of an inch, but all of them have to be sawed.

You draw your design on a flat piece of wood if you wish it, and then you saw out the wood you don't want. After you've got the design sawed, then you go to work with your carving tools and shape the thing into leaves and flowers, and round off the parts you don't want square, and square the parts you want square, and leave depressions, emphasizing by outlining it, and just use your own imagination. I don't have much originality.

For instance the gadget that's holding that perfectly beautiful white and green piece of jade - I had dinner once with President Syngman Rhee in Korea, and while I was sitting with him before dinner in a perfectly beautiful chair the carving on the back of that chair fascinated me and impressed itself on my mind. That little thing is a replica of the back of Syngman Rhee's chair.

The rest of them are the same - they're suggested from something.

Q: But the home is almost like living in the middle of an art museum, except it's so beautiful and homey and comfortable. I did want to comment on that, and I know it's mostly the result of your artistry. So you are an artist as well as a technician.

I've been interested in this interview as we've gone along because it seems to me that you have developed your character in the interview. As well as relating incidents that happened you have been able to bring out in the various assignments you've had the development of your own character.

How would you describe your character as of this present moment?

Smoot: Character-wise I think I'm more humanitarian than anything else. I'm very considerate of other people, I've always been that way.

I am not competitive, competitive in the sense of playing cards or a game. I don't particularly care if I lose, it doesn't bother me.

I don't want to ever have a feeling - and this is probably not very good, that I'm better than somebody. If I'm better than somebody I want them to find it out, and not by my having to prove it.

Q: You said that I think in the first interview I had with you - when you first went to the Academy.

Smoot: Yes. I was not very good in athletics at the Academy, and I should have been because I had a good strong physique. I was a strong young man, strong and well built, and fast. I could beat anybody on the track, but I didn't want to. I wasn't interested in it.

I play golf now, and I love golf. I play with a foursome and they take it so seriously. We wager a quarter, and you'd think that we were playing for a million dollars. It doesn't bother me in the least. As a matter of fact I would far prefer to give my competitors the quarter to start with and go ahead and play golf.

I play golf and like it, because I'm playing against myself, and I am my one and only competitor.

So if there is any competitiveness in my system it's with me, me myself. I don't like competition. I don't like unpleasantness. I don't like arguing. I would be a very poor debater, very poor — I would hate that type of thing.

I find that I can control people and always have been able to control people, not by the fear of punishment but more by the hope of reward. People always want to be recognized for what they do.

I take much more pains to give somebody a pat on the back, and I look for somebody that I can, and I look for a reason that I can, and pick them up that way. Then you've got them in the palm of your hand. It's so much better than to go around with a whip.

Q: I think you might write a book on the issue, Admiral.

Tell me, and this is going to conclude our interview, what do you consider in the development of your career, your life, your personality, your character, as the outstanding incident or accomplishment?

Smoot: I think probably the thing that caused a definite path to be followed was probably an incident when I went to submarine school, because it was there that I first learned that I really could do anything that I wanted to do in terms of thinking and brains, and finally ended up standing 'one' in that place.

It was a shock to me to find out that there were quite a few people who were senior to me who were rather derogatory about the business of standing one, and it had been awfully important to me.

I thought at the time -- were they jealous of me because I stood one? Did they want to stand one? And if they did, what are they going to get out of it?

I went to them and said, "What have you been lambasting me about? I didn't do anything to you." They said, "Oh no, all you did was just spend night and day working like the devil so you could stand one." I said, "What else is there to do?" And they said, "You can be a fellow among fellows, can't you?"

I said, "How do you go about being a fellow among fellows? Do you want me to act stupid when I'm not stupid? Is that the idea? Do you want me to put myself on your level? You didn't stand one. What am I supposed to do -- become popular by bringing myself down to you? Why don't you try to bring yourself up to me? Why don't you try that and see what happens?"

Those two fellows looked at me in a different light. They went away and I heard them sort of mumbling to themselves. They were gone for ten or fifteen minutes and they came back and shook my hand and said, "We made a mistake, you've got something."

I didn't think I had something very much. It didn't occur to me at the time that that was a rather significant feature of the way I was going to be, but it is.

Q: Yes, it is an illuminating incident.

Now on the other hand, did you have something which you would consider yourself a weakness or something you wish you hadn't done?

Smoot: Oh yes, sure, many. I've made lots of mistakes.

The weakness that I have is that if I'm convinced about something and think it's right, I will state my case completely and I will state why I think it. But if for reasons that I think are rather poor reasons somebody else decides that that's not the way they're going to go, and if they're in authority to do it that way and have got several people behind them, I'll drop the case. I won't follow through unless it's fatal.

If it's going to be a fatal thing then I'll just say, "Okay have it your own way, but you're going to be sorry, youre wrong." But I won't tell them they're wrong on small matters or things like that.

In other words it's another facet of my not being competitive — I'd rather drop out of a small matter and let them have their way rather than try to fight right through with mine when it's not really going to amount to anything in the end anyway.

If I get my principle across and I know my principle and I tell them it's wrong, I'm through, I won't fight for it, unless it's going to hurt somebody. If it's going to hurt somebody or something, yes, I'll fight for it.

What it is – I am not a very firm type of a guy. I will be very firm if there's a principle involved, but I can't be unpleasant about it. I'd far rather say, "This is my opinion, I think it's right, you go your way and I'll go mine."

Q: Those are both interesting comments of your own evaluation of yourself. History and your biography and ultimate uses of your biography may come to different conclusions.

I think you're the first person who I've interviewed whose character came through clearest, and I have found it extremely interesting. I appreciate the time you've taken. I think it's a fine biography and I hope the Institute agrees with me.

I hope you are happy when you get it back for correction and additions. I'm putting this on the tape to remind you that you will go through the voluminous material you have and select representative pictures because the Institute will be glad to have them.

Index for

Series of Interviews with

Vice Admiral Roland N. Smoot, USN (Ret.)

Administration - Deputy CNO for; study of the future of the navy, etc., 282-283; Smoot named at request of Adm. Felt, 291-292

USS ALBERT T. GRANT - DD: Lags in battle of Suragao St., target for U. S. fire, 135-138; reactions on board, 139; taken in tow, 140

ALHENA - Supply ship, 100-103; torpedoed, 104; towed by DD MONSEEN, 104-107

Atomic Bomb - reactions to dropping on Japan, 182-183

USS AULICK - DD: first command, 48; condition of ship in mothballs, 49-50; difficulties with turbines, 52-54; practice docking, 58-59; new A/S gear installed, 59-60

Badger, Admiral Oscar Charles, 184, 192, 200, 205-207

Battle of Eastern Solomons, 99-100

Braisted, RADM Frank Alfred: in command of Sound School, 111-113; refusal to let Smoot leave, 112-114

British Base - DD swap: U. S. DDs prepared for delivery at Halifax, 60-62; the turnover, 62-63

Brown, Capt. Wm. D.: commanding officer of BB MISSOURI, 259-262; 265; distress of his wife over grounding, 265

Burhans, RADM A. D., skipper of PORTLAND, 110

Burke, Adm. Arleigh: names Smoot to Taiwan Defense Command, 293-295

Cape Cod Canal, 77-80

Career Building, comments on, 277, 279-280

Carney, Adm. Robert B., 198, 200-201; effect on Smoot's assignment, 202

CASCADE, Headquarters Ship, 123

USS CHASE - DD, 15-16

Chiang Ching-Kuo, son of Chiang Kai-shek, 320; takes Smoot on a secret journey to inspect Special Forces under his command, 321-324; outlines the Gimo's plan of action, 324, 326-327

Chiang Kai-shek: The Gimo, 296-297; 308-310; 319; 329-330; requests Smoot's tour of duty be extended, 333; decorates Smoot, 336

Chiang, Madame, 301-302, ff; tells Smoots about farewell party, 336

Chinese Manners and Customs, 306-308, 335-337

Civil Service Commission - on Oahu: survey of available workers, 43-44; discrimination against the Japanese 45-46

SS CLEVELAND, Smoot's homeward trip from Taiwan, 336-339

Convoy Duty - North Atlantic - Iceland - U.K., 66-75

CRU DIV 3, command in Japanese water, 272; Smoot relieved of command, 276

Cruise, VADm. Edgar Allen (nickname - Batt), 120

USS DES MOINES, 245-246

DESRON 56: Smoot in command, 154, 175, 200

Destroyers - Unit commander, 178; assigned as screen to Fast Carrier Task Force, 178; "delousing stations" established, 180-181

Doolittle, Gen. James H., 82-84, 92

Doyle, Admiral Austin K., turns over Taiwan Defense Command, 300

Drumright, The Hon. Everett F., U. S. Ambassador to Nationalist China, 331-332

EINAWETOK, 118

Eisenhower, President Dwight D., visit Taiwan, 328-329

E-ring, Pentagon, 280-281

Felt, Adm. C. D., Vice CNO, 284, 291, 299, awards DSM, 336

Guadalcanal, participation in battle, 92-97

Guantanamo, 248

Halsey, Fleet Adm. Wm., 18, 216; San Bernadino Strait, 145-146; plans for surrender party, 192; ashore after surrender, 198

Hird, Captain Harry, 41

Holloway, Adm. James L., Jr., commander of cruisers, U. S. Atlantic Fleet, 267; begins using computers in BuPers, 270; offers Smoot job as head of P.G. School, 280; 285

Homosexuals, problems attendant on, 118-121

HORNET, USS, CV: DD MONSEEN and her squadron, escorts for Doolittle raid on Tokyo, 82-84

Houston, home port of Caribbean Neutrality Patrol, 58-59

Hu, S. K., Military aide to President Chiang, 312

ICELAND, 67-68, 72-73, 76

Iron Bottom Bay, 92

Iwo Jima, 158-159

Kamikaze, attacks on fleet off Okinawa, 163-173; shock results for personnel, 168; battle fatigue as result, 177

Kauffman, VADM (Reggie) James L. - Squadron Commander, 51, 56-57, gets Smoot sprung from Sound School at San Diego, 113; puts Smoot in command of Task Unit of inter-island bombardment DDs, 116-117; gives Smoot orders to set up DD base at Einewetok, 118-119

Kerama Retta, landing on, 161; NEWCOMB towed there, 167

King, Fleet Adm. E. J., 18, 110, 112

Kurita, Vice Adm. T. (Japanese), story of his turn around at
    Leyte Gulf, 143-145

Kwajalein, base for DDs harrassing Japanese in bypassed islands, 117

Leahy, Fleet Adm. William D., 18

USS LEARY - DD: Battle of Suragao St., 136-137, Smoot and staff
    transfer to her after Newcomb damaged, 167

Libby, VADM R. E., 122-125

Lingayen Gulf Operation, 151-153, incident of man overboard, 152-153

Long Beach, California, 276-277

USS LOUISVILLE, fires at DD GRANT in battle of Suragao Strait, 136

MacArthur, Gen. Douglas, incident involving a hospital ship, 199-200

Manus, R and R after Leyte, 149-150

Mao Tse-tung, 325

Martin, Adm. Beauty, 175

MARYLAND - BB, 36-37, ordnance in use, 38-39

McClain, RAdm. Tex, 235-239

Midshipman Cruise, Chief of Staff to Task Force commander,
    vicissitudes of, 235-238

Midway, Battle of, 87

Mindoro, 149

Mine Force Commander, 276-277; problems with new minesweepers, 278

USS MISSOURI - BB, surrender ceremony in Tokyo Bay, 196-197, 239;
    goes aground at Norfolk, 254, 263-264; morale factor for
    wives of officers, 266

MONSEEN, USS - DD, 64-66; convoy duty in North Atlantic, 66-69; rescues torpedoed DD, 69-71; stands watch on BB TIRPITZ in North Atlantic storm, 72-75; 76; failure to rendezvous with BB WASHINGTON off Cape Cod Canal, 77-80; escort for HORNET on Doolittle raid, 82-84; not fully equipped for action at Midway, 88; participation in Battle of Guadalcanal, 90-97; rescues torpedoed supply ship ALHENA, 104-107; 108; gets new skipper, 109

Morrow, The Hon. Dwight W., four rules of life as ascribed to him, 227-228, 230

USS NARWHAL, duty on, 29-33; an experimental deep dive, 31-32

Navy Selection System, introduced, 36, 39

Neutrality Patrol, 58-60

NEWCOMB - DD, Smoot takes command of DesRon 56 on board NEWCOMB, 123; summary of impressions on engagements, 125; Battle of Leyte, Gulf, 127-138; credit for sinking enemy BB, 139-140; difficulties with refueling, 141-143; kamikaze attack on in Linguyen Gulf, 151; kamikaze attack on her at Okinawa, 164-166; out of battle, 172

Newport News Shipbuilding Co., 244

Nimitz, Fleet Adm. Chester, 18, 84-85, Coral Sea planning, 85-86, 88-89

Officer Distribution - Director of, 215-222; problems involved in captain assignments, 222; reduction of personnel, 223-225; job as an 'Admiral maker,' 228; influence peddling, 229-230; coordination of efforts at officer detailing, 233-234;

illustration of failure of system, 239-240; comments on failure of the system as it pertained to Captain of BB MISSOURI at time of her grounding, 259-260

Okinawa, 161-163, concerted attack of kamikaze, 163, 'call fire for DDs, 173-174; Japanese tactics, 174; Smoot goes ashore, 175

Ormoc Convoys, 147-148

Pearl Harbor, 75

Pearl Harbor Shipyard, duty there, 41-42; pre-WW II enlargement, 43; personnel plans, 43-44; apprentice school established, 44

Personnel - Assitant CNO for, 281-283, 285-286, preparation of Budget, 287-288; contingency funds, 289

Personnel Control : Smoot becomes Assistant Chief of Naval Personnel for Personnel Control, 267-272; naming of selection boards, 268; comments on selection process, 269 ff

Personnel matters, contrast between battleships sailor and small ship's sailor, 40

Port Director, Yokosuka, 198-199; incident involving hospital ship, 199-200; visits to various parts of Japan, 202

Post Graduate School, 24, at Penn State U., 25-26; Smoot is forced to re-write his thesis, 27-29

Puller, Gen. 'Chesty': rescue of Puller and his men from Japanese trap, Guadalcanal, 101-103

Rodgers, VAdm. Bertram Joseph, 158; in command of support force for Okinawa, 163; puts Smoot in command of attack group of DDs, 167, 169

USS S-7, Smoot has duty on, 20-21

USS S-26, Smoot has duty on, 20-21; considers this duty beginning of his career, 22

Sabatori, Henry, 339

Salazar, Premier Antonio de Oliveira, bestows Medal of Order of Aviz, 337

San Bernadino Sprait, 130

Sasebo, 273, 277

Savo Island, first battle of, 96-99, 134

Shima, Vice Adm. K. (Japanese), battle of Suragao Strait, 144

Smith, Adm. H. P., takes over command of BB MISSOURI after grounding, 264

Smith, VAdm. Hoke, 252-254, names new skipper for BB MISSOURI, 264

Smoot, Senator Reed, 3-5

Smoot, VAdm. Roland: early history, 1-5; Naval Academy, 6-14; family background, 1-4; concept of personal leadership, 8-10; religious background, 11; makes j.g., 23; Lt., 24; studies horography, 26; selection for Lt. Cdr., 47; illness forces hospitalization, 109-110; selection for Commodore, 175; retirement and activities thereafter, 339-349

Smoot, Mrs. Roland, works with wives of officers on board grounded MISSOURI, 265-266, 299-301, 330-331, 333

Sound School, 110; Smoot sets up school at request of Adm. King, 110-111

Spruance, Adm. Raymond, 146

Stump, Adm. Felix, 295

www.ingramcontent.com/pod-product-compliance
Lightning Source LLC
Chambersburg PA
CBHW082149070526
44585CB00020B/2150

Yokosuka: preparations for landing, 184; landing operations, 186-187; prisoners freed, 187-189; 190-192; attitude of Japanese Naval Officers at base, 196; post surrender attitudes of Japanese people, 197; 203-204; British landing party, 207; British looting, 208-210; surrender ceremony for all Japanese DDs in Yokosuka, 211-214

Young, Brigham, 2

Yu Tai Wei – Minister of Defense, 300, 302, 317-318

Submarine School, Smoot attends, 18-19

Mt. Suribachi - on Iwo Jima, 159

Taipei, 298, 303, 308

Taiwan Defense Command, 295; historical background, 296, telephone bugging of quarters, 303-305, communist shelling of offshore islands, 312-313, U. S. Forces take over military defense of Taiwan during crisis, 314-319, problems of heavy social life on Taiwan, 328, attends Cabinet meetings at invitation of President, 330, made an honorary citizen of Taiwan, 332-333

TENNESSEE, USS - BB, 133

Thach, Adm. John S., 236, 239

TIRPITZ - German BB, 72-73; U. S. and British forces mass off Iceland to intercept, 72-73

Tongatabu, rehearsal for Guadalcanal landing, 90

Tulagi, 94, 96, 98

Tyree, RAdm. David Merrill, Commander CruDiv 3, 273

USS NEWPORT NEWS - Cruiser, building in Newport News Shipyard, 232, 240-242, selection of staff, 242-243, putting her in commission, 244, gift of silver service, 244, life of commanding officer, 246-251

Wang Shu Min, General: Chief of the General Staff on Taiwan, 300

WASHINGTON, USS - BB, off Cape Cod Canal, incident involving MONSEEN, her designated escort, 77-80

Wilmer and Chews, prep school, 4-5

Womble, RAdm. John P., Jr., 201

Wong, General Tiger, Chairman, Joint Chiefs of Staff on Taiwan, 317-318